Borges and Translation

The Bucknell Studies in Latin American Literature and Theory
Series Editor: Aníbal González, Pennsylvania State University

Dealing with far-reaching questions of history and modernity, language and selfhood, and power and ethics, Latin American literature sheds light on the many-faceted nature of Latin American life, as well as on the human condition as a whole. This series of books provides a forum for some of the best criticism on Latin American literature in a wide range of critical approaches, with an emphasis on works that productively combine scholarship with theory. Acknowledging the historical links and cultural affinities between Latin American and Iberian literatures, the series welcomes consideration of Spanish and Portuguese texts and topics, while also providing a space of convergence for scholars working in Romance studies, comparative literature, cultural studies, and literary theory.

Titles in Series

Borges and Translation

The Irreverence of the Periphery

Sergio Waisman

Lewisburg
Bucknell University Press

Associated University Presses
2010 Eastpark Boulevard
Cranbury, NJ 08512

The paper used in this publication meets the requirements of the American National Standard for Permanence of Paper for Printed Library Materials Z39.48-1984.

Library of Congress Cataloging-in-Publication Data

Waisman, Sergio Gabriel.
  Borges and translation : the irreverence of the periphery / Sergio Waisman.
     p. cm. — (Bucknell studies in Latin American literature and theory)
  Includes bibliographical references and index.
  ISBN 0-8387-5592-5 (alk. paper)
  1. Borges, Jorge Luis, 1899—Contributions in translating and interpreting.
2. Translating and interpreting—Argentina—History—20th century. I. Title.
II. Series.
PQ7797.B635Z949   2005
868'.6209—dc22   2004011310

Contents

Acknowledgments

I WOULD LIKE TO THANK MY PROFESSORS, COLLEAGUES, FRIENDS, AND family without whose invaluable support this book would not have been possible. To Francine Masiello and Gwen Kirkpatrick, for their wisdom and guidance, their unequivocal support of the value of translation, their generosity, and serving as role models through the examples they set as thinkers and teachers. To Tulio Halperín Donghi, for everything he taught me about Argentine history. To my other professors at Berkeley—especially Emilie Bergmann, Anthony Cascardi, and Dru Dougherty—who challenged and encouraged me during my years as a graduate student. To Daniel Balderston, for everything having to do with Borges and his support of this project from beginning to end. A warm thanks to the Tuesday night *Finnegans Wake* group in Berkeley, especially John Bishop, Dan Schiff, and Karen Callaway. And I want to acknowledge Ricardo Piglia for the privilege of being one of his translators, and our conversations about literature and translation.

To Kathleen Kish and Gustavo Segade, for helping make my time at San Diego State University propitious for working on translation, and giving me the opportunity to teach translation courses.

An earlier version of chapter 5 appeared as "Borges Reads Joyce: The Role of Translation in the Creation of Texts," *Variaciones Borges* 9 (2000); and an earlier version of the epilogue appeared as "Ethics and Aesthetics North and South: Translation in the Work of Ricardo Piglia," *MLQ* (*Modern Language Quarterly*) 62.3 (September 2001).

Thank you to Marta and Eduardo who gave me, among many other things, two distinct languages and cultures. And to Maureen and Emma, who make it all worthwhile.

Borges and Translation

Introduction

Ningún problema tan consustancial con las letras y con su mo-
desto misterio como el que propone una traducción.

[There is no problem as consubstantial to literature and its modest mysteries as that posed by a translation.][1]
                        —Jorge Luis Borges, "Las versiones homéricas"
                                    [The Homeric Versions] (1932)

This book studies the importance of translation in the work
of Jorge Luis Borges, the importance of Borges for translation theory, and the highly productive fertilizations that can result from the
cross between these two fields. In Argentina's twentieth century,
there is arguably no other writer for whom translation is as integral
a part of his or her literary production as it is for Borges. In one
way or another, Borges was an active translator throughout his life;
significantly, this was an activity that he always kept close to his
other literary endeavors. In fact, as Borges develops his narrative
techniques in the 1930s, which culminate in his best-known fictions
of the 1940s and early 1950s, his theories of translation become
inseparable from his theories of reading and of writing. Translation
and writing, in Borges's texts, become nearly interchangeable practices of creation, of hermeneutic inquiry, and of aesthetic and ethical reflection. In the process, Borges defies the notion that
translations are necessarily inferior to originals and valorizes an irreverent practice of mistranslation that lends an unexpected freedom to writers in the periphery. Borges's position destabilizes the
concept of a "definitive text" and challenges the supposed primacy
of the center from where it comes, thus expanding the potential for
writers in Latin America to create new literatures.
    Translation—like any act of writing—is always undertaken from
a specific site: the translator's language, but also the entire cultural
and sociohistorical context in which translators perform their task.
Translation is not solely the transposition of a text from one linguis-

tic system into another; it is also, at the very least, the rewriting of a text from one literary system into another, from the source's context into that of the target language.[2] When one translates, one translates into a language's very specific place and time. As Lawrence Venuti argues in *The Scandals of Translation*: "The possible motives and effects [of translation] are local and contingent, differing according to major or minor positions in the global economy" (158).

Translators—like writers—have at their disposal the array of texts that have come before them to use as a library of styles and forms from which to "borrow." If we find it impossible (or perhaps simply reductive and unproductive) to consider a literary text outside its cultural and historical context, we quickly realize that the issue is doubly complex for a translation. When we consider a translation, we must take into account the context of the source text, that of the target text, and, most important, the distance between the two. It is in this distance—in a Babel of linguistic, temporal, and spatial displacements—that everything happens: texts and cultures are transmitted or lost, renegotiated, reexamined, and reinvented.

The variety of ways by which a nation's writers, readers, and translators establish a relationship with this distance is, of necessity, a major aspect of that nation's cultural identity. Translation is one of the driving forces in the development of any literature and has a tremendous effect on how that literature defines itself locally and globally. As Octavio Paz has observed:

> La historia de cada literatura y de cada arte, la historia de cada cultura, puede dividirse entre imitaciones afortunadas e imitaciones desdichadas. Las primeras son fecundas: cambian al que imita y cambian a aquello que se imita; las segundas son estériles. (*Los hijos del limo* [The Children of the Mire] 123)

> [The history of every literature and of every art, the history of every culture, can be divided between fortunate and unfortunate imitations. The former are fruitful: they change the one imitating, as well as that being imitated; the latter are sterile.]

This distinction helps explain why sometimes influence and translation are interpreted as positive, renovative forces, whereas at other times, they are said to lead to derivative and inferior copies of the original material.

In nineteenth- and twentieth-century Latin America, translation

has a special importance, as it affects how emerging national literatures are founded and renovated with respect to Western European
and U. S. traditions.[3] This importance is magnified by the sensitive
nature of the issue of originality in Latin America, where political
and cultural independence are often linked. In this study, I will
argue that the role of translation varies fundamentally from one culture to another; a difference that is magnified, in this case, by the
disparities between Latin America—as part of a geopolitical periphery—and Western Europe (and later the U.S.)—seen as symbolic as well as real centers of power.[4] But what exactly is at stake
in such a claim? What can it contribute to our understanding of Argentine literature in particular, and to translation and critical literary theory at large? And to what extent is the periphery not only
geopolitical, but also—and especially for Borges—a theoretical
space delineated to challenge many of our basic suppositions about
translation and literature, and the relationships between them?

Throughout this book, as I analyze Borges's contributions to the
theorizing of translation *and* the contributions of Borges's theories
of translation to the study of Argentine literature, I follow three
main strategies. The first is to consider Borges's theories of translation within the specific Argentine context in which they are developed. The second is to study Borges's theories of translation as an
integral part of his entire literary discourse. The third is to situate
Borges's theories of translation in a transnational context by placing them in textual dialogue with other twentieth-century thinkers
who have written on the subject (including Walter Benjamin,
Roman Jakobson, and Jacques Derrida), and in a broader modernist
context by comparing Borges's use of translation with that of writers such as T. S. Eliot, and especially with that of James Joyce. Including a writer's translations, as well as a writer's reflections on
translation, as part of his or her overall literary production, and not
as a separate, isolated activity, reveals the role that translation plays
in that writer's aesthetics and, by extension, in writing *per se*. There
is no essential difference between the "original" writings and the
translations of a writer's discourse. It is especially important not
to forget this fact when talking about writers/translators from the
margins, where translation is a way to renovate local traditions and
to remap previously established center–periphery and North–South
hierarchies, as well as the transnational issues associated with these.

Current scholarship in the field of translation studies in the hu-
manities falls into roughly two main categories. One focuses on

translation in relation to the study of language and meaning;[5] the other takes a more culturally based approach.[6] In both cases, studies tend to base their conclusions on the implications of translation for Western European and U.S. literatures.[7] Although clearly important in and of themselves, these approaches seldom consider how translation functions in the periphery and why this might differ from how it is used in the center.[8] Among other objectives, this book seeks to fill this gap by presenting a new perspective to contemporary debates on translation that will be of interest to research in the North and the South alike.

To delineate a theoretical framework for translation in the periphery, we begin in chapter 1 by discussing the context in which Borges develops his ideas on the topic. Why is translation so central to the history of Argentine literature and what is Borges's role in this history? To answer these questions, we go briefly back to Argentina's nineteenth century and to several key moments of national foundation (particularly the Salón Literario of 1837 and Domingo F. Sarmiento's *Facundo* of 1845), where we find the seeds of the polyglot nature of the literature of Argentina's twentieth century. This polyglossia flourishes in the Buenos Aires of the 1920s and 1930s, a place and time rife with numerous translation projects. As we will also examine in chapter 1, writers in this avant-garde period find new ways to cross the foreign and the local to redefine what it means to be Argentine. As an active participant in this scene, it is precisely during these years that Borges develops his ideas about translation, reading, and writing.

In chapter 2 we trace the development of Borges's theories of translation through a close reading of his three main essays on the topic: "Las dos maneras de traducir" [The Two Methods of Translation] (1926), "Las versiones homéricas" [The Homeric Versions] (1932), and "Los traductores de *Las 1001 Noches*" [The Translators of *The 1001 Nights*] (1935). In these, Borges challenges the notion that translations are necessarily inferior to the original and suggests that the concept of a "definitive text" is a fallacy. What happens when Borges suggests that so-called originals are as much "drafts" as translations are? How does this affect our thinking about translation and about literature in general? What does it mean for a writer from Argentina to propose such an irreverent idea? Chapter 2 addresses these questions by placing Borges's arguments in textual dialogue with both traditional and more contemporary translation theories.

The development of Borges's theories of mistranslation coincides almost perfectly with the development of his narrative techniques in the early- to mid-1930s. To illustrate the extent to which rewriting, misreading, and mistranslating become interconnected practices for Borges, we dedicate the first part of chapter 3 to Borges's *Historia universal de la infamia* [Universal History of Infamy] (1935). In the texts of this book, anticipating a move he perfects in the stories of *Ficciones* (1944) and *El Aleph* [The Aleph] (1949), Borges reworks selected pre-texts through linguistic and cultural appropriations and displaces them toward the margins to create unexpected meanings in an Argentine context. We then turn to "Pierre Menard, autor del *Quijote*" [Pierre Menard, Author of the *Quixote*] (1939), arguably Borges's most insightful commentary on the relationships among reading, writing, and translation. Anticipating reader response theories by at least thirty years, "Pierre Menard" teaches us that, through changes in the context, even the same words in the same language can gain entirely new meanings—and that this can occur, paradoxically, without necessarily losing the old meanings. This lesson is especially profitable for a writer from the margins, since a shift in context is precisely what happens when one takes a pre-text out of Europe or the U.S. and displaces it—reinscribes it, mistranslates it—into a Latin American context. We conclude chapter 3 with an analysis of another story, "Examen de la obra de Herbert Quain" [An Examination of the Work of Herbert Quain] (1941), and two later essays, "Sobre el *Vathek* de William Beckford" [Regarding the *Vathek* by William Beckford] (1943) and "El enigma de Edward FitzGerald" [The Enigma of Edward FitzGerald] (1951), which round off Borges's theories of translation.

By the early 1950s, Borges had completely changed the landscape of Argentine letters, not only through his fiction and poetry, but also through his ideas about and uses of translation. In his 1951 essay "El escritor argentino y la tradición" [The Argentine Writer and Tradition], Borges posits that the very condition of marginality—in both a literal and a figurative sense—allows Latin American writers to take from any and all traditions with irreverence. In chapter 4, we further explore the consequences of Borges's theories of mistranslation by drawing direct correlations between "El escritor argentino y la tradición" and Borges's practice of writing as translation. I discuss several stories, including "La muerte y la brújula" [Death and the Compass] (1942), "La busca de Averroes" [The

Search of/for Averroes] (1947), and "El Sur" [The South] (1953) to analyze how Borges works with displacements and contradictions in a remapping of difference that makes use of the potential of innovating from the margins. To demonstrate the extent to which the effects of translation are fundamentally different in the periphery than in the center, we consider the strong contrast between Borges's use of Dante as a pre-text in "El Aleph" [The Aleph] (1947) and T. S. Eliot's nearly opposite use of the same pre-text in *The Waste Land*.

In chapter 5 we consider how Borges reads, in the broadest sense of the term, one foreign writer in particular: James Joyce. Borges's textual dialogue with Joyce incorporates translation, numerous readings, and several rewritings, making it particularly apt as an analysis of how Borges's theories of reading, writing, and translation work together in response to a single writer. Throughout his dialogue, Borges skillfully exploits his similarities and differences with the Irish Modernist to "create" an ambivalent version of Joyce, as a particular kind of precursor (in terms of Borges's 1951 "Kafka y sus precursores" [Kafka and His Precursors]). The Joyce who Borges prefers is the one who, like Borges, constantly challenges the Metropolis and establishes an irreverent position with respect to its canons in order to innovate verbally and formally. Borges's reading of Joyce begins with his 1925 translation of the last page of *Ulysses*; includes reviews and commentaries; and takes us through a discussion of metempsychosis in "El acercamiento a Almotásim" [The Approach to Al'Mu-tasim] (1936), and an analysis of representation and verisimilitude in "Funes el memorioso" [Funes the Memorious] (1942). We also look briefly at the role that translation and polyglossia play in Joyce to better understand Borges's responses to him and to compare the importance of translation in both writers. This leads to a further consideration of the possibilities and limits, if any, of translation.

Then, after the conclusion to the book, I include an epilogue in which I illustrate the major implications of Borges's theories of translation in contemporary Argentine literature by applying them to a discussion of the work of Ricardo Piglia. In his texts, Piglia updates the techniques of both Borges and Roberto Arlt to create narratives in which translation functions as an act of resistance in the periphery. These narratives, these simulacra without a fixable origin, serve to challenge official discourses—whether they be of the state in the 1970s and 1980s, or of the neoliberal market in the

1980s and 1990s. Furthermore, from a more personal point of view as one of Piglia's translators in the U.S., I discuss the ethical and aesthetic issues that a translator from the center faces when translating someone like Piglia, given the uses that he makes of Argentina's long tradition of (mis)translation.

To question originality in the periphery, to make use of mistranslation and textual appropriation, is never mere literary technique. Rather, as we will see, it can form part of a distinctive challenge to a center that seeks to define and protect such originality for itself and its traditions. To translate from the margins puts at stake every aspect of that writer's/translator's relationship with the context of the source text, both culturally and politically; it is a loaded move, and one particularly deserving of critical attention.

From the nineteenth century to the 1920s and 1930s, from the 1940s and 1950s through contemporary times, a study of Borges and translation provides us with a productive and insightful way to approach Argentine literature. Borges shows us how mistranslation—like misreadings; like the blurring between fiction and criticism, or between apocryphal and veridical citations; like all manner of creative infidelities—can create a privileged site from which writers can innovate and from which they can define and renovate their literatures. Borges's texts contain crucial contributions to the theorizing of translation in the South, as well as numerous challenges to the way translation is currently theorized in the North. This combination makes a study of Borges's theories of translation relevant not just for Borges and Latin American specialists, but for anyone interested in the central role of translation in modern culture and literature.

1

Argentina and Translation: Delineating a Cultural Context

INTRODUCTION

To TALK ABOUT ARGENTINA AND TRANSLATION—TO SEE HOW TRANS-lation theory can provide a new lens through which to reexamine Argentine literature—we must define what we mean by both trans-lation and Argentine literature. Both terms are considerably more complicated than they might at first appear to be. To delineate the cultural context in which Borges produced his theories of transla-tion—to study Borges's contributions to the theorizing of transla-tion—we must also understand why the pairing of the two is so natural and so productive.

A central characteristic of Argentine literature, like that of most Latin American nations, has been a lasting preoccupation with de-fining its place among other Occidental traditions. In the simplest of terms, this obsession is born from Argentina's history as a Spanish colony, intensifies through the period of Independence and the na-tion-building efforts of the nineteenth century, and is renewed con-stantly as the country continues to experience itself in a peripheral position, politically, economically, and culturally, to Western Eu-rope and the United States. Writers and intellectuals have always sought, in one way or another, to identify what it means to be "Ar-gentine," even as the issue has remained a mark of the literature itself. What topics and themes are allowed of Argentine writers? What forms and styles are available to them? Should themes and dictions be limited to the "local," or can they also include the "uni-versal"? In other words, how can an Argentine writer, or any Latin American writer for that matter, produce literature in the periphery that is not considered derivative of the center and that does not re-produce an act of cultural imperialism?

A key to addressing these questions lies in how translation has been utilized and conceptualized by Latin American writers, and in Argentina most prominently by Jorge Luis Borges. Translation from a periphery is not the same as translation in the center—just as any act of writing is different in the margins than it is in the center. We must thus find a working definition of translation that reflects the crucial role that it has held in the literatures of peripheral nations. We must find a way to talk about translation that allows us to understand Borges's theories of translation and the importance of these to Argentine literature.[1]

In his 1959 essay "On Linguistic Aspects of Translation," Roman Jakobson defines three kinds of translation, "three ways of interpreting a verbal sign: it may be translated into other signs of the same language, into another language, or into another, nonverbal system of symbols." The first of these he terms "intralingual translation or *rewording*"; the second "interlingual translation or *translation proper*"; and the third "intersemiotic translation or *transmutation*" (114; emphasis in the original). When most people say translation, they usually mean "translation proper": the transposition of a text from one language to another. When I talk about translation in this study, I will sometimes mean translation in this sense. But I also want to consider translation in a much broader sense, as a linguistic, literary, and cultural process of transformation, as a rereading, recontextualizing, and rewriting of all or part of one or more pre-texts.

In recent years, "translation" as a critical concept has been utilized in much broader terms than merely as "translation proper." The expanded possibilities that scholars in a wide range of fields have found in translation theory are due, in large part, to the usefulness of thinking of translation as a metaphor for reading and writing.[2] Translation, in fact, can be thought to include all sorts of transformations, such as imitation, variation, paraphrase, pastiche, substitution, and permutation, as well as citation, reference, and allusion. As George Steiner argues in *After Babel*, these transformations are transmitted through history and across languages and cultures in a process that is arguably the same as that found in "translation proper" (436–95). In this book I propose that we think of translation not only in the sense of "translation proper," but also in broader terms, terms that include Steiner's conception of translation as analogous to cultural transformation. But even this is not enough. For what we gain when we think of cultural and artistic reproductions and transformations as modes of translation is an awareness of the difference and distance involved in these processes. In other words, looking at cultural transformations through the lens of translation theory brings to the forefront issues of difference and otherness, as well as a series of hermeneutic, aesthetic, and ethical considerations.[3] Thus, to talk about Borges and translation we must also consider what translation means for a Latin American writer, for someone working in a language and a nation situated in the margins—theoretically conceived and articulated as such. To this end, throughout this book, as we explore these and other issues, we will analyze Borges's ideas about, and applications of, translation in an Argentine, as well as a transnational, context.

Too often, translation—in the sense of "translation proper"—is judged to lead to inferior, secondary copies of the original. This traditional view, which maintains a nearly sacred privileging of the original, assumes that there is always a loss associated with translation. Such devaluing of translation is especially problematic for Latin American writers, whose national literary traditions emerge and develop as reflections and refractions—as a series of distorted translations—of Western Europe and its traditions. Translation has completely different cultural political implications for "younger" literatures than it does for "older" ones; and the motivations and effects of translation are fundamentally different for writers in the margins than it is for those in the center.[4]

In this respect, the practice and the theorizing of translation in Latin America are closely linked to issues of center–periphery and the relationship between world literatures, cultures, and languages. Translation in the periphery—"translation proper" as well as translation in a broader sense—is both problematic and full of potential, as it raises issues of influence, originality, and subjectivity. At stake for the periphery in the practice and the theorizing of translation is the foundation and renovation of national literary traditions and the related issues of identity and representation. As Frances Aparicio observes: "El acto de traducir se puede proponer en Hispanoamérica como metáfora de la búsqueda de una literatura nacional, mediante la cual los autores leen y transforman los textos extranjeros en sus propias creaciones literarias, bajo cada una de sus improntas singulares" [The act of translation, in Spanish America, can be posited as a metaphor for the search for a national literature, in which authors read and transform foreign texts into their own literary creations, according to each of their individual impressions] (27).[5]

With this in mind, we begin in this chapter with a discussion of the importance of translation in the history of Argentine literature. This will allow us to delineate the cultural context within which Borges develops his ideas on translation and Borges's role in shaping this context. We will then be able, in subsequent chapters, to situate Borges's position in relation to Argentine literature and to other literary and theoretical traditions.

The literature of Argentina's twentieth century, beginning with the avant-garde period of the 1920s and 1930s, has a definite polyglot nature, with an unusual combination of international/cosmopolitan and local/*criollo* tendencies.[6] These contradicting forces have coexisted in an uneasy—but at times very productive—tension through contemporary times. Argentina's most accomplished literature has often resulted from a cross between a process of intralingual translation of local culture and history, and a process of interlingual translation of European texts and styles.[7] The seeds of this irreverent combination can be traced to Argentina's nineteenth century, where translation and bilingualism were actively put to use in projects of nation foundation. Therefore, to understand the role of translation in Argentina's twentieth century, including its importance in Borges, we will take a brief look back at Argentina's nineteenth century. In particular, we will consider two moments of nation foundation: the Salón Literario of 1837 and Domingo F. Sarmiento's *Facundo: civilización y barbarie; vida de Juan Facundo Quiroga* (1845).[8] A reading of Sarmiento through Borges, facilitated by Ricardo Piglia, will suggest a way by which Argentina's entire nineteenth century can be reread through Borges's theories of translation.

In the second half of this chapter, then, we will focus on Argentina's avant-garde period and the cultural context in which Borges began his main literary production. Buenos Aires in the first half of the twentieth century was home to a vigorous, multilingual cultural life, rich in publishing opportunities, with some of the most vibrant avant-garde activities in the Americas. This vital cultural context also fed off of recent immigrants and numerous foreign visitors, as diverse as F. T. Marinetti, José Ortega y Gasset, Henri Michaux, and Witold Gombrowicz, among others. By analyzing some of the activities of the publications *Proa*, *Martín Fierro*, and *Sur*, where Borges was a major contributor, we will see the constitutive role of translation in debates on Argentine identity and subjectivity. The translation politics and practices of these and other periodicals, as well as the specific approaches of their writers/translators (including Borges's), demonstrate a variety of ways by which translation can function as a site of renovation in the margins.

The need for a new critical conception of translation in this book arises from the innovative practices and theorizing of translation by Argentine writers themselves, and especially by Borges. The need for a new critical conception of translation derives from a belief that there are by far more similarities than differences between "translation proper" and so-called "original" compositions. It arises from Borges's challenge to the notion of a "definitive text," and from his suggestion that a translation's merits often reside, paradoxically, in its creative infidelities instead of its fidelities. It arises from Borges's use of irreverence and displacement and from the fact that Borges develops his ideas in a specific cultural context, in Argentina, in a geopolitically peripheral nation. And, in turn, that this context itself, this margin—claimed and mined as a particularly productive position by Borges himself—is a key element in Borges's theories and uses of translation.

THE SEEDS OF MISTRANSLATION: A LOOK AT ARGENTINA'S NINETEENTH CENTURY

The seeds of the polyglot nature of Argentine literature are found in the nineteenth century, where translation and bilingualism function as protagonists in the founding of a national literary tradition. In Argentina, as in the rest of Spanish America, the political and economic break with Spain is accompanied by a search for cultural independence. As Borges states in "El escritor argentino y la tradición": "La historia argentina puede definirse sin equivocación como un querer apartarse de España, como un voluntario distanciamiento de España" [The history of Argentina can be defined unequivocally as a desire to separate from Spain, as a voluntary distancing from Spain] (OC I: 271). This leads to a look toward European literatures outside the Iberian Peninsula and immediately brings the act of translation to the forefront as an agent in the process of independence. Translation is thus linked, from the beginning, with cultural independence and with the related questions of the founding of a national tradition. In this sense, translation is also linked from the beginning with issues of identity and representation. As Mary Louise Pratt observes: "The end of Spanish colonial rule entailed a full-scale renegotiation of relations between Spanish America and Northern Europe—relations of politics and economics, and with equal necessity, relations of representation and imagination" (112).[9]

When the Salón Literario of 1837 formed to establish the basis for a national literature for Argentina, its members made clear that cultural independence from Spain was essential, as they turned their focus to French Romanticism and other Western European traditions.[10] In his address to the Salón Literario, Juan María Gutiérrez (1809–78), a founding member, states:

> Nula, pues, la ciencia y la literatura española, debemos nosotros divorciarnos completamente con ellas, emanciparnos a este respecto de las tradiciones peninsulares, como supimos hacerlo en política, cuando nos proclamamos libres. Quedamos aún ligados por el vínculo fuerte y estrecho del idioma; pero éste debe aflojarse de día en día, a medida que vayamos entrando en el movimiento intelectual de los pueblos adelantados de Europa. Para esto es necesario que nos familiaricemos con los idiomas extranjeros, y hagamos constante estudio de aclimatar al nuestro cuanto en aquéllos se produzca de bueno, interesante y bello. (*El tabaco que fumaba Plinio* 365)

> [Invalid, then, are Spanish science and literature, we must divorce ourselves entirely from them, we must emancipate ourselves in that respect from Peninsular traditions, as we were able to do in the matter of politics, when we proclaimed ourselves free. We remain tied still through the strong and tight bond of language; but it will loosen day by day, to the extent that we begin to join the intellectual movement of the advanced nations of Europe. To this end we must become familiar with foreign languages, and constantly study how to acclimate ours to what there is in them that produces good, interest, and beauty.]

The last remaining connection between the new South American nation and Spain is the Spanish language itself. Gutiérrez suggests that turning to other languages—becoming multilingual—is the way to finalize the freedom initiated with the Independence Movement.[11] Translation would thus function to import other traditions and permit Argentina to join "the intellectual movement of the advanced nations of Europe," as Gutiérrez puts it. By the same token, Gutiérrez states: "Y si hemos de tener una literatura, hagamos que sea *nacional*; que represente nuestras costumbres y nuestra naturaleza . . ." [And if we are to have a literature, let us make it a *national* one; so that it may represent our customs and our nature . . .] (*El tabaco que fumaba Plinio*, 365; emphasis in the original). Gutiérrez's message is loud and clear: if Argentina is to found a literature, it must look both abroad and within, it must translate the foreign as well as its own customs and traditions.[12]

This dual vision, initiated by the Salón Literario of 1837, reaches a zenith with the work of Domingo F. Sarmiento (1811–88). In his autobiographical texts—beginning with *Mi defensa* (1843) and throughout *Recuerdos de Provincia* (1850)—Sarmiento presents reading and translation as complementary activities in a process of adapting—of transforming—the foreign for his South American context. Sarmiento often speaks of reading, in fact, as a form of translation, in this sense of adapting the European for his South American stage, as he is "buscando la aplicación de aquellos resultados adquiridos a la vida actual, traduciendo el espíritu europeo al espíritu americano, con los cambios que el diverso teatro requería" [searching for the application to everyday life of those acquired results, translating the European spirit into the American spirit, with the changes that the difference in setting required] (*Recuerdos*, 181; Molloy's *At Face Value*, 26).[13]

A key point here is that for Sarmiento and for the other members of the Generation of 1837, translation was not only a way to access foreign (mostly French) texts and ideas, it actually served to actively fertilize—and ultimately create—Argentine culture, by encouraging the mix of the foreign with the local. As Carlos Altamirano and Beatriz Sarlo have said:

> Sarmiento defended not just the legitimacy but the necessity of polyglotism and, concurrently, the right to contaminate American Spanish. . . . The Generation of 1837 claimed (and on this point Sarmiento adopted the same perspective), for the first time in the history of Argentine culture, the right to contaminate peninsular Spanish in order to make it Argentine through the use of other European languages. ("The Autodidact and the Learning Machine," 161)

On the one hand, this position explains the Gallicisms found throughout much of the writings of Argentina's nineteenth century. On the other, this approach lays the groundwork and provides the initial model of what would become the multiple polyglot crosses and combinations of Argentina's twentieth century.

Significantly, Borges is arguably the first twentieth-century

writer to consider the nineteenth century in these terms, as he looks
there for the origins of Argentine literary irreverence, especially in
the work of Sarmiento. In his 1944 "Prólogo" to *Recuerdos de provincia*, for example, Borges clearly identifies Sarmiento's place in
Argentina's nineteenth century:

> Ningún espectador tiene la clarividencia de Sarmiento. . . . Sabe que
> nuestro patrimonio no debe reducirse a los haberes del indio, del gaucho
> y del español; que podemos aspirar a la plenitud de la cultura occidental,
> sin exclusión alguna. . . . En un incompatible mundo heteróclito de pro-
> vincianos, de orientales, y de porteños, Sarmiento es el primer argen-
> tino, el hombre sin limitaciones locales. (*OC* IV: 123)

> [No other observer has the perspicacity of Sarmiento. . . . He knows that
> our patrimony must not be reduced to the fortunes of the Indian, the
> gaucho and the Spaniard; that we can aspire to the plentitude of Occi-
> dental culture, without any exclusions. . . . In an incompatible, heteroge-
> neous world of provincials, of Orientals [i.e., Uruguayans], and of
> *porteños*, Sarmiento is the first Argentine, the man without local limita-
> tions.]

Anticipating an argument he would later develop in "El escritor argentino y la tradición," Borges suggests that Sarmiento is the "the
first [or foremost] Argentine" precisely because he does not feel
restricted to local topics. Sarmiento does not avoid the gaucho, of
course, since his *Facundo* is the story of the most (in)famous of
gauchos; rather, Sarmiento does not limit himself to the local. Sarmiento—like Borges, we might say—is not afraid to write about
any topic in Western culture, and this very fact is what most makes
him an Argentine. The implication is that from its very beginnings
Argentine literature emerges and thrives in the tension between the
foreign and the local, between the interlingual translation of European literatures and languages and the intralingual translation of
local *criollo* traditions.

Such points of contact between Borges and Sarmiento suggest a
way to reread Argentina's nineteenth century through translation
theory.[14] Ricardo Piglia illustrates what such an analysis might look
like in his essay "Sarmiento the Writer." The crux of Piglia's text
lies in his insights into the first page of Sarmiento's *Facundo*,
which begins with the epigraph: "On ne tue point les idées." The
phrase comes from a sentence by Diderot. Sarmiento misquotes it,
mistranslates it, and attributes it to another thinker altogether, For-

toul.[15] Is it possible for one of the most intelligent and prolific intellectuals of Argentina's nineteenth century, Piglia asks, to commit such an error accidentally? The answer must be no. Instead, Sarmiento's misquotation, according to Piglia, opens up "a line of equivocal references, false quotations, and apocryphal erudition which is a sign of Argentine culture at least up to the time of Borges" (132). And this line of mistranslation, we can add, does not end with Borges at all, but extends all the way to contemporary Argentine literature, including Piglia himself.[16]

When Sarmiento rewrites the French phrase of the epilogue of the *Facundo* as "A los hombres se degüella; a las ideas no" [Men are beheaded; ideas are not], he enacts an important geographic and linguistic recontextualization. By introducing the concept of beheading, an image not in the original, Sarmiento takes the idea from the French (with irreverence) and rewrites it (displaces, mistranslates it) in a context that now alludes to Rosas's *mazorca*—without losing the "original" meaning about the strength and perseverance of ideas during times of tyranny.[17] The confusion that Sarmiento's act produces in Rosas's government is the very difference between languages and cultures that translation and displacement always foreground. But whereas it causes fear and anxiety for the "barbarians," as Sarmiento calls them, it creates a field of opportunity within which Sarmiento, and his peers from the Generation of 1837, can proceed to write the foundations of Argentine literature.[18]

Sarmiento later explains what is needed to found a national literature, in chapter 2 of part 1 of the *Facundo*:

> Si un destello de literatura nacional puede brillar momentáneamente en las nuevas sociedades americanas, es el que resultará de la descripción de las grandiosas escenas naturales, y sobre todo de la lucha entre la civilización europea y la barbarie indígena. . . . (21)

> [If a flash of national literature might glow for a moment in the new American societies, it is that which will result from the description of the grand, natural landscapes, and above all from the battle between European civilization and indigenous barbarism. . . .]

In this metatextual allusion, Sarmiento all but asserts that the *Facundo* itself can serve as Argentina's foundational text. Furthermore, the battle between the "European civilization" and the "indigenous barbarism" to which Sarmiento refers here and throughout the *Facundo* is analogous to the cross between intralingual translation (of local traditions and dictions) and interlingual translation (of foreign traditions, rewritten and recontextualized) that would become a trait of Argentine literature in both the nineteenth and the twentieth centuries.

In this sense, what Sarmiento does with the opening epigraph is a microcosm of what he does throughout the *Facundo* and a central part of his entire cultural project: he takes what he needs from French literature and political philosophy with irreverence and places it in a dialectical relationship with local Argentine culture—from an Argentine point of view—to establish a new South American subjectivity. This displaces the center as a way to legitimize the literature of the periphery. Sarmiento appropriates the foreign and Americanizes it (i.e., *lo acriolla*), thus setting the stage for the foundation of Argentine literature.[19] Herein, then, lie the seeds of the avant-garde crosses—of the irreverence and displacement—of the 1920s and 1930s and of Borges's theories of (mis)translation.

Babel on the Shores of the Río de la Plata: The 1920s and 1930s

Borges lived in a multilingual environment and was exposed to European as well as Argentine cultures practically from birth. Borges grew up bilingual, speaking and reading English as well as Spanish at home as a child, and he had access to his father's library, which was well stocked with books in several European languages and from different literary traditions. But this did not preclude Borges from also being fully immersed in Argentine literature and history. Very different, local writers such as Evaristo Carriego and Macedonio Fernández, for example, were both friends of his father's, and Carriego was a regular visitor at the house during Borges's childhood.[20] The foreign and the local coexisted in Borges's background—his mother's side of the family included several heroes from Argentina's wars of independence and the civil wars; his paternal grandmother was English—and Borges seemed to realize from the beginning that there was no need to choose between one or the other. Or perhaps that it was even truer to the Argentine spirit to incorporate the foreign in representations of the local.

Borges spent an influential part of his adolescence with his family in Europe, as the Borgeses lived in Switzerland from 1914 to

1919 and in Spain from 1919 to 1921 and in 1923. While in Europe, Borges learned French, German, and Latin, read widely, did several translations, wrote some of his earliest poems and essays, met a number of Spain's leading writers and thinkers, and participated in major literary salons in Seville and Madrid, where he was an important contributor to Spain's avant-garde Ultraismo movement.[21] When Borges returned with his family to Buenos Aires for good in 1923, he rediscovered his native city and found a perfect milieu to continue exploring his already broad literary interests.

The 1920s and 1930s, when Borges came of age as a writer in Argentina, were an era in which translation and the relationship of the Argentine tradition to foreign literatures were a major part of the cultural context of the nation, and especially of the capital, Buenos Aires. The desire to join the modern world in the economic and technological arenas was echoed by a renewed drive to modernize culturally and to import the most "advanced" literary and artistic developments, namely from Europe. Simultaneously, there was an accompanying move to recover national traditions, the historical and cultural traits that had defined the "Argentine" in the nineteenth century and through the celebrations of the Centenary of 1910. In this manner, the place of the new as well as the old was thoroughly questioned, debated, and reevaluated.

Borges actively participated and quickly became a major contributor to this literary world. His contributions to the cultural milieu of the 1920s and 1930s include the appropriation of European avant-garde ideas and their inclusion in the development of Argentine Ultraismo, his activities as a translator from a very young age, his work as an editor in avant-garde journals, and the production of his own texts, including poetry, essays, reviews, prologues, and, beginning in the mid-1930s, short stories. Borges's interests, experiences, and skills made him especially well suited to explore, along with his contemporaries, both national and international literary traditions and, more important, the combination of these from an Argentine perspective. He led his generation in renovating Argentina's literature by effecting a series of dialogic crosses between local/*criollo* and cosmopolitan/international tendencies and by demonstrating that such intersections have always been at the core of Argentine literature. In the 1920s and 30s, the local and the European—intralingual and interlingual translation—coexisted in a tension that was experienced as deeply problematic, but also produced extremely important cultural innovations.

As we have seen, Argentina's nineteenth century featured a strong tradition of bilingualism, dating back at least to the Salón Literario of 1837 and Sarmiento. But after the waves of immigration at the turn of the century, Argentine writers in the twentieth century experienced a cultural transition, as they repeatedly found themselves in a multilingual society. Although French remained the second language of preference for the educated elite for many years, by the 1920s one could hear in the streets of Buenos Aires Spanish spoken with Italian, Yiddish, Galician, German, English, or Arabic accents, among others.[22] Faced with the challenges and confusion of a modern, South American Babel, writers sought some manner of synthesis—a figurative, unifying Tower—in the projects of literary magazines and in their own work. Or, when such synthesis was not possible, they sought a way to transform tension into potential, to transform the margin into a new, modern center, but always into a distinctively *Argentine* modern center.

In *Una modernidad periférica*, Beatriz Sarlo describes Buenos Aires's avant-garde period as a site of a Latin American "culture of mixture." Sarlo speaks of a series of crosses—between *criollismo* and *vanguardia*, between local and cosmopolitan intentions, between traditional Argentine and imported European literatures—that create the cultural context of the avant-garde.[23] And Sarlo mentions the importance of translation in the literature of the time: "Podría decirse, sin exagerar, que en los años veinte y treinta los escritores argentinos eligen de todas partes, traducen y el que no puede traducir lee traducciones, las difunde, publica o propagandiza" [One could say, without exaggerating, that in the 1920s and 1930s Argentine writers select from everywhere, that they translate and if they cannot translate they read translations, they disseminate, publish or publicize them] (43). Sarlo's assertion is accurate, but I believe that we need to go even further in our estimation of the role of translation in Argentina's avant-garde and in Argentina's literature in general. To this end, I propose that we rethink the literary production of Argentina's 1920s and 1930s in terms of a dialogic cross between processes of intralingual and interlingual writing as translation.

Thinking of Buenos Aires's "culture of mixture" in these terms underscores the extent to which translation drove the innovations of the avant-garde. Furthermore, it suggests an approach by which the place of translation in the entirety of Argentine literature can be studied, an approach that helps account for the linguistic, cultural, and political tensions that abound in Argentine literature in particular and in Latin American literature in general. By rephrasing the tensions and intersections of the 1920s and 1930s in terms of a dialectical relationship between intralingual and interlingual translation, we can better understand the cultural context of Borges's literary discourse. We can thus delve deeper into a number of issues that are intimately linked with translation in the margins—issues of influence and originality, of identity and representation—and study how these play out in the development of Argentine literature.

INTRALINGUAL AND INTERLINGUAL TRANSLATION
IN ARGENTINE JOURNALS

The importance of translation in Argentine literature is well demarcated in the history of its cultural journals and magazines. During the avant-garde period, translation of European letters and ideas played a major role in nearly every single publication, regardless of its ideological or aesthetic position. Such a practice was not entirely new. Nineteenth-century periodicals often included a traditional "European letters" section that was primarily informational in nature: what had been published, by whom, where, and so on. These sections extended into the early twentieth century, especially in the journal *Nosotros* and the cultural pages of the daily newspaper *La Nación*. The manner in which publications during the 1920s and 1930s approached foreign literature, however, completely changed the terms under which Argentine intellectuals dialogued with the European, as they began to incorporate the foreign into local polemics and to recontextualize fragments of other traditions to renovate their own.

One of the earliest examples of the cross between intralingual and interlingual translation is found in the small journal *Proa*. Not coincidentally, Borges was one of *Proa*'s leading editors during the journal's most important period, the two years (1924–26) of its second series. (The other editors were Brandan Caraffa, Ricardo Güiraldes, and Pablo Rojas Paz.) Based on the preferences of its editors, *Proa* undertook an unsystematic practice of translation, even as it published new, local writers, including the editors themselves.[24] In a sense, the lack of a clear system of what was translated—or rather a system based solely on the editors' interests—is part of *Proa*'s break with more traditional journals. By selectively taking from European sources, *Proa* demonstrated an irreverent attitude, as its editors displaced the translated/fragmented material to present it in a Río de la Plata context.

Proa expressed a new aesthetics that combined cosmopolitan, avant-garde sensibilities with traditional, *criollo* references, vocabulary, and syntax. As Beatriz Sarlo has said:

> Frente al perfil tradicional de . . . [la clásica sección 'letras europeas'], *Proa* practica cortes y organiza no un muestrario de lo publicado sino un sistema de lo nuevo; no difunde ni a todos los autores ni a todos los textos: *refuncionaliza la literatura europea en el contexto de la renovación rioplatense*. (*Una modernidad periférica*, 116; emphasis added).

> [Faced with the traditional profile of the . . . [classical section of 'European letters'], *Proa* practices ruptures; it organizes not a display of what has been published, but a system of the new; it disseminates neither every author nor every text: *it refunctionalizes European literature within the context of Río de la Plata renovation*.]

By publishing articles about some of the latest trends in European art and literature in translation side by side with the new Río de la Plata avant-garde, *Proa* becomes an early site of Argentine polyglossia.

This combination of intralingual and interlingual writing as translation is broader in scope and even more pronounced in the journal *Martín Fierro* (1924–27). The very name of the journal, in fact, captures the tension between the local and the foreign. Even as *Martín Fierro* published the new movements from Europe, it also looked back at traditional Argentine roots. Specifically, it sought to reclaim José Hernández's classic gauchesque poem from the patriotic readings it had received during the time of the Centenario. Hernández's *Martín Fierro* represents the epitome of the line of nineteenth-century Argentine literature that works with intralingual translation of local dialogue and traditions. By naming their journal after Hernández's poem, the new generation claim Hernández as their own, even as they suggest that the tradition of the gauchesque is only one facet of Argentine identity. The other was the modern, cosmopolitan literature the *martinfierristas* were now writing and publishing. This produces both a modernization of Hernández's *Martín Fierro* and an Argentinization (i.e., *un acriollamiento*) of modern international art and literature.

The magazine presented avant-garde movements from Europe,

but also from Argentina itself, and at times from other places in Latin America. On the pages of *Martín Fierro* we find, side by side, a reevaluation of local Argentine traditions, articles about and translations of European writers, other cultural material from Latin America, and poetry and articles by Argentine writers in a marked Río de la Plata diction. The polyglossia at the center of the *Martín Fierro* project defines a tension with which Argentine writers would negotiate throughout the twentieth century. And it is precisely this tension—negotiated through rereading, rewriting, and mistranslation—which has led to the production of some of the best, most innovative literature in the Río de la Plata region, including that of Borges himself.

Martín Fierro's contradictions and dualities are seen clearly in the magazine's famous "Manifiesto" (presented in the fourth issue, in 1924).[25] Written by Oliverio Girondo (1891–1967), one of Argentina's leading avant-garde poets, the text declares *Martín Fierro* to be the site and purveyor of the "new":

> "MARTIN FIERRO" siente la necesidad imprescindible de definirse y de llamar a cuantos sean capaces de percibir que nos hallamos en presencia de una NUEVA sensibilidad y de una NUEVA comprensión, que, al ponernos de acuerdo con nosotros mismos, nos descubre panoramas insospechados y nuevos medios y formas de expresión. (*Revista Martín Fierro*, 25)

> ["MARTIN FIERRO" feels the imperative need to define itself and to call to those capable of perceiving that we find ourselves before a NEW sensibility and a NEW comprehension, that, as we agree amongst ourselves, it opens for us unexpected views and new modes and forms of expression.]

But the editors and contributors of the magazine also firmly root themselves and the site of the "new" in their Río de la Plata context, especially with respect to their linguistic, cultural, and geographic identity:

> "MARTIN FIERRO" acepta las consecuencias y las responsabilidades de localizarse, porque sabe que de ello depende su salud. . . .

> "MARTIN FIERRO" tiene fe en nuestra fonética, en nuestra visión, en nuestros modales, en nuestro oído, en nuestra capacidad digestiva y de asimilación. (*Revista Martín Fierro*, 25)

["MARTIN FIERRO" accepts the consequences and the responsibilities of localizing, because it knows that its health depends on it. . . .

"MARTIN FIERRO" has faith in our phonetics, in our vision, in our modalities, in our ear, in our digestive and assimilative capacity.]

The Argentine perspective ("our vision, . . . our ear") and point of view ("our modalities"), the language of the Río de la Plata region ("our phonetics"), is utilized by *Martín Fierro* to appropriate ("our digestive and assimilative capacity"—i.e., the capacity to rewrite, to mistranslate) European trends. This then becomes a space of potential which Borges, among others, actively sows and harvests.

The development of this space involved issues of identity and representation, as the *martinfierristas* reconsidered what it meant to be "Argentine." The question is raised explicitly by *Martín Fierro* in their "Primera Encuesta" [First Poll] (1:4; May 15, 1924), in which the editors asked: "1. ¿Cree Ud. en la existencia de una sensibilidad, de una mentalidad argentina? 2. Si Ud. cree en la existencia de una sensibilidad, de una mentalidad argentina, ¿cuáles son sus características?" [1. Do you believe in the existence of an Argentine sensibility, of an Argentine mentality? 2. If you believe in the existence of an Argentine sensibility, of an Argentine mentality, what are its characteristics?] (*Revista Martín Fierro*, 28). The results are published in the next issue (1:5–6; May 15–June 15, 1924). The answer to the first question is a resounding yes: Argentine writers and intellectuals of the time definitely believe that there is such a thing as an "Argentine sensibility." The answer to the second question, regarding what constitutes the "Argentine sensibility," is much more diverse. In their responses, the participants often mention nineteenth- and early twentieth-century Argentine writers, making it clear that the current debate includes a rereading of Argentina's past. Several, including Ricardo Güiraldes and Pablo Rojaz Paz, emphasize that a defining characteristic of the "Argentine sensibility" is a power of assimilation—thus highlighting the acculturation of the foreign that contributed a key element to the *Martín Fierro* project.[26] In this issue, as in others throughout the journal's existence, the new and the old, the European and the local, are juxtaposed on the same pages. It is this very polyglossia, in actuality, which functions as the best answer to *Martín Fierro*'s inquiry about what constitutes the "Argentine sensibility."

Furthermore, *Proa* and *Martín Fierro* are not the only periodicals in which we see the importance of translation during this pivotal period in Argentine letters. The central place of translation is also witnessed in publications with completely different ideological and aesthetic positions. This is the case with the leftist *Claridad* project, which had a broader and more popular distribution than *Martín Fierro*.[27] Under the direction of Antonio Zamora, *Los Pensadores* and *Claridad* magazines, as well as the *Claridad* publishing house, heavily used translation to appropriate texts and ideas from Europe and the Soviet Union as part of its work to provide a leftist education to its readership.[28] The first one hundred issues of *Los Pensadores*, for example, were primarily translations of left-wing European writers and intellectuals, including Anatole France, Knut Hamsun, and Emile Zola (King, 25; Masiello's *Lenguaje e ideología*, 56).[29] In the cultural context of the 1920s and 1930s, as Argentines worked to redefine and renovate their literature, translation—the rewriting of the foreign in an Argentine context—abounded, regardless of political ideologies or aesthetic preferences, and became a key part of the cultural production of the period itself.

VICTORIA OCAMPO AND *SUR*'S CULTURAL IMPORTATION MACHINE

Taking advantage of the space established by the *martinfierristas*, *Sur* begins its reign as *the* cultural journal of Argentina in 1931, a position it holds until the late 1950s. As critics have noted, in more ways than one, translation lies at the core of the *Sur* project.[30] By displacing texts from the Metropolis to the margins, by appropriating them through translation, by recontextualizing them within a framework of the South—literally and figuratively—*Sur* demonstrates that a politics of cultural importation can contribute to (re-)creating a center in the circumference. *Sur* is also relevant in the context of our study because of its defining place in Argentine (and Latin American) letters through several decades of the twentieth century, and because Borges published numerous texts in *Sur*, including many of his best known stories and essays, as well as a number of fascinating, lesser known articles and translations.[31]

Modeled after journals such as the *Revista de Occidente*, *The Criterion*, and the *Nouvelle Revue Française*, *Sur* was founded and directed by Victoria Ocampo to establish a two-way dialogue of "high" culture that could function as a bridge between South America and Europe. The second part of this objective, the exportation of the best local talent to Europe succeeded only on a limited scale, through Victoria Ocampo's personal friendships and with the "discovery" of Borges in France in the early 1960s.[32] The first aspect of *Sur's* objective, on the other hand, was certainly realized, as the journal (and the press created to accompany it) consistently published poetry, fiction, and nonfiction in translation, thus helping to incorporate the European into the cultural context of the "South" throughout its considerable duration.

Also, although *Sur's* discourse did not reach Europe in a significant manner, a number of Latin American writers outside Argentina, including Octavio Paz, Gabriel García Márquez, Guillermo Cabrera Infante, Mario Vargas Llosa, and Carlos Fuentes, have acknowledged that they first read many European and U.S. writers in translation for the first time in *Sur* (King, 77, 144). The texts that *Sur* imported through translation could then be appropriated by Latin American writers through their individual styles and preferences. In addition, a certain acculturation occurred within the very pages of *Sur*, as Argentine and other Latin American writers were published together and on a par with their European and U.S. counterparts.

An important consideration in any critical reading of *Sur's* translations is the selection process of what was translated and by whom.[33] Most of *Sur's* editorial decisions depended on a few individuals, and Victoria Ocampo's preferences and personal relationships always played a major role in this process. Victoria Ocampo's tastes were idiosyncratic. She followed mostly the developments in French letters, and her preferences became more conservative with time. Still, despite attacks from some of Argentina's intellectuals, Victoria Ocampo's editorial decisions represent an unusual reading and displacement of European and U.S. traditions. This necessarily led to the presentation of a skewed image (i.e., a rewriting, a mistranslation) of foreign writers in a Río de la Plata context.

It is also worth noting the double role of legitimization that translation holds for Victoria Ocampo as a Latin American female intellectual. Victoria Ocampo even wrote some of her own texts in French—in part to escape the male-dominated scene that Spanish represented for her, in part to legitimize her efforts by appropriating the language of the center.[34] Victoria Ocampo's move toward French and translation frees her from the gender restrictions of the patriarchal structures of Argentina and from the expectations placed upon Latin American writers by center–periphery hierarchies. Victoria Ocampo always displayed more irreverence and impatience with Argentine, *criollo* traditions than with European ones, as she valued the European almost to a fault. But her project of cultural importation also created a substantial displacement of the foreign toward the margins, while the uses other writers and readers made of her efforts remained inevitably beyond her control.

Although Borges stayed on the periphery of its editorial decisions, *Sur* provided an important forum for Borges to publish articles and essays on a broad range of topics, as well as translations and fiction. Borges also undertook several translation projects for *Sur*'s press: *Un cuarto propio* (*A Room of One's Own*) and *Orlando, una biografía* (*Orlando, A Biography*) by Virginia Woolf (1936 and 1937), *Perséphone* by André Gide (1936), and *Un bárbaro en Asia* by Henri Michaux (1941). Borges's main role in *Sur*, in any case, is the presence of his texts in the pages of the journal. In this manner, writers and other intellectuals in Argentina and throughout Latin America soon found themselves exposed to and dialoguing with Borges's texts, including his theories of reading, writing, and translation. This important readership thus had access, through *Sur*, not only to key Argentine and Latin American writers, and to foreign writers in translation, but also to Borges—to his irreverent creativity and to the hugely important cultural and political implications that his writings represent for writers in the margins.

Foreign Visitors in a South American Babylonia

Another important influence on the context in which Borges developed his theories of translation is the many visitors who passed through Argentina during this time, and whose intellectual pursuits and literary endeavors included numerous translation projects and activities. The visitors came from throughout the world and interacted with local Argentines, including recent immigrants, thus contributing to the cultural mix of the country in the first half of the twentieth century. Two Latin American men of letters who spent a number of years in Buenos Aires and with whom Borges and other Argentines had considerable contact were Alfonso Reyes, who was the Mexican ambassador in Argentina beginning in 1927,[35] and the Dominican Pedro Herníquez Ureña. And both *Martín Fierro* and later *Sur* maintained a tradition of hosting foreign writers in Argentina, including, among others, F. T. Marinetti in 1926 (hosted by *Martín Fierro*), and numerous visits hosted by *Sur*, including the PEN Club meeting in Buenos Aires in 1936 (King, 64–68).

Buenos Aires was home to many Spanish exiles during that country's civil war, among them the poet Rafael Alberti and Guillermo de Torre, the critic and writer who founded the publishing house Losada and married Borges's sister Norah in 1928. A number of French writers were exiled in Buenos Aires during World War II, including André Malraux and Roger Callois. Henri Michaux visited Argentina on several occasions; in 1935 Borges met Michaux and soon thereafter translated *Un bárbaro en Asia* for *Sur*. About this project, Borges has remarked that he translated the book into Spanish "no como un deber sino como un juego" [not as a duty but as a game] (*OC* IV: 479). Translation as a game, as experimentation, as a process of discovery of self and other: Borges's comment applies to his own playful attitude toward translation and reflects Argentina's polyglot culture, particularly in Buenos Aires, during this period.

Also important was the intermittent presence of the Spanish philosopher José Ortega y Gasset, who was a major influence on Victoria Ocampo and the founding of *Sur*, but with whom Borges did not see eye to eye. The differences between Borges and Ortega extended to how the two thinkers viewed translation. Ortega first published his essay on the topic, "Miseria y esplendor de la traducción" [Misery and Splendor of Translation], in Argentina, in the newspaper *La Nación* (May–June 1937). Ortega's position in this text is radically different from Borges's theories of translation. In "Miseria y esplendor de la traducción," Ortega strongly privileges the original, as he argues that translations should be literal, as close to the original as possible, "ugly," and be accompanied by many footnotes.[36] Borges, as we will study in depth in the following chapters, believes in the creative potential of translation, in an irreverent displacement away from the center necessary for the production of new texts in the periphery.

Perhaps the most interesting contribution by a visitor to twentieth-century Argentine culture is that of the Polish modernist Witold Gombrowicz (1904–69), who lived in exile in Argentina from 1939 to 1963.[37] While in Buenos Aires, in a highly unusual process that has become legendary in Argentine literary history, Gombrowicz had a group of writers who did not know Polish translate his novel

Ferdydurke into Spanish in 1946. The group was led by another visitor, the Cuban writer Virgilio Piñera; they worked at times through French and with Gombrowicz's broken Spanish. This story presents us with an incredible scene of confusion and creation, of adaptation and transformation, which can be seen as emblematic of the innovative role of translation in the literatures of the periphery.

In a brief text entitled "Un cadáver exquisito" [An Exquisite Corpse], Gombrowicz describes the city of Buenos Aires, in which he lived for so many years, and the multitudes among which he was lost as a virtual unknown. Underneath the sardonic tone with which he treats his poverty of the time lies an image of what must have been a veritable Babel of languages and cultures:

> Jamás he sido tan poeta como en esa época, por las calles desbordantes de gente, completamente perdido (perdido en la multitud y perdido también en lo que a mi suerte se refería). Enjambre, hormiguero, multitudes, luces, estrépito ensordecedor, olores, y mi pobreza era un goce; mi caída, un levantar vuelo. Me dejé arrastrar sin vacilaciones, sin problemas, a aquella *confusión de lenguas diversas*, y llegué a ser uno de ellos. (*La Buenos Aires ajena*, 263; emphasis added)

> [I was never more of a poet than during that time, in the streets overflowing with people, completely lost (lost in the multitude and lost also in what pertained to my luck). Crowds, swarms, multitudes, lights, deafening clamor, smells, and my poverty was a delight; my fall, a taking of flight. I allowed myself to be dragged along without hesitation, without problems, through that *confusion of diverse tongues*, until I became one of them.]

Gombrowicz portrays a city with a capacity to absorb visitors, exiles, and immigrants in its "confusion of diverse tongues" until the individuals became part of Babel itself. That is, until they became Argentine, until they became a constitutive part of the mix that is Argentine culture and literature.

CONCLUSION: TRANSLATION IN CONTEXT

In the chapters that follow, as we undertake a full analysis of Borges's theories of translation—as we study the importance of translation in Borges *and* Borges's contributions to the theorizing of translation—we must keep in mind the cultural and sociohistorical context in which these theories were developed. If we do not, we risk losing some of the most relevant implications of Borges's work. In fact, I believe we should never forget the context in which translation theories are articulated, just as we should never forget the context in which any literary text is produced. In his case, what Borges brings to translation theory is, as much as anything else, a shift in context—an irreverent displacement toward a Latin American margin. If we take Borges out of his Argentine context and perspective, a context and perspective that he worked hard to shape and expand, we would be erasing key elements of his contributions.

As we will see, Borges consistently challenges preconceived cultural political notions by positing that the margins are not necessarily limiting for writers, just as translations are not necessarily inferior to originals—and that, in both cases, quite the contrary can be true. The very act of writing in the margins reiterates a difference between center and periphery. Such difference does not cause anxiety in Borges; instead, it suggests a field of potentiality. Translation affords writers in the margins with the possibility of rereading, rewriting, and recontextualizing originals from the center. In other words, it allows them to make use of displacements, to take with irreverence, to (re)create texts with new meanings in new contexts—which is to say in their own Latin American contexts—and to do so, paradoxically, without necessarily losing the "original" meanings of the source texts. Displacement and irreverence: key factors in Borges's conception of the potential of literature, key factors in Borges's theorizing of translation. Keeping Argentina's specific cultural context in mind, then, we turn now to Borges's challenges and contributions to our understanding of both literature and the theorizing of translation. Or, better yet, to Borges's challenges and contributions to our understanding of literature through the theorizing of translation.

2

Borges on Translation:
The Development of a Theory

INTRODUCTION

DESPITE A SIGNIFICANT EXPANSION IN CRITICAL WRITINGS ABOUT translation in recent years, anthologies that bring together essays on the topic have tended to exclude Borges's texts, and analysis of Borges's contributions to translation studies remains surprisingly limited.[1] Likewise, even with the existence of a handful of useful articles and one recent book, the importance of translation for Borges has not been sufficiently studied to date by Borges scholars.[2] Part of this can be explained by the difficulty involved in interpreting Borges's ideas on translation, since their analysis, and in turn their incorporation into translation theory, is far from an obvious task. Complicating the matter, Borges himself never explicitly states a theory of translation, just as he never explicitly articulates a theory either of reading or of writing; his comments are typically elliptical, complex, and often purposefully paradoxical or even contradictory, techniques that disarm the reader as they challenge our suppositions about translation and originality. In addition, Borges has even said, in at least one interview, that he does not believe in, and that he does not hold, a theory of translation.[3] But what Borges objected to was limiting himself to any specific overarching methodology of translation, any program that insists that the translator follow a particular approach (such as a literal or a paraphrase approach). In fact, as we will see, Borges consistently values diverse, even opposing translation methodologies. Furthermore, Borges's essays on translation, and his use of translation in the creation of his own works, is evidence that Borges does indeed have a theory of translation—not only in relation to the practice and valorization

41

of the craft, but also in the much broader sense of the theoretical, literary, cultural, and philosophical potentiality of translation.

The first step toward understanding Borges's theory of translation is to deduce, or to extrapolate, such a theory from Borges's main writings on the topic. It is also crucial to place Borges's ideas on translation within the context of twentieth-century translation theory—all the while keeping in mind the specific cultural context from where Borges's literary production arises. To these ends, this chapter traces the development of Borges's theories of translation through a contextualized and comparative reading of his main essays on the topic: "Las dos maneras de traducir" (1926), "Las versiones homéricas" (1932), and "Los traductores de *Las 1001 Noches*" (1935). Such a reading will allow us to delve into the unexplored intersections between Borges scholarship and translation studies, for it is here—when we simultaneously consider the importance of translation in Borges *and* the contribution of Borges's ideas to translation theory—that we find the most surprising and useful insights, whether one is interested in Borges, in Argentine and Latin American literature, in issues related to translation and transnational relationships, or in any combination thereof.

Borges's writings on translation contain challenges to many of the basic tenets of translation theory, as they present a complete reformulation of how the relationship between source and target texts and cultures is usually understood. In particular, most theories of translation strongly privilege the original over the translation, assuming that translation is always accompanied by loss and that there are always limits to what is translatable. This privileging of the original is commonly expressed through an impossible demand for fidelity to the source text, a demand that inevitably sets the translation up for failure. It is precisely these kinds of suppositions that Borges consistently questions and defies.

Fidelity, as critics have observed, is the basic underlying question in just about every theory of translation and remains a major issue in translation studies today. As George Steiner states:

> It can be argued that all theories of translation—formal, pragmatic, chronological—are only variants of a single, inescapable question. In what ways can or ought fidelity to be achieved? What is the optimal correlation between the A text in the source-language and the B text in the receptor-language? The issue has been debated for over two thousand years. (275)

Through an inversion that forces us to reconsider the very concepts of fidelity and originality, Borges shifts the emphasis to the translation, as he suggests that there are no "definitive texts," only drafts and versions. This magnifies the potential of translation—an idea especially relevant given that Borges challenges the concept of a "definitive text" from a South American margin, thus problematizing the center–periphery dichotomy.

The twentieth century has seen significant variations in how translation is theorized, particularly with respect to concepts of fidelity and the relationship between source and target texts and languages. The major break with traditional translation theory occurs with Walter Benjamin's 1923 seminal essay "The Task of the Translator." Benjamin's text is crucial not only for the new approach it brings to translation theory—as he demonstrates that a theory of translation is a theory of language—but also for the influence it has on a number of thinkers in the last twenty-five years: most famously on Jacques Derrida and Paul de Man, and subsequently on Lawrence Venuti, Joseph Graham, Barbara Johnson, Philip E. Lewis, and Gayatri Spivak, among others.[4]

In "The Task of the Translator," Benjamin uses translation to develop a theory about the relationship between languages and the way that meaning is constituted within language. For Benjamin, translation reveals that originals are not isolated and self-sufficient; rather, that there is much instability in how they convey meaning. Translation thus complements the original, revealing its foreignness, but also seeking to resolve it. In the process, translation reveals a glimpse of a "pure language" which lies behind all languages. This idealization is a utopic, Adamic concept: it imagines translation as a way to restore what is missing in the original, and as a way to repair the disaster at Babel.

Despite the new ground that Benjamin opens, especially through the readings provided by Derrida and de Man, the nearly sacred place of the original is never completely dislodged. Borges, on the other hand, irreverently challenges the place of the original, suggesting a theory of mistranslation, an aesthetics of theft and infidelity. These ideas, placed in textual dialogue with Benjamin and Derrida, have important literary and philosophical implications. In addition, when Borges's theories are compared with the branch of contemporary translation studies that focuses on cultural-political issues,[5] they reveal how translation—how mistranslation—can be a powerful site of innovation and resistance for the periphery.

As we analyze Borges's essays on translation, we must also keep in mind that, when he wrote them, Borges was an active translator of fiction and poetry from English, French, and German.[6] In fact, it is safe to say that Borges was involved in the practice of translation throughout his life: from his translation of the last page of James Joyce's *Ulysses* in 1925, to his translations of G. K. Chesterton, Edgar Allan Poe, Herman Melville, Francis Ponge, Virginia Woolf, Franz Kafka, and William Faulkner in the 1930s to 1940s, to his work with Anglo-Saxon in the late 1950s and 1960s, to his version of Walt Whitman's *Leaves of Grass* in 1969. To see some of the ways that Borges puts his theories of (mis)translation into practice in his own translations, we will briefly consider, toward the end of this chapter, Borges's translations of the American Modernist poet e. e. cummings (a partial one from 1937, another from 1944).[7]

The development of Borges's theories on translation are so interwoven with the development of his fiction, that the processes of translation, reading, and writing in Borges become nearly interchangeable. Borges does not consider Babel to represent a loss. Multiplicity and difference is *not* a disaster for Borges, but a field of potentiality. In "Las dos maneras de traducir," "Las versiones homéricas," and "Los traductores de *Las 1001 Noches*," we find the idea that literature is always translatable—and, even more striking, that literature *is* translation.

"LAS DOS MANERAS DE TRADUCIR": TESTING THE LIMITS OF TRANSLATION

From his very first words on the topic, Borges suggests that there is no reason to believe that a translation is necessarily inferior to the original—an idea to which he will return time and again, and which constitutes a central element of his theories of translation. The 1926 essay "Las dos maneras de traducir" (first published in *La Prensa*, later collected posthumously in *Textos Recobrados*) opens with the following statement:

> Suele presuponerse que cualquier texto original es incorregible de puro bueno, y que los traductores son unos chapuceros irreparables, padres del frangollo y de la mentira. Se les infiere la sentencia italiana de *traduttore traditore* y ese chiste basta para condenarlos. (*TR*, 256)

[It is often presupposed that any original text is so purely good that it is not correctable, and that translators are an irreparable bunch of bunglers, fathers of cattle feed and lies. They are indicted with the Italian sentence *traduttore traditore* and that joke is enough to condemn them.]

As opposed to those who hold such presuppositions, Borges presents his own thoughts on the potential of translation: "En cuanto a mí, creo en las buenas traducciones de obras literarias (de las didácticas o especulativas, ni hablemos) y opino que hasta los versos son traducibles" [As far as I am concerned, I believe in good translations of literary works (let us not even speak of didactic or speculative ones), and it is my opinion that even verses are translatable] (*TR*, 256). This statement, along with the rest of the article, sets the defiant tone of Borges's stance on translation. In future texts, such defiance will become a point of departure for Borges's questioning of the original—not only in "translation proper," but in literature in general.

Although full of humorous touches, this oft-ignored article deals with serious issues in translation, aesthetics, and cultural context. The language of the text, full of *porteño* localisms, coincides with Borges's writings of the time, especially his verbal experiments in *El tamaño de mi esperanza*, published that same year.[8] The attention Borges pays to etymology is an interest that would accompany him throughout his life, and is also related to his own production of poetry at the time (his second book of poetry, *Luna de enfrente*, appeared the year before; his third, *Cuaderno San Martín*, would come out three years later, in 1929).

The focus of "Las dos maneras de traducir" is on the translatability of poetry. As an example of his belief that poetry can be successfully translated, Borges discusses the Venezuelan Pérez Bonalde's version of "El cuervo" ("The Raven") by Edgar Allan Poe. Borges acknowledges the possible objection that this translation will never be to Argentines what the original in English is to U.S. readers. But Borges provides an ingenious response to this kind of traditional critique of translation. He states that the same could be said of how a Chilean might read Evaristo Carriego (the minor Argentine poet about whom Borges would write a pseudobiography in 1930), in contrast to how Borges reads him as a fellow *porteño*—although both would be reading him in Spanish. Borges thus indicates an important aspect of all texts, originals and translations alike: that they have different values for different readers, even if the readers speak the same language. For a non-Argentine, Spanish-speaking reader of Carriego, "[para] un forastero . . . su caudal representativo será menor" [for a foreigner . . . its representative wealth will be less] (*TR*, 256).

This point alludes to the temporal and spatial displacements that exist between the time and place a text is written, and when and where it is read. By focusing on shifts in meaning that occur as a text is displaced through time (diachronically) and space (synchronically, geographically), Borges is beginning to develop a fluid conception of texts with relation to their contexts and readers. Borges is already aware that translation always involves such temporal and spatial displacements with respect to the original, just as the original does with respect to the time and place of its original production, and that this makes translation an ideal metaphor for writing, as well as a perfect point of departure to consider issues of aesthetic value and cultural difference.

This line of thought leads Borges to a discussion of how the meaning and interpretation of words change, even within the same language, from country to country, from one individual reader to another, and from generation to generation (*TR*, 256–57). Borges provides a series of examples, all in Spanish, to show that *how* texts are read and understood varies with time, place, and, most important, reader. Borges thus emphasizes the importance of the reader and the context of a text (the context in which a text is read, when, and by whom) in determining that text's meaning. By using Argentine examples, including the aforementioned implied parallel between Evaristo Carriego and Edgar Allan Poe, Borges also provides a specific South American context to his discussion.

Next, Borges describes the two possible ways of translating, referred to in the title of the article: "Una practica la literalidad, la otra la perífrasis. La primera corresponde a las mentabilidades románticas, la segunda a las clásicas" [One practices literalness, the other paraphrase. The former corresponds to Romantic, and the latter to Classical, mentalities] (*TR*, 257–58). Borges associates the practice of paraphrase with Classicism because, as he explains, Classicists are interested in the work of art, and not in the artist. According to Borges, they seek absolute perfection in translation at the cost of all "los localismos, las rarezas, las contingencias" [localisms, rarities, contingencias], and are thus willing to leave behind what is associated with the artist: the specific elements of the poetic voice, his words, syntax, and metaphors, even.

Romantics, on the other hand, are interested in the artist, they revere the poetic subject, at the cost of the work of art: "Esa reverencia del yo, de la irremplazable diferenciación humana que es cualquier yo, justifica la literalidad en las traducciones" [That reverence of the I, of the irreplaceable human differentiation that exists in any I, justifies the literalness of the translations] (*TR*, 258). In this formulation, every one of the artist's words is essential for the Romantic and must be translated literally, even at the cost of the overall work. Although he criticizes its search for perfection in art, Borges's tone reveals a strong preference for Classicism and a clear condemnation of Romanticism. In the course of the argument, Borges distances himself as much as possible from Romanticism's idealization of the poet and his every word by arguing that a literal translation can never, regardless of its claims, be faithful to the original.[9]

The two opposing methods to which Borges refers—metaphrase and paraphrase—are the ones that have been postulated in nearly every treatise on translation dating as far back as Cicero and Horace.[10] With variations, translation treatises have always debated how translations should be faithful to the original by following one or the other of these approaches. Although he does not delineate its history in "Las dos maneras de traducir," the Classicist stance on translation to which Borges refers derives from the relationship writers and scholars had with antiquity during the Renaissance, as they held that translation was desirable and that the reworking of the "spirit" of the classics was the best way to renovate their own culture and infuse it with the grandeurs of Greco-Roman times. In the words of John Dryden, who, in his Preface to *Ovid's Epistles* (1680), coined the terms "metaphrase" and "paraphrase" now used for the two opposing approaches, this would indicate a preference for paraphrase, for "translation with latitude," in which "sense" is more important than specific wording (Dryden, 17).

The preference for literalness, on the other hand, can be traced in modern times to the 1813 essay "On Different Methods of Translating" by Friedrich Schleiermacher (1768–1834). Schleiermacher articulated the metaphrase–paraphrase dichotomy in slightly different terms, referring to the distance between the reader and the target and source texts. He argued that a translator can either bring the target text closer to the reader, or bring the reader closer to the source text. The former would be equivalent to a paraphrase (or a domesticating translation), whereas the latter equates to a metaphrase (or a foreignizing translation).[11] The argument in favor of literalness, which derives from a strong privileging of the original, extends all the way to today, and can be found in broadly different thinkers and writers.[12]

Borges disagrees with arguments in favor of literalness, stating that claims of "traslaciones literarias de obras antiguas" [literary transpositions of ancient works] never go further than the prologue: "El anunciado propósito de veracidad hace del traductor un falsario, pues éste, para mantener la extrañez de lo que traduce se ve obligado a espesar el color local, a encrudecer las crudezas, a empalagar con las dulzuras y a enfatizarlo todo hasta la mentira" [The announced objective of veracity makes the translator a liar, for, in order to maintain the oddity of what he is translating, he finds himself forced to thicken the local color, to make what is crude even more so, to make the sweet more sickly, and to emphasize everything to the point of lying] (*TR*, 258). According to Borges, literal translations belie their own objectives. In this first essay on translation, Borges considers the two poles of this dichotomy (metaphrase v. paraphrase, letter v. spirit), and leans as far away from the literal as possible.

In the process, Borges not only challenges the premise that translation is always accompanied by loss, he also questions the idea that translation is not truly possible because there are too many essential differences between languages for translation to succeed. The greater the complexity of the original, the argument goes, the closer the tie between matter and form, between letter and spirit, and the greater the loss in translation. The epitome of this premise lies with poetry. As George Steiner observes: "Traditionally, the weight of the argument bears on poetry. Here the welding of matter and form is so close that no dissociation is admissible" (253). Arguments following this line of thought have been made repeatedly by thinkers through time, from St. Jerome to Dante, Du Bellay, Diderot, Dr. Johnson, Rilke, Nabokov, and Robert Frost (Steiner 253–54).

In the twentieth century, the theoretical justification for the belief that poetry cannot be translated is perhaps best articulated by Roman Jakobson. Although Jakobson allows that didactic or speculative translations are possible, he states that "poetry by definition is untranslatable." Jakobson's argument is that poetry is governed by "paronomasia": the relationship between phonemic and semantic units (e.g., puns and other plays on words) (Jakobson 150–51). Because translation of poetry necessitates a disassociation of the link between the phonemic and the semantic, Jakobson argues, it is accompanied by a loss of either content or form, and of the connections between them.

But is there really such a clear distinction between the difficulties associated with the translation of poetry and that of other forms? If so, where and how should such boundaries be drawn? Is not most prose also heavily dependent on the close association between matter and form, between *what* a text says and *how* it says it? Careful consideration, in fact, suggests that poetry is an extreme example of the broader question of whether translation is possible at all. As Steiner argues: "Attacks on the translation of poetry are simply the barbed edge of the general assertion that no language can be translated without fundamental loss. Formally and substantively the same points can be urged in regard to prose" (255).

Borges's defiant notion in "Las dos maneras de traducir" that translations are not necessarily inferior to the original sets the stage for a position that will turn just about every premise of traditional translation theory on its head. And the fact that Borges speaks of the translatability of poetry already suggests a formulation in which translation can be seen as a potential site of gain, and not necessarily one of loss. For if poetry is the litmus test of translatability, and Borges finds poetry translatable, then there is no inherent failure associated with translation, on the contrary. The full implications of these ideas become evident in Borges's two main essays on translation—"Las versiones homéricas" and "Los traductores de *Las 1001 Noches*"—to which we now turn.

"LAS VERSIONES HOMÉRICAS": THE FALLACY OF THE "DEFINITIVE TEXT"

"Las versiones homéricas" (first published in *La Prensa* on May 8, 1932, then included in *Discusión* that same year) begins with the memorable assertion that: "Ningún problema tan consustancial con las letras y con su modesto misterio como el que propone una traducción" [There is no problem as consubstantial to literature and its modest mysteries as that posed by a translation]. As opposed to "escrituras directas" [direct writings], Borges adds, "la traducción parece . . . destinada a ilustrar la discusión estética" [translation seems . . . destined to illustrate aesthetic discussions] (*OC* I: 239). In other words, to talk about translation is to talk about aesthetics, and there is perhaps no better point of entry into literature and "its modest mysteries" than the study of translation.

As a number of critics have observed, when Borges reads, he writes. Borges's writings are made up of a series of readings, of a web of intertextualities, of "textual rubrics," as Sylvia Molloy has called them.[13] In this sense, when Borges talks about literature, he is talking about his own literary production; or, better yet: he is producing his own literature. Likewise, when Borges talks about aesthetics through translation—and the central role of translation in any discussion of literature—we can deduce that Borges is talking about the aesthetics of his own writings, and the central role that translation plays within them. In this sense, studying translation in Borges does not limit us to an isolated aspect of his work; rather, it introduces us to one of the most important ones. From its opening statements "Las versiones homéricas" points the way for such a hypothesis.

Early in the essay Borges states that the various translations of an original represent multiple perspectives of an unstable object:

> ¿Qué son las muchas [versiones] de la *Ilíada* . . . sino diversas perspectivas de un hecho móvil, sino un largo sorteo experimental de omisiones y de énfasis? (No hay esencial necesidad de cambiar de idioma, ese deliberado juego de la atención no es imposible dentro de una misma literatura.) (*OC* I: 239)

> [What are the many [versions] of the *Iliad* . . . if not diverse perspectives of a movable event, if not a long experimental assortment of omissions and emphases? (There is no essential need to change languages, that deliberate game of attention is not impossible within the same literature.)]

The idea of the mobility of the original, of the original as a "movable event," is quite subversive, as it questions the notion of a fixed and stable original, and suggests a mutability inherent in all texts.

From this, Borges establishes an extremely fluid conception of the relationship between texts, including originals and translations:

> Presuponer que toda recombinación de elementos es obligatoriamente inferior a su original, es presuponer que el borrador 9 es obligatoriamente inferior al borrador H—ya que no puede haber sino borradores. El concepto de *texto definitivo* no corresponde sino a la religión o al cansancio. (*OC* I: 239; italics in the original)

[To presuppose that every recombination of elements is necessarily inferior to its original, is to presuppose that draft 9 is necessarily inferior to
draft H—as there can be only drafts. The concept of the *definitive text*
corresponds only to religion or fatigue.]

This statement challenges just about all traditional theories of translation, which have always privileged the original—read: "definitive
text"—and assumed that translations are the inferior of the two. If
all texts are "drafts," there can be no original, no "definitive text,"
to measure up to.[14] The "superstición de la inferioridad de las traducciones" [superstition of the inferiority of translations] (*OC* I:
239), as Borges calls it, is shown to be just that: a superstitious belief in something that does not exist. It is not that translations are
necessarily superior to the original, either. Rather, Borges suggests
that translations are as legitimate as originals, and that this is the
case because both are actually "drafts." In this reformulation, traditional preconceptions of why one (i.e., the original) might be favored over the other (i.e., the translation) no longer apply. In
addition, Borges's challenge of the "definitive text" allows for a
shift in value from the original to the translation, and for the legitimization of the new version—in a new context, in Latin America
—as a rewriting of one or more pre-texts.

As these initial reflections suggest, Borges's provocative statements about the "concept of the definitive text" raise all manner of
questions. For what exactly is a "definitive text" or, for that matter,
an "original"? In what sense can all texts be said to be "drafts"?
What happens when our preconceptions about the relationship between texts are thus shaken by a writer in South America? How
does this affect what we believe about tradition and influence, about
the transmittal of culture, about representation and subjectivity,
about center and periphery? The implications are vast. In the case
of Borges, the idea that the "definitive text" is a fallacy will become a key aspect of the intertextual system of quotations, citations, and allusions, both veridical and apocryphal, found
throughout his fictions. Furthermore, it is in part this problematizing of originality, this idea of literature as a constant reworking of
previous texts, that has appealed so strongly to poststructuralist the-
orists (such as Foucault, Barthes, Blanchot, and Genette) and left
such a strong mark on contemporary literature (from Italo Calvino
to Thomas Pynchon, among others).

Borges suggests that literature is a series of multiply reflected versions, a textual hall of mirrors in which it is impossible to differentiate the original being reflected from its many reflections. But perhaps we should say "refractions," using André Lefevere's term, since translation is always a literary transformative process, even when it occurs within the same language.[15] We are reminded here of the "juego con espejos que se desplazan" [game of shifting mirrors] that unfold in "El acercamiento a Almotásim."[16] The simulacra overtake the original, the original loses its privileged place as a solid source at the center; what is left is translations of translations, without an identifiable origin. Every text is a rereading of a previous text, constituted of a network of references, citations, and allusions, an infinite system of intertextualities without a single, stable core. The structure is like the inside of "La biblioteca de Babel": interchangeable rooms, all alike, all different.

The implications of Borges's questioning of the "definitive text" in "Las versiones homéricas" become clearer when he discusses the issue of the translation of the classics. In this regard, he states: "Con los libros famosos, la primera vez ya es segunda, puesto que los abordamos sabiéndolos. La precavida frase común de *releer los clásicos* resulta de inocente veracidad" [With famous books, the first time is already the second, since we approach them already knowing them. The cautious common saying of *rereading the classics* turns out to be of an innocent veracity] (*OC* I: 239; emphasis in the original). There is no such thing as an original reading of the classics. We are always somehow already rereading a classic because we have encountered some previous incarnation of it—a refraction—in other stories, texts, or versions. But the fact that one already knows a classic before one reads it does not imply that the previous text is the one privileged. Instead, Borges leans toward a configuration in which all versions are legitimate and full of potential. Value—and even influence, as we see in "Kafka y sus precursores"—are not determined by chronology. The different existing translations of Homer, Borges states, are all "sinceras, genuinas y divergentes" [sincere, genuine and divergent] (*OC* I: 240). This idea is suggested in the very title of the essay: "The Homeric *Versions*."

Borges observes that not knowing the source language of the original is precisely the condition that allows a reader to enjoy a vast number of versions of it. In fact, it is notable that Borges compares only translations of the *Iliad* and the *Odyssey* and that he makes no attempt to refer back to the original. By deviating from the traditional approach of comparing the original with the translation, Borges avoids the unproductive practice of simply listing what is lost in translation. In addition, in his own case, "la *Odisea*, gracias a mi oportuno desconocimiento del griego, es una librería internacional de obras en prosa y verso" [the *Odyssey*, thanks to my opportune ignorance of Greek, is an international library of works in prose and verse] (*OC* I: 239–40). Borges works with paradox here to turn an apparent lack—not knowing the source language—into an unexpected gain—the potential to create multiple versions in the target language. In addition, this statement points to the importance of the reader and the context in creating this "international library" of Homeric versions. As Frances Aparicio has observed, by not knowing Greek, "el lector goza del desconocimiento y la ambigüedad entre el lenguaje del autor, del traductor y de la época en que se escribió" [the reader enjoys the not-knowing and the ambiguity between the language of the author, of the translator and of the time period in which it was written] (116). It is a case of the advantage and potential gain—not loss—of translation for Borges.

Borges goes on to explain how this gain, the "riqueza heterogénea y hasta contradictoria," [heterogeneous and even contradictory wealth] of the different Homeric versions is achieved. In the case of Homer, it is due to the "dificultad categórica de saber lo que pertenece al poeta y lo que pertenece al lenguaje" [the categorical difficulty of knowing what belongs to the poet and what belongs to the language] (*OC* I: 240). Borges uses the example of Homeric adjectives to illustrate what he means by such a difficulty. He argues that it is quite likely that certain adjectives which are always attached to certain nouns in Homer are analogous to prepositions in modern Spanish (*OC* I: 240). These epithets thus belong to the language at that historical moment (as the use of prepositions does in modern Spanish), and not entirely to the poet. Therefore it is impossible to determine on which end of the spectrum the emphasis lies in Homer: nearer the poet, the meaning, the spirit of the text (as Homer "intended" it to be); or nearer the language, the grammar and syntax (inherent in the language at that moment in time; the language within its historical and cultural context) that determines *how* a text means. This vast uncertainty in the original is precisely what opens the way for the numerous possible versions of texts: "Nada de mayor posible riqueza para los que traducen" [There is no greater possible wealth for translators] (*OC* I: 241).

This distinction brings us back to the issue of the context in which a text exists, and to the relationship between meaning and time. In other words, on the diachronic nature of how texts are read. As George Steiner has said: "One thing is clear: every language-act has a temporal determinant. No semantic form is timeless. When using a word we wake into resonance, as it were, its entire previous history. A text is embedded in specific historical time; it has what linguists call a diachronic structure" (24). Borges speaks of the difficulty in determining what belongs to the poet and what belongs to the language. This is analogous to speaking of the difficulty in determining between text and context, between meaning and *how* language means through time.[17]

Although Borges chooses Homer in part because the distance between meaning and grammar, between content and language, is so pronounced, the point is widely applicable. All texts are mobile, it is impossible to know what the original means, because we cannot separate any text from its context; we cannot separate texts from language and from *how* language signifies at the time and place it is utilized. Or, rather, it is in the attempt to make such a separation, in the space and tension between "what belongs to the poet and what belongs to the language," that potential is created, that the doors are opened to the many, diverse Homeric versions: "A esa *dificultad feliz* debemos la posibilidad de tantas versiones, todas sinceras, genuinas y divergentes" [It is to that *joyful difficulty* that we owe the possibility of so many versions, all sincere, genuine and divergent] (*OC* I: 240; emphasis added). This space, achieved through multiple displacements—rhetorically established through the use of paradox and ambiguity—creates the potentiality of translation.

THE NEWMAN—ARNOLD POLEMIC: FRAMING FIDELITY

Before discussing the specific Homeric versions themselves, Borges introduces the Newman–Arnold polemic as a frame for his comparisons. In 1861–62, the Victorian poet/critic Matthew Arnold (1822–88) and the critic/translator Francis W. Newman (1805–97) (Cardinal Newman's brother) engaged in a drawn-out debate over the two main opposing approaches to translation most often postulated in discussions on the topic. Although the details of their specific arguments are now nearly forgotten, their debate echoes the main issues and positions traditionally taken in translation theory:

whether a translation should be faithful to the letter or to the spirit of the original, with the assumption that it is impossible to be faithful to both.[18] In his 1856 translation of the *Iliad*, Newman undertakes a literal approach. Arnold critiques Newman's metaphrase and argues in favor of paraphrase.[19]

Newman and Arnold take very well defined opposing positions, which allows Borges to summarize their arguments into the sharp dichotomy he had already referred to in "Las dos maneras de traducir," and then to depart from there.[20] Although Newman and Arnold represent opposing and contradictory approaches to translation, Borges paradoxically suggests that both are actually valid. Borges does this by identifying the value, in terms of the pleasures obtained by the reader, of each kind of translation. Newman's approach (the metaphrase) offers "los agrados de los continuos y pequeños asombros" [the pleasures of continuous and small surprises]; whereas Arnold's (the paraphrase) offers "los agrados de la uniformidad y la gravedad" [the pleasures of uniformity and gravity] (*OC* I: 241). Furthermore, Borges qualifies the debate as "hermosa" [beautiful] and asserts that it is more important than either of its interlocutors. By using this vocabulary (the "pleasures" of either technique, the "beauty" of the polemic), Borges turns a debate about methodologies of translation into a debate on aesthetics and value. This slant continues in the next part of the essay, as Borges compares six versions of one passage from the *Odyssey*. He proceeds in order from the most to the least literal of the translations, commenting on individual styles of the translators and identifying, in each, the kind of aesthetic "pleasures" that accompany the corresponding manner of translating (*OC* I: 241–43).[21]

After comparing these Homeric versions, Borges asks which is the most faithful. Until this point, Borges has mostly sidestepped the question of fidelity as it is traditionally treated by stating that translations are not necessarily inferior to the original, and suggesting that the concept of the "definitive text" is a fallacy. But now he faces the question of fidelity head-on. The answer, he states—once again in paradoxical terms—is: "ninguna o todas" [all or none]. If fidelity must be to what belongs to "las imaginaciones de Homero, a los irrecuperables hombres y días que él se representó" [the imaginations of Homer, to the irretrievable men and times that he represented], then none of these versions is faithful from our point of view, for we cannot possibly aim to reproduce Homer's cultural and historical context. Such an effort would be equal to a kind of "original repetition," or perfect mimesis, which is impossible even without changing languages. Whereas if fidelity must be to Homer's intentions ("a sus propósitos" [to his objectives]—to the essence, to the meaning of the text) then all of these can be said to be faithful, except for the literal ones, for they derive their aesthetic value entirely from "[el] contraste con hábitos presentes" [the contrast with current uses] of language. In other words, if fidelity is to be not only to the poet's intentions (to the essence, the meaning of the text), but also to *how* the poet intended those intentions to come across—to both meaning and *how* a text means, to both text and original context—then fidelity is not possible. However, all versions—save the literal ones—could be considered faithful to the poet's intention, to the essence or meaning of the text.

Literal translations, for Borges, derive their value only from the contrasts in language that they present with contemporary usage. Although they might be interesting, literal translations are something of an oxymoron for Borges. As he states in "Las dos maneras de traducir," claims to literalness always make of the translator a liar ("un falsario") (*TR*, 258). This idea contrasts sharply not just with Newman's position, and with the Romantic favoring of metaphrase alluded to in "Las dos maneras de traducir," but also, in more recent times, with very different thinkers and writers, such as Jakobson and Nabokov, both of whom strongly believe that literal translation is always possible (and preferable, in the case of Nabokov).[22] In addition, by saying that all of the Homeric versions, except the most literal ones, are in a way faithful to the poet's intention, Borges reiterates his belief that translation is not necessarily accompanied by loss. Instead, he identifies an unexpected gain in the multiplicity of possible versions, in the "international library" of reproductions.

Borges's take on the issue of fidelity reveals a complicated playfulness and the insightful sensibilities of an active translator. It is not enough to speak of fidelity in general. We must ask to what elements of the source text the translator is expected to be faithful, and not only how he/she should achieve such faithfulness but, perhaps more importantly, why? How is the translator's ability to achieve fidelity related not only to the value of the source text, but also to its very originality? Does the translator not, in a way, actually "create" what is "original" about the source text—in a move analogous to how writers "create" their precursors, as Borges explains in "Kafka y sus precursores"—by deciding which elements of the source merit an attempt at "faithful reproduction," however such a thing is defined?

Borges finally answers his rhetorical question regarding the relative fidelity of the Homeric versions: "No es imposible que la versión calmosa de Butler sea la más fiel" [It is not impossible that Butler's calm version is the most faithful] (*OC* I: 243). The choice of Butler's calm and understated version, which captures the spirit of the original but makes no attempt to translate the letter, is surprising at first, and is surely meant to come off as such. Butler's version is by far the least literal, the one that most paraphrases the original to present an essential (and essentialized) Homer. We get the sense that Borges would rather not have to choose between Newman and Arnold, between fidelity to the letter and fidelity to the spirit, since Borges sees all translations as valid, divergent versions with potential aesthetic value. But if he were forced to choose, he would choose Arnold's point of view. Still, Borges's wording in announcing Butler's paraphrase as possibly the most loyal is ambiguous at best, leaving the question partially unresolved for now.

Certainly Borges's tendency is to avoid any overly simplistic demands for fidelity, demands that inevitably lead to failure and to supposedly inferior copies of the original—a position with which Borges strongly disagrees. Borges's irreverence toward the "definitive text" represents a direct challenge to traditional conceptions of fidelity and of the supposed power of the original. This fact is further illustrated by a brief comment that Borges includes in his "Prólogo" to Néstor Ibarra's translation of Paul Valéry's *El cementerio marino* (*Le cimetière marin*) (Buenos Aires: Schillinger, 1931), a text published just prior to "Las versiones homéricas."[23] Borges states:

> . . . Invito al mero lector sudamericano—*mon semblable, mon frère*—a saturarse de la estrofa quinta en el texto español, hasta sentir que el verso original de Néstor Ibarra:
>
> > *La pérdida en rumor de la ribera*
>
> es inaccesible, y que su imitación por Valéry:
>
> > *Le changement des rives en rumeur,*
>
> no acierta a devolver íntegramente todo el sabor latino. (*OC* IV: 152)

> [. . . I invite the mere South American reader—*mon semblable, mon frère*—to immerse himself in the fifth strophe of the Spanish text, until he feels that the original verse by Néstor Ibarra:

> *La pérdida en rumor de la ribera*

is inaccessible, and that its imitation by Valéry:

> *Le changement des rives en rumeur,*

does not accurately hit upon the entirety of its Latin flavor.]

In a formulation in which there are only "drafts," Valéry's verse can be seen as an imitation, and Ibarra's as the original. There is nothing sacred about the original for Borges: the "definitive text" does not hold a sacred or privileged place, and the aesthetic value of originals and translations is not determined by chronological order. Borges frames this inversion with the false modesty "I invite the mere South American reader," thus linking determinations of originality and aesthetic value with identity and location. In other words, it is "merely" but specifically "a South American reader" who dares question the original to arrive at a new conception of the relationships among texts, authors, and literatures. It is "merely" but significantly a "South American reader" who challenges such notions—notions established and maintained in the center—to reformulate them from the margins.

THEORIZING TRANSLATION IN THE TWENTIETH CENTURY: BORGES, BENJAMIN, DERRIDA

To further explore the implications of "Las versiones homéricas," especially Borges's suggestion that the "definitive text" is a fallacy, we turn now to a brief comparison of Borges's essay and Walter Benjamin's "The Task of the Translator." The first point of contact between the two is that both utilize translation to access a discussion of aesthetics. Borges opens his essay, as we have seen, with the explicit statement that: "There is no problem as consubstantial to literature and its modest mysteries as that posed by a translation. . . . Translation seems . . . destined to illustrate aesthetic discussions" (*OC* I: 239). Similarly, translation for Benjamin appears to be better suited to articulate a philosophy and criticism of literature than poetry itself (de Man 81–82). Benjamin finds in translation an ideal form to consider the fundamental relationship between languages; translation allows him to set aside the issue of meaning, which he cannot do in a direct discussion of poetry. As Joseph Graham has said: "Benjamin suggests how translation could—and urges it should—contribute significantly to something like a theory of meaning for language" (24).

But how might one articulate "a theory of meaning for language"? Benjamin's answer is that translation allows us to see both the differences and the similarities among languages. This leads him to formulate the complex and elusive notion of a "pure language," which can be thought to lie hidden, invisible, behind all languages. Translation, by making contact with what languages have in common, releases an echo of the existence of this "pure language." Benjamin argues that "translation . . . ultimately serves the purpose of expressing the central reciprocal relationship between languages" (73–74). To illustrate his idea, Benjamin draws an analogy between the different languages and a fractured vessel, in which each language contributes a fragment toward the whole (79).

As critics have noted, Benjamin's formulation is nearly mystic in its use of the Kabalistic tradition. Benjamin's "pure language" resembles an Adamic utopia in which speech equals meaning. And the image of a reconstructed vessel resonates strongly with the myth of the Tower of Babel, wherein the concept of a "pure language" is akin to a messianic call for translation to repair the disaster at Babel. The tone of the essay implies a religious imperative to translate, to recover a universal that existed before the fall of the Tower.

These ideas contrast with the key section of "Las versiones homéricas":

> To presuppose that every recombination of elements is necessarily inferior to its original, is to presuppose that draft 9 is necessarily inferior to draft H—as there can be only drafts. The concept of the *definitive text* corresponds only to religion or fatigue. (*OC* I: 239; italics in the original)

By comparing drafts named with two apparently unrelated symbols—H (the eighth letter of the modern Roman alphabet) and 9 (the ninth numeral of the decimal system)—Borges moves from one symbolic system to another, easily and with pleasure. Apparently, for Borges, the fall of the Tower of Babel is *not* a failure, but a site of opportunity; multiplicity and difference are *not* a disaster, but a field of potentiality.

Borges's formulation invites us to consider literature as a series of drafts/refractions, which can extend indefinitely, precisely because the source is not necessarily "definitive" and because the translations are not necessarily inferior. This translation-driven, open-ended series, like an unresolved and unresolvable chain of signifiers, need not have the imperative to work toward a "pure language," as it does in Benjamin. In Borges, all drafts—translations as well as so-called originals—may acquire aesthetic value, as in the "pleasures" he identifies in the various Homeric versions. The value of these texts can come from a variety of sources: from a comparison with other translations, from the contrast with the standard uses of language at a given point in time, from how they affect our views of other texts, from their status as an independent creation, or—and perhaps more likely—from a combination of all of these. But the point is that the value of any given "draft" does not depend, and is not determined, by a "definitive text"; the translation need not try to fix a broken vessel to be legitimate and potentially valuable.

In contrast, for Benjamin, translation has an unrealizable yet utopic objective. For this reason, it serves to reveal an inherent instability and disjunction in the original, between meaning and language, which we would not have been aware of were it not for the translation. There is no way to know how far an original is from Benjamin's "pure language" until a translator demonstrates the failure of translation, thus revealing the distance between source and "pure language." The process of translation reveals this fault (or lack) in the original, even as it suggests the potential of reaching the "pure language." This implies that translation can serve to compensate for such a lack.[24] The translation provides a fragment for the fractured vessel, which is to say for the reconstruction of Babel.

The instability of the original—which, according to Benjamin, can only be revealed by translation—is not unlike Borges's formulation of Homer as a "movable event." As we recall, Borges asks rhetorically: "What are the many [versions] of the *Iliad* . . . if not diverse perspectives of a movable event, if not a long experimental assortment of omissions and emphases?" (*OC* I: 239). Borges and Benjamin coincide here on the mobility of the original. But mobility is freer in Borges's conception of literature, in which the original seems to disappear in a game of shifting mirrors, one forgets which is the original and which the translation, the "definitive text" is destabilized, and the original loses its power of determination. Borges finds this mutability to exist in all texts, even without the necessity of changing languages; translation does not represent the "afterlife" of the original, as Benjamin argues (Benjamin, 73), but exists on a potentially equal plane with it.

Furthermore, the irreverence and playfulness (in Roland Barthes' sense of the word) in Borges's text contrasts sharply with Benjamin's messianic tone.[25] The wording of the phrase "The concept of the *definitive text* corresponds only to religion or fatigue," for example, creates a humorous analogy between religion—and a belief in the existence of definitive, sacred texts—and fatigue. Benjamin, in contrast, treats poetry as a sacred, ineffable language, as precisely that which cannot be translated. In other words, in a "sacred text"—which poetry approaches—language and content are inseparable, so that translatability remains predetermined by the original.

For Benjamin, a translation must touch the original lightly at a small point of its meaning, then pursue its own course "according to the laws of fidelity in the freedom of linguistic flux" (Benjamin, 81). Benjamin, much like Borges, sees the trap behind traditional demands for fidelity: "Fidelity in the translation of individual words can almost never fully reproduce the meaning they have in the original. . . . [And] it is self-evident how greatly fidelity in reproducing the form impedes the rendering of the sense" (Benjamin, 79). But Benjamin's solution is very different from Borges's, as he seeks a "demand for literalness" which contributes to his idea of translation as "complementation" and his formulation of a "pure language":

> A translation, instead of resembling the meaning of the original, must lovingly and in detail incorporate the original's mode of signification, thus making both the original and the translation recognizable as fragments of a greater language, just as fragments are part of a vessel. . . . The significance of fidelity as ensured by literalness is that the work reflects the great longing for linguistic complementation. (Benjamin, 79)

The idea that literalness, and specifically syntactic literalness (Benjamin, 79–80), can lead to "linguistic complementation" contrasts with Borges's position in "Las versiones homéricas." When Borges values literalness, it is for the kinds of aesthetic "pleasures" it might provide, and *not* because it leads to a fidelity grounded in linguistic complementation. If anything, Borges values the linguistic *difference* that literalness reveals, since, in terms of fidelity, he

finds literal translations to be the least faithful. Benjamin's complementation, in this sense, is quite different from Borges's conception
of literature—of all texts, originals and translations alike—as valid,
divergent versions. The complementation in Borges, if we wish to
call it that, is not with a determining original, but, in a much looser
formulation, among the different versions themselves, with value
placed on difference as such.

When he considers the uncertainty between what belongs to the
poet and what belongs to the language in the Homeric versions,
Borges finds "[un] contraste . . . intenso y . . . abismal" [an intense
and abysmal contrast] (*OC* I: 241) between them. Interestingly,
Benjamin also uses the word "abyss" in his discussion of translation, but what it connotes for him is quite different. The contrast
between the two here is related to what happens when one begins
to abandon fidelity and what Benjamin holds to be the much more
sacred place of the original. Benjamin discusses Hölderlin's translations of Sophocles to illustrate his ideas of literalness, fidelity,
and complementation, praising them, in part, for their particularly
light touch of meaning: "In them the harmony of the languages is
so profound that sense is touched by language only the way an Aeo-
lian harp is touched by the wind" (Benjamin, 82). But this causes a
problem for Benjamin, for the translation has strayed too far from
the original, and the original meaning is in danger of becoming irre-
versibly lost. Something sacred is revealed precisely at the point at
which it is about to be lost.

The risk of the diffusion of meaning produces an anxious reac-
tion in Benjamin: "Hölderlin's translations from Sophocles were
his last work; in them meaning plunges *from abyss to abyss* until
it threatens to become lost in the bottomless depths of language"
(Benjamin, 82; emphasis added). The disarticulation of the original
suggested by this process, as Paul de Man argues, is essentially de-
structive. Paradoxically, this may be precisely the glimpse of the
"pure language" for which Benjamin longs. De Man identifies
"pure language" with pure form: language entirely freed of the illusion of meaning. But the anxiety arises because the translation suggests an "abyss," a "bottomless depth," and reveals an alienation
that is at its strongest in relation to our own original language (de
Man, 84).

This is the clearest example of how Benjamin's shift from a demand for fidelity to a view of translation as a supplement to the
original remains problematic in "The Task of the Translator." Ap-

parently, a translation can only approach the desired "pure language" by sacrificing too much meaning of what remains, for Benjamin, a sacred original. Despite the shift from traditional conceptions of fidelity to one of complementation, translation is still measured against the original, and always comes up short.

For Borges, on the other hand, this "abyss" may be vertiginous, but it is not threatening. Rather, it is rife with possibility, in versions that are all "sincere, genuine and divergent." There is no anxiety associated with this veritable explosion of possible versions diverging from an ultimately unknowable—and unprivileged—original. The translator does not—cannot—fully know the original (in the sense of what belongs to the poet and what belongs to the language), even as he tries to transpose the text to a new context (his own language in his own time and place). Just as there is no exhaustion in Borges's fictions, there is no implication of loss (of meaning, as in Benjamin) from original to translation.

Benjamin's essay represents a significant break from past translation theories, as he turns away from traditional questions of fidelity toward viewing translation as a complement of the original. But the shift from a requirement for fidelity to a concept of supplementation remains problematic and unresolved for Benjamin: the fragmentation of the vessel on the one hand, the illusion that it can be reunified on the other. This move toward seeing translation as a complement is where Derrida takes up Benjamin. There are several important points of contact between Derrida's reading of Benjamin and Borges to consider here. There is much resemblance, in particular, between Borges's break with traditional demands for fidelity and his conception of literature as a series of "drafts" (i.e., versions of versions), and Derrida's formulation of *difference* in texts and of translation as complementation.[26] As Frances Aparicio has observed:

> Antes que Derrida, ya Borges había intuido el valor de lo diferencial y la condición de complemento que se establece entre un primer texto y el segundo, ya sea una traducción intranlingüística o entre dos lenguas. . . . [Borges anticipa] lo que los desconstruccionistas, entre otras cosas, reafirman hoy: la interrelación complementaria entre textos y entre lenguas. (23)

> [Before Derrida, Borges had already intuited the value of difference and the condition of complementarity that is established between a primary

and a secondary text, whether through intralingual or interlingual translation. . . . Borges anticipates what deconstructionists affirm today, among other things: the complementary interrelation between texts and languages.][27]

In his reading of Benjamin, Derrida focuses on the importance of the sacred in relation to translatability. For Benjamin, the sacred text is untranslatable because in it meaning and letter cannot be disassociated (Benjamin, 82; *The Ear of the Other*, 104). The sacred lies at the core of what Derrida considers the paradoxical nature of translation—that it is both necessary and impossible, a necessity as impossible ("Des Tours de Babel," 170–72). This derives from Derrida's analysis of the myth of Babel. In the moment that God condemns the Shems to a multiplicity of tongues, he creates this paradoxical need and impossibility of translation (*The Ear of the Other*, 100–104). To highlight his argument, Derrida uses the example of the necessity and impossibility of translating the proper name of Babel itself: the name that means confusion but must remain a proper name as the name of God. Babel thus embodies, for Derrida, the paradoxical nature of translation (its necessity/impossibility) as it applies to a sacred text itself: the name Babel as the example and embodiment of this necessity/impossibility.

In *The Ear of the Other's* "Roundtable on Translation," Donald Bouchard asks Derrida if it is ". . . necessary to have sacred texts and . . . [if] . . . a perfect translation [is] possible" (146). Derrida responds that the sacred text ". . . is an event, and that is what Benjamin means. One always has to postulate an original. . . . Every time the event of an untranslatable text occurs, every time there is a text that is not totally translatable. . . , it gets sacralized" (147–48). When dealing with such sacralization, the sacred is untranslatable, so that:

> One is dealing with poetry. This is why Benjamin refers literature or poetry to a religious or sacred model, because he thinks that if there is something untranslatable in literature (and, in a certain way, literature is the untranslatable), then it is sacred. (148)

This leads to Derrida's assertion that "There is Babel everywhere" (149). But Derrida also clarifies that this limit of translation for Benjamin, this untranslatability that is the sacred—"the sacred text in which the sense and the letter can no longer be dissociated"—is

also the *pure* translatable—"the place and the appeal for translation" (150). Here, then, is Derrida's version of the "pure" language
that Benjamin believes exists behind all languages but can only be
glimpsed through translation.

Derrida works with a series of paradoxes to deconstruct traditional assumptions about translation: translation is necessary yet
impossible; the sacred is untranslatable yet literature may just be
the untranslatable. Still, the emphasis on sacralization holds us back
from a complete rupture with a dependence on the original: "One
always has to postulate an original," Derrida insists. In this sense,
Derrida's reading of Benjamin remains deterministic, and although
translation is seen as complementary, the original still maintains a
place of privilege. This contrasts with Borges's defiance of the "definitive text"—read, in this case, as the sacred—and with the irreverent tone in which Borges presents his defiance. Borges's
humorous comparison between religion and fatigue is an important
break with the determination of the original and the sacralization of
literature; it allows Borges to see all texts as "drafts," versions
flowing without the constraints of "superstitions" about the supremacy of the original, nor limited by arguments of untranslatability. For Borges, if Babel is said to be everywhere, then its presence
is joyful and productive. In this sense, Borges's challenge to the
concept of the "definitive text" can be seen as an irreverent rejoic-
ing in the potential of Babel on the shores of the Río de la Plata.

"Los traductores de *Las 1001 Noches*": The Valorization of Creative Infidelities

Borges goes on to explore the possibility—the potential gain—
that accompanies translation in his 1935 essay "Los traductores de
Las 1001 Noches."[28] In a text that anticipates reader–response theory by at least thirty years, Borges demonstrates the importance of
the displacements that occur when one goes from an original to a
translation, and how these displacements create the potential for
new and unexpected meanings. Through a surprising reading of
several versions of *The Thousand and One Nights* (the collection
Alf Layla wa-Layla), Borges completely bypasses traditional requirements for fidelity, and develops a theory of *mis*translation with
powerful implications for Latin American writers.

In "Los traductores de *Las 1001 Noches*," much as he had done

in "Las versiones homéricas," Borges compares only the translations of the *Nights*; he makes no attempt to refer back to the original, except through what the translators themselves have to say
about it. Once again deviating from the traditional approach of
comparing the original with the translation, Borges displays a pro-
fane attitude toward the concept of a "definitive text." As he looks
at the series of European versions of the *Nights*, Borges considers
how each translator varies from the previous one, making it clear
that he is discussing versions of versions, without assuming that any
is necessarily inferior to the original. Paradoxically, on the contrary, this approach does not detract from Borges's lifelong appreciation of *The Thousand and One Nights*. In fact, the appearance
of the *Nights* as multiple, legitimate variations may very well be an
important aspect of what appealed so strongly to Borges about this
text, since any story of *The Thousand and One Nights* and its inheritance is ultimately a story about the translation of the *Nights*.

"El Capitán Burton"

Borges points out that when we think of the *Arabian Nights*, we
invariably turn to the first translation of the text into a European
language; that is, Jean Antoine Galland's version of 1704–17.
Borges is drawn to the fact that the original *Nights* is a translation,
and refers to Galland as the "fundador" [founder]. Galland's version establishes the stories that everyone in the Occident thinks of
when they think of the *Nights*: "El hombre de Europa o de las Amé-
ricas que piensa en *Las 1001 Noches*, piensa invariablemente en esa
primera traducción" [When someone from Europe or the Americas
thinks of *The Thousand and One Nights*, he invariably thinks of that
first translation] (*OC* I: 397).[29]
But Galland's version contains several stories that have never
been found in any "original" version of the *Nights*, including some
of the more famous tales, such as "Aladdin" and "Ali Baba"
(Irwin, 17). Galland's new stories then become such an integral part
of the *Nights*, Borges reminds us, that none of the translators who
have followed dares to omit them. *The Thousand and One Nights* is
thus seen as an original—Galland's version was then translated into
numerous languages, including Arabic—but one that is a translation of a previous text, which is itself a compilation of anonymous
stories of unknown origin. The idea of any solid original, in the
traditional sense of the term, is thoroughly destabilized.

The next version that Borges considers is that of Edward Lane (1840), whose version includes a major project to exclude everything that he found morally objectionable. Borges argues that Lane, despite his many years among the Arabs, is unable to do away with his "pudor británico" [British reserve]. This makes his version "una mera enciclopedia de la evasión" [a mere encyclopedia of evasions]: evasions executed through a long series of footnotes, in which Lane explains that he has left something out, but only alludes to what he has omitted by justifying the omission. Thus, as Borges states, whereas "Galland corrige las torpezas ocasionales por creerlas de mal gusto" [Galland corrects the occasional awkwardness because he believes it to be in poor taste], "Lane las rebusca y las persigue como un inquisidor" [Lane gleans them out and pursues them like an inquisitor] (*OC* I: 399).

In their different ways, as Borges illustrates through numerous examples, "es muy sabido que [las versiones de Galland y de Lane] *desinfectaron* las *Noches*" [it is well known that Galland's and Lane's versions *disinfected* the *Nights*] (*OC* I: 400; emphasis added). But Borges does not object to Galland's and Lane's omissions and changes in and of themselves; he does not critique Galland's and Lane's paraphrastic domestications. In fact, according to Borges, Galland is able to capture the essence of *The Thousand and One Nights* and manages to convey its magic and wonder for a European readership (*OC* I: 401). It is Lane's moral rationale for such modifications, his "subterfugio puritano" [puritanical subterfuge], which Borges condemns.

The verb "to disinfect" is noteworthy here, as it implies that there is something "dirty" or "diseased" in the original Arab text and language, reminding us of Galland's and Lane's strong Orientalism.[30] Borges alludes to such Orientalism without any condemnation of it. Borges's use of "disinfecting" to describe the act of translation indicates that a version that rewrites and domesticates the original, such as Galland's or Lane's, always keeps the two languages considerably more apart than a literal translation. In these terms, a freer translation (i.e., a paraphrase) avoids "contamination" of the target language from the source language, whereas a literal translation is more likely to incur it. (We will return to Borges's relationship to the Orientalist tendencies of the translators of the *Nights* in the last section of this chapter.)

In the course of this argument, Borges once again utilizes the Newman–Arnold polemic as a frame to compare the various trans-

lations. His outline of their positions—the former advocating a literal approach (metaphrase), the latter a freer one (paraphrase)—and
the possible aesthetic pleasures ("agrados") associated with each,
is almost identical to that in "Las versiones homéricas." But this
time Borges makes an important addition; he states:

> Ambas [conductas] son menos importantes que el traductor y que sus
> hábitos literarios. Traducir el espíritu es una intención tan enorme y tan
> fantasmal que bien puede quedar como inofensiva; traducir la letra, una
> precisión tan extravagante que no hay riesgo que la ensayen. Más grave
> que esos infinitos propósitos es la conservación o supresión de ciertos
> pormenores; más grave que esas preferencias y olvidos, es el movi-
> miento sintáctico. (*OC* I: 400)

> [Both behaviors are less important than the translator and his literary
> habits. To translate the spirit is such an enormous and phantasmal inten-
> tion that it may very well remain as inoffensive; to translate the letter is
> such an extravagant precision that there is no risk that it be undertaken.
> More serious than those infinite objectives are the conservation or the
> suppression of certain details; more serious than these preferences and
> omissions, is the syntactic movement.]

These comments problematize the metaphrase–paraphrase dichotomy, as Borges posits that the translator's preferences and omissions are more important than the impossible objectives of
attempting either a literal translation or one meant to translate the
spirit of the original. This shift allows Borges to focus on the translator's work as a (re)writer—how he/she is able to manipulate the
"syntactic movement" of language—and leads to a valorization of
translation as a creative effort in and of itself. It is the translator's
individual "literary habits"—like a writer's—and *not* the sacred
status of the original, that must be taken into account in the final
analysis.

With this in mind, Borges turns to Richard F. Burton's translation
of *The Thousand and One Nights*.[31] He begins by summarizing Burton's life and work (*OC* I: 401–3), stating: "Aventuro la hipérbole:
recorrer *Las 1001 Noches* en la traslación de Sir Richard no es
menos increíble que recorrerlas 'vertidas literlamente del árabe y
comentadas' por Simbad el Marino" [I risk the following hyperbole: to traverse *The Thousand and One Nights* in Sir Richard's
transposition is no less incredible than to traverse them 'voiced literally in Arabic and commentated' by Simbad the Sailor] (*OC* I:

403). How does Burton achieve this effect? What are his "literary habits"? What "syntactic movement" makes the version by Burton so special for Borges? The answer Borges provides is paradoxical: Burton achieves an effect of hyperfidelity by executing a series of creative infidelities. The key lies in a certain irreverence toward the original and the potential created by the temporal and spatial displacements between the original and the translation, between one version and the next.

Borges tells us that when Burton set out to translate the *Nights,* one of the main problems that he had to resolve was how to interest nineteenth-century British gentlemen in thirteenth-century Arabian serialized stories (Borges calls them "novelas por entregas"). The problem lay with the difference between the two audiences, between those who would have heard the original stories in thirteenth-century Arabia and those who were to read Burton's nineteenth-century version in London, as their interpretations were bound to differ widely (*OC* I: 403–4). As in "Las dos maneras de traducir" and "Las versiones homéricas," Borges again reveals his astute awareness of the importance of the reader in the reception of any text.[32]

The issue becomes how to translate a text from one context to another. As is evident by Borges's argument, it is the context (including class, race, ethnicity, religion, gender, time period, historical, political, and cultural conditions), and not just the language, that changes as one goes from source to target text. But the issue of text/context in translation is problematized by the need to take the reader into account. The readers (listeners might be more appropriate) of the Arabian version were: "pícaros, noveleros, analfabetos, infinitamente suspicaces de lo presente y crédulos de la maravilla remota" [rogues, novelty seekers, illiterates, infinitely distrustful of the present and credulous of the distant marvel]; whereas those of Burton's intended audience were: "señores del West End, aptos para el desdén y la erudición y no para el espanto o la risotada" [gentlemen from the West End, apt at disdain and erudition and not at awe and boisterous laughter] (*OC* I: 404).

What is the best way, then, to translate, to transpose, *The Thousand and One Nights*—or any work, for that matter—from one context and audience to another? How does Burton resolve his objective of making the *Nights* appealing to his target readership? As Borges tells us, Burton makes countless substitutions; he uses a wide-ranging, contradicting, and disparate vocabulary, including an

abundance of neologisms and foreign terms; he completely rewrites
the first and last stories; and he undertakes numerous alterations,
omissions, and interpolations. Borges then concludes, in what is the
most important twist of "Los traductores de *Las 1001 Noches*," that
these changes are actually for the best. They represent, he says:
"Un buen falseo, ya que esas travesuras verbales—y otras sintácticas—distraen el curso a veces abrumador de las *Noches*" [A good
falsity, since these verbal antics—as well as other syntactic ones—
distract the sometimes wearisome course of the *Nights*] (*OC* I:
405).[33] They are falsifications, made unashamedly—irreverently—
which improve on the original. Paradoxically, the merit of the translation, as Borges sees it, lies in its *infidelities*.

Burton's falsifications inaugurate a crucial move that explains
why Borges values Burton to such an extent, here and elsewhere in
his writings. This point in the essay represents a leap in Borges's
theories on translation toward the valorization of mistranslations,
of translations whose merit resides in their very infidelities. Burton
becomes the perfect figure of the translator/recreator for Borges: a
translator who irreverently (re)writes the original in order to (re)-
create a version capable of supplanting/displacing it. In this sense,
Borges creates Burton as his precursor, in terms of "Kafka y sus
precursores."[34] In fact, what Borges values about Burton's version
of the *Nights*, with its rewritings and alterations, sounds precisely
like the poetics of Borges's own stories, beginning with *Historia
universal de la infamia*, as we will see in the next chapter.

"El Doctor Mardrus"

In the next section of "Los traductores de *Las 1001 Noches*,"
Borges discusses the 1889 version of *The Thousand and One Nights*
into French by J. C. Mardrus, whom Borges sees as perfecting the
move toward creative infidelities inaugurated by Burton. This is
made even more paradoxical, however, by the fact that Mardrus
claimed to be the most truthful and literal of the translators of the
Nights, as seen in the subtitle itself of Mardrus's translation: *Versión literal y completa del texto árabe* [Literal and Complete Version of the Arabic Text] (*OC* I: 406). But Borges provides
numerous examples in which Mardrus clearly changes and rewrites,
and others in which Mardrus adds and complements for a perceived
lack in the original: "Continuamente, Mardrus quiere completar el
trabajo que los lánguidos árabes anónimos descuidaron. Añade pai-

sajes *art-nouveau*, buenas obscenidades, breves interludios cómicos, rasgos circunstanciales, simetrías, mucho orientalismo visual" [Continuously, Mardrus wants to complete the work that the languid, anonymous Arabs neglected. He adds art nouveau landscapes, good obscenities, brief comic interludes, circumstantial traits, symmetries, much visual Orientalism] (*OC* I: 409).

Borges not only proves that Mardrus's version is far from being literal, he also states that: "En general, cabe decir que Mardrus no traduce las palabras sino las representaciones del libro: libertad negada a los traductores, pero tolerada en los dibujantes" [In general, it should be said that Mardrus does not translate the words but the representations of the book: a liberty that is denied translators, but tolerated in painters] (*OC* I: 409). The idea that Mardrus's translation resembles a painted version of a preexisting text is reminiscent of Jakobson's definition of intersemiotic translation. According to Jakobson, an intersemiotic translation, or "transmutation," is "an interpretation of verbal signs by means of nonverbal sign systems," such as a musical or pictorial representation of a poem (Jakobson, 145). But for Jakobson each kind of translation—the intralingual, the interlingual, and the intersemiotic—is distinct and separate. Borges's comments challenge such clear-cut distinctions, as they suggest a blurring of the line between the interlingual and the intersemiotic.[35] Borges finds a freedom in Mardrus more characteristic of intersemiotic translations than of "translation proper," as Mardrus reads the original, then "paints" his version of it in a new language and context through his own "habits of the translator," his own "syntactic movement." Borges's suggestion that translation can be both interlingual and intersemiotic, that it can be both "translation proper" and "transmutation," challenges Jakobson's rigid schematic and implies the need for a new model altogether.

But how does such a blurring, such an expansion of the concept of what is possible in translation, occur? Borges's response is that the greatness of Mardrus lies not in his supposed literalness and fidelity, but rather in the creative infidelities that lead to his transmutative translation: "Celebrar la fidelidad de Mardrus es omitir el alma de Mardrus, es no aludir siquiera a Mardrus. Su infidelidad, *su infidelidad creadora y feliz*, es lo que nos debe importar" [To celebrate Mardrus's fidelity is to omit Mardrus's soul, it is to not even speak of Mardrus. It is his infidelity, his *creative and joyful infidelity*, with which we should be concerned] (*OC* I: 410; empha-

sis added). By postulating that it is mistranslation—that it is, paradoxically, the infidelities and not the degree of fidelity—which
lends merit to a translation, Borges inverts the relationship between
fidelity and value, and frees himself from the constraints of traditional translation theory. Borges's move does away with superstitions of limitations and untranslatability. The valorization of
Burton's and Mardrus's falsifications is a sophisticated extension
of Borges's belief that translation is more than possible, that it is a
site for potentiality and gain—a gain clearly linked to the creative
infidelities of the translator/recreator.

It is worthwhile to note that Borges's challenge to traditional
concepts of fidelity anticipates a line of recent criticism in translation theory. Contemporary critics who present deviations from accepted beliefs of fidelity, as Barbara Johnson discusses in "Taking
Fidelity Philosophically," mostly make use of the territory opened
by Derridean theory.[36] Johnson describes the traditional view on
fidelity as that of a translator: "Once bound by contracts to love,
honor, and obey . . . [which they] inevitably betray." She adds that
the translator, traditionally, is a "faithful bigamist, with loyalties
split between a native language and a foreign tongue," who is "necessarily doubly unfaithful" even as he/she pushes against the limits
of fidelity (142–43). Derrida's concept of *difference* within texts
and languages reveals a tension between letter and spirit already
present in the original itself. It is to this tension, Johnson argues,
and not to either the letter or the spirit, to which it is necessary to
be faithful (146–47). Borges, as we have seen, intuits such a difference as early as "Las versiones homéricas," in which he argues that
the innumerable options available to the translator arise from the
difficulty in determining what belongs to the poet and what belongs
to the language. The possibilities presented by this tension already
found in the original, combined with the freedom to omit, change,
add, rewrite, and falsify as necessary, lead to Borges's conception
of limitlessness in translation.

One contemporary critic in particular whose ideas resemble Borges's valorization of creative infidelities is Philip E. Lewis.[37]
"The Measure of Translation Effects," Lewis speaks of an "abuse
principle" that takes advantage of the inevitable infidelities always
found in translation: "The real possibility of translation . . . points
to a risk to be assumed: that of the strong, forceful translation that
values experimentation, tampers with usage, seeks to match the
polyvalencies or plurivocities or expressive stresses of the original

by producing its own" (41). Such abuse, Lewis argues, does not sacrifice traditional requirements of fidelity and intelligibility, because the translation itself compensates for losses, justifies the differences, and supplies for the inevitable lack in the process (41–42). This leads Lewis to postulate a "new axiomatics of fidelity," in which what is at stake is "what the translation itself contributes"; in other words, the "abuse, committed by the translator, whereby the translation goes beyond—fills in for—the original" (42).

Lewis concludes, however, that such a translation is possible only in theory: "No doubt the project we are envisaging here is ultimately impossible" (43). Borges, on the other hand, both theorizes and proves the possibility and potential of such translations. In fact, the kind of "abuse" imagined by Lewis, and his description of the risks associated with the "real possibility of translation," are very much like the mistranslation that Borges celebrates in Burton and Mardrus. They are also very much like the recreations that Borges himself perpetrates as a translator and, in a way, like the creative infidelities that he incorporates into the poetics of his own fictions.

Another contemporary critic who considers the effects of infidelities is George Steiner, in his chapter "The Hermeneutic Motion" from *After Babel* (312–435). There, Steiner discusses "betrayals" that lead either upwards or downwards, by which he means translations that are either better or worse than the original, in which there are either gains or losses. But Steiner strongly values those translations that manage to be more or less equivalent to the original, neither more nor less than it. Borges, for his part, would never consider an augmentation to be a betrayal. Or, better yet, he would consider it to be precisely the kind of betrayal where we find the innovative potential of translation.

"Enno Littmann"

In the third and final part of "Los traductores de *Las 1001 Noches*," Borges briefly discusses the four German versions of the *Nights*. Borges looks at these translations in light of what he has just established about the potential of creative infidelities. Of the first German translation, Gustavo Weil's version (1839–42), Borges praises only the infidelities. He states: "Sus *interpolaciones* me merecen todo respeto" [His *interpolations* are entirely worthy of my respect]. After giving several brief examples of these, he adds:

"Esas buenas *apocrifidades* no son indignas de Burton o Mardrus" [These good *falsifications* are not unworthy of Burton or Mardrus] (*OC* I: 410; emphasis added). "Interpolations" and "falsifications": key aspects of Borges's valorization of mistranslations, but also of the intertextual system of quotations, citations, and allusions, veridical as well as apocryphal, which make up Borges's fiction, beginning with *Historia universal de la infamia*.

After briefly considering the versions by Max Henning (1895–97) and Félix Paul Greve (1879–1948), Borges turns to Enno Littmann's (1923–28), which was meant to replace them. According to major sources, as Borges reports, it is the best one available; but Borges disagrees:

> [Littmann] es siempre lúcido, legible, mediocre. Sigue (nos dicen) la respiración misma del árabe. Si no hay error en la Enciclopedia Británica, su traducción es la mejor de cuantas circulan. Oigo que los arabistas están de acuerdo; nada importa que un mero literato—y ése, de la República meramente Argentina—prefiera disentir. (*OC* I: 411)

> [Littmann is always lucid, legible, mediocre. He follows (we are told) the very breath of Arabic. If the Encyclopedia Britannica is not mistaken, his is the best translation available. I understand that the Arabists agree; it does not matter at all that a mere man of letters—and one from the Republic merely of Argentina at that—prefers to dissent.]

Especially notable here is that the false modesty with which Borges expresses his objection is so closely linked with him being from Argentina. Being Argentine—and not from the Metropolis, where the *Encyclopedia Britannica* is written and where Orientalists reside—leads to a dissenting evaluation of what constitutes a good translation. At stake for translators and writers from the periphery, Borges suggests, is how they incorporate previous traditions—that is, the legacy of the past—through irreverent rereadings and rewritings of previous texts. As texts travel, their value is altered and geographic and political distance become as large a factor in their possible interpretations as linguistic difference. Distance and displacement, as Borges illustrates, lead to transformation—and not necessarily to loss and inferior copies, as the traditional translation theories of the center would have us believe. Recontextualization toward the margins—in this case toward Borges' *argentinidad* [Argentineness]—complicates our notions of value.

In addition, as Borges explains, Littmann does not make use of any of the styles or literatures available to him from past German traditions (*OC* I: 412). This contrasts sharply with the translators whom Borges values, namely Burton, Mardrus, and even Galland. For example, Borges tells us that Burton's *Nights* contains echoes of John Donne's hard obscenity, of Shakespeare's and Tourneur's gigantic vocabulary, of Swinburne's archaic fiction, and so on: "En algún modo, el casi inagotable proceso inglés está adumbrado en Burton" [Somehow, the nearly inexhaustible process of English is shaded in Burton] (*OC* I: 411). But Littmann's version, because it is too honest and too literal, because it does not take any risks, make changes, omissions, or additions, is rendered into a German that does not incorporate any of the literary tradition to which Littmann had access when he translated the text.

Drawing from the literary tradition of the translator's language, then, becomes the last element needed to establish the potential of the new version. To fully realize the possibilities of what Borges calls creative infidelities, the translator—like the writer—must take from tradition as necessary. A translation that does not undertake this process remains, like Littmann's, unsatisfactory and, even worse, innocuous. Separating language from its literatures sterilizes and devalues it. Translators—like writers—have at their disposal the entire tradition contained in the language in which they are working from which to "borrow."

To illustrate his point, Borges leaves us at the end of "Los traductores de *Las 1001 Noches*" with a seductive daydream. What would have become of the *Nights*, he asks, if only someone like Kafka had (mis)translated them with the kind of distortion available in German literature: "Según la deformación alemana, según la *Unheimlichkeit* de Alemania?" [According to the German deformation, according to the German *Unheimlichkeit*] (*OC* I: 412). The eruption of the term for the uncanny in German ("Unheimlichkeit") foregrounds, through a linguistic interpolation, precisely the kind of taking from tradition (from the uncanny aspects of German literature that Kafka drew upon to create his nightmarish tales) which Borges believes is always available in language, and which translators and writers have access to if they are to innovate. In other words, it is this use of the tradition of the target language that allows translators and writers to create versions which are valuable recreations of the pre-text(s), recreations containing meanings which are, paradoxically, both new and the same as those in the source text(s).

In his own translations, Borges, not surprisingly, makes decisions that illustrate and bring to bear the potential of translation that he discusses in "Las versiones homéricas" and "Los traductores de *Las 1001 Noches*." In Borges's translations, we often find, for example, precisely the kinds of creative infidelities and rewritings which he valorizes in certain translators of the *Nights*. Borges the translator finds a variety of techniques to displace and recreate the source text, reinscribing it into a specific *rioplatense*—and, in fact, Borgesian—context. As an example of this, we look briefly now at two of Borges's translations of the poet e. e. cummings.

BORGES TRANSLATES CUMMINGS:
HYPERFIDELITY AND SOUTH AMERICAN APPROPRIATION

Borges translated three poems by the American Modernist poet e. e. cummings (1894–1962): one strophe from "a clown's smirk in the skull of a baboon" as part of an essay on cummings (in 1937), and two other poems—"Buffalo Bill" and "somewhere I have never traveled"—in their entirety (with the collaboration of Adolfo Bioy Casares, in 1944). In the first of these, Borges rewrites cummings completely by rendering just a fragment of the poem into prose; but in the two other translations, he takes nearly an opposite approach, as he finds unexpected ways to recreate analogous innovations in Spanish to those found in the originals. Thus, working with the same poet, in one case Borges completely deforms the source text; whereas, in the other two translations, Borges stays very close to the form—even bending the Spanish as necessary to resemble the source—but still makes key lexical changes which lend his versions a decidedly *rioplatense* flavor. In the process, Borges displaces and appropriates; paradoxically, with these creative infidelities Borges achieves a certain hyperfidelity to the source.

Borges's first reading of cummings is a "Biografía sintética" ["Synthesized Biography"] published in *El Hogar* in 1937 (*Textos cautivos*, 162–63). The essay includes a severe condemnation of typographical experimentation in poetry in general, and in cummings in particular.[38] Instead of the typographical and the visual, Borges emphasizes what he considers to be the more important features of cummings's work: the surprises in the imagery and the unexpected word choices, or cummings's unsettling word combinations.[39] As part of his arguments in the essay, Borges presents a translation into prose of the third stanza of "a clown's smirk in the skull of a baboon" (from *W [ViVa]* [1931]). Borges's version reads as follows:

> La cara terrible de Dios, más resplandeciente que una cuchara, resume la imagen de una sola palabra fatal; hasta que mi vida (que gustó del sol y la luna) se parece a algo que no ha sucedido. Soy una jaula de pájaro sin ningún pájaro, un collar en busca de un perro, un beso sin labios; una plegaria a la que faltan rodillas; pero algo late dentro de mi camisa que prueba que está desmuerto el que, viviente, no es nadie. Nunca te he querido, querida, como ahora quiero. (*Textos cautivos*, 163)[40]

The irreverence in Borges's partial rewriting of "a clown's smirk in the skull of a baboon" is quite marked: first, by translating only one stanza out of four, which completely removes it from the context of the original; second, by providing a prosification, which eliminates precisely the formal experiments and typographical games which Borges critiques in the essay; and third, by inserting this fragmented prosification into his own text about cummings, by which Borges exaggerates the act of displacement and appropriation that always accompanies a translation. These moves lead to a complete recontextualization of the North American poet, as cummings is displaced and presented to an Argentine readership in a version "created" by Borges and inscribed within Borges's poetic discourse.

However, although Borges's version is an extreme rewriting of the original (a fragment of a longer poem, rendered in prose in the context of Borges's essay)—although it is a severe domestication of the source text toward the South—the translation also contains a few details that take the reader in the other direction. Namely, Borges seeks to recreate in Spanish the lexical innovations found in cummings's poem. For example, Borges translates "undead" (in the verse "he is undead who,living,noone is") as "desmuerto" (in the line "está desmuerto el que, viviente, no es nadie"). In the same line, in fact, Borges "corrects" cummings's play with the spacing, while creating a neologism in Spanish that reproduces the effect that cummings frequently draws by adding the prefix "un-" to nouns that do not usually accept them.[41] This draws a distinction between the typographical games for which Borges did not have much patience, and the lexical experimentation which he found much more sophisticated, and which he sought to reproduce and highlight in his own version of cummings.

In another translation of a poem by cummings, his version of "Buffalo Bill" (from *Tulips and Chimneys* [1923]; translated with Bioy Casares for *Sur* in 1944), Borges takes quite a different approach, especially with respect to form. Here Borges not only recreates compound words as necessary, he also remains fairly loyal to the visual and structural aspects of the original, helping to reproduce the shifts in rhythm that are so potent in the text. Thus, Borges's version both sounds and looks like cummings; however, the poem is subtly but significantly displaced toward an Argentine context, as illustrated by a lexical detail of "Buffalo Bill" ["Búfalo Bill"]:

Poem:

Buffalo Bill's
defunct
            who used to
            ride a watersmooth-silver
                                    stallion
and break onetwothreefourfive pigeonsjustlikethat
                                                Jesus

he was a handsome man
                            and what i want to know is
how do you like your blueeyed boy
Mister Death (*Poems*, 50)

Poema:

Búfalo Bill
muerto
            que solía
            montar un padrillo
            plateado y suave como el agua
            y romper unadostrescuatrocinco
palomassimplementeasí
                                    ¡Jesús!

Era un hombre apuesto
                        y quiero saber si
le gusta su muchacho de ojos azules
Señor Muerte. (*Sur*, 87)

At first sight, the poem seems a wonderful re-creation of the original; it appears to strive for literalness, particularly as a formal transposition of the source text. There is a key word in the translation, however, which works against any idea of strict literalness. The word in question is that utilized by Borges and Bioy Casares for Buffalo Bill's "stallion": "padrillo" (line five in the original; line four in the translation). A more "neutral" Spanish word choice would have been "semental" or "garañón." But by translating the "watersmooth-silver stallion" as a "padrillo plateado y suave como el agua," Borges and Bioy Casares perform an act of linguistic acculturation that places Buffalo Bill—and e. e. cummings's modernist rendition of this American legend—in the Argentine Pampas.

The irreverent displacement in Borges's (and Bioy Casares's) version of "Búfalo Bill" is subtle but poignant. And the effects— here and throughout Borges's work as a translator—are surprising, for it is precisely when Borges uses creative infidelities, when he displaces and recontextualizes the source text, that, paradoxically, the translation most succeeds. This creates a certain hyperfidelity, as the key elements of the "original" seem to be best recreated precisely when the translator is least faithful. Translation, thus conceived and executed, has the potential to shift just about any theme and style to Borges's South, in a move that opens any and all pretexts for rereading and rewriting in a new Latin American context.

BORGES AND DOMESTICATING TRANSLATIONS: ORIENTALISM FROM THE MARGINS?

The comments in Borges's essays on domesticating translations, and his own uses of it as a translator, require further consideration, especially in light of recent work in translation studies that has critiqued such techniques. Throughout "Los traductores de *Las 1001 Noches*," Borges does not at all deny that the Europeans whose translations he compares domesticate the *Nights* to make them more interesting to their contemporaries back home. This is especially the case for those versions that Borges most praises: Galland's, and especially Burton's and Mardrus's. Borges says, for example, that Galland "domesticaba a sus árabes . . . para que no desentonaran irreparablemente en París" [domesticated his Arabs . . . so they would not be irreparably out of tune in Paris] (*OC* I:

399). And it is precisely in Burton's and Mardrus's manipulation of the *Nights* that Borges locates the value of their creative infidelities.

The fact that Borges approves of such acculturation of the Near Eastern stories of the *Nights* might suggest that he is taking an Orientalist position.[42] A few critics, not referring to Borges, but to translation overall, have recently condemned this practice of domestication. Lawrence Venuti, most prominently, has argued against translations that read fluently in the target language, which try to make it seem as if the text were written in English, and not in the foreign language. He argues that such "transparency" effaces "the linguistic and cultural difference of the foreign text . . . [and] performs a labor of acculturation" that becomes part of a project of cultural imperialism ("Introduction," 4–5).

But what exactly is involved in Borges's approval of such domestication? On one level, Borges suggests that the processes involved in domestication—the translator's preferences and alterations and the resulting acculturation—are present in all translations. When he compares Galland's version with Burton's, Borges states: "Ambos, diversamente, *deforman*: el original es menos ceremonioso que Galland y menos grasiento que Burton" [Both, diversely, *deform*: the original is less ceremonious than Galland and less greasy than Burton] (*OC* I: 398; emphasis added). Borges never assumes that a translation will do anything other than "deform" the original. Such manipulation always occurs in translation as texts are displaced from one context to another. The distance between the original, Middle Eastern context and Galland's eigteenth-century Paris, or Burton's nineteenth-century London, is an opening within which the translator/recreator can practice all manner of changes, omissions, and interpolations to recreate the text. Borges strongly suggests that this is potentially a much richer way to translate than Littmann's innocuous and ineffective neutral attempt.

On another level, the issue of domestication is made considerably more complicated by the fact that Borges is speaking from the margins, from Argentina, and not at all from the center of empire. In fact, Venuti's criticism of domesticating translations, which is certainly valid and important in relation to the history of translation into English, does not apply very well to the case of translations into Spanish and Portuguese in Latin America.[43] In the U.S. or in Western Europe, a fluent translation that recontextualizes the original and erases any evidence of its "foreignness" can be interpreted as part of a project of cultural imperialism, as a domestication that reinforces power relationships between center and periphery. But the ethics and the aesthetics of translation are fundamentally different in the periphery than they are in the center. To use a crude metaphor: it is not the same when a king steals from a serf as when a serf steals from a king—at least the consequences are not the same. Techniques that in the center contribute to projects of cultural imperialism can, in the periphery, function as a form of resistance, as a redrawing of political as well as literary maps. In Latin America, a domesticating translation can represent an appropriation from the Metropolis through linguistic acculturation, and a way to challenge not only the supposed supremacy of the original, but also of the cultural political power of the society in which it was produced. This makes Borges's concept of creative infidelities that much more important, as it creates a displacement towards the margins and suggests a new way to think of center–periphery dichotomies.

This play with transnational relationships, and the cultural political assumptions that accompany them, resurfaces in a late essay that Borges dedicates to *The Thousand and One Nights*, in the collection *Siete noches* [Seven Nights] (1980). Challenging the stability of a Western center from his South American margin, Borges states:

> La cultura occidental es impura en el sentido de que sólo es a medias occidental. Hay dos naciones esenciales para nuestra cultura. Esas dos naciones son Grecia (ya que Roma es una extensión helenística) e Israel, un país oriental. . . .
> ¿Qué es el Oriente? Si lo definimos de un modo geográfico nos encontramos con algo bastante curioso, y es que parte del Oriente sería el Occidente o lo que para los griegos y romanos fue el Occidente, ya que se entiende que el Norte de África es el Oriente. . . . Al decir Oriente creo que todos pensamos, en principio, en el Oriente islámico. . . .
> Tal es el primer sentido que tiene para nosotros y ello es obra de *Las mil y una noches*. Hay algo que sentimos como el Oriente . . . que [yo] he sentido en Granada y en Córdoba. (*OC* III: 235–36)

> [Occidental culture is impure in the sense that it is only half Occidental. There are two nations that are essential to our culture. Those two nations are Greece (since Rome is a Hellenistic extension) and Israel, an Oriental country. . . .
> What is the Orient? If we define it geographically we come across something quite curious, which is that part of the Orient is actually the Occident, or what was the Occident for the Greeks and the Romans,

since it is understood that North Africa is part of the Orient. . . . When
we say Orient I believe that we all think, in the first place, of the Islamic
Orient. . . .

That is the first meaning that it has for us and this is due to *The Thousand and One Nights*. There is something that we feel as the Orient . . .
which I have felt in Granada and in Córdoba.]

Borges shows that our definitions of Occident and Orient depend
on each other, and on each other's texts and translations. The exact
geographies of Occident and Orient are undeterminable, much like
originals and translations are unstable and open for rewriting in
Borges's conception of literature.

Significantly, Borges repeatedly connects this idea with issues of
identity:

¿Y cómo definir al Oriente . . . ? Yo diría que las nociones de Oriente
y Occidente son generalizaciones pero que ningún individuo se siente
oriental. Supongo que un hombre se siente persa, se siente hindú, se
siente malayo, pero no oriental. Del mismo modo, nadie se siente latinoamericano: nos sentimos argentinos, chilenos, orientales (uruguayos).
(*OC* III: 236)

[And how to define the Orient . . . ? I would say that the notions of
Orient and Occident are generalizations, but that no individual feels Oriental. I suppose that a man feels Persian, or Hindu, or Malayan, but
not Oriental. Likewise, no one feels Latin American: we feel Argentine,
Chilean, Oriental (Uruguayan).]

The uncertainty surrounding the definitions of Occident and Orient
is increased by the humorous reference to the fact that in the Río
de la Plata region an "Oriental" is someone from Uruguay. Such
comments underscore the subjective nature of the borders between
East and West, North and South. The tension between Occident and
Orient, between center and periphery, is displaced toward and reconsidered from the shores of the Río de la Plata. By redrawing
geographical maps from South America, Borges redraws political
and cultural maps, opening new territories for Latin American
writers.

We reach these conclusions, in large part, by considering Borges's essays on translation in the context in which they were produced. This context, whether it be Argentina or anywhere else in
Latin America, remains one of political, economic, and cultural

marginality with respect to Western European and U.S. centers. As has been said, it is due to this very tension between center and periphery that translation has been and remains today such an important theme and metaphor, as well as a crucial practice, in Latin American literatures. Borges's concept of creative infidelities, combined with his irreverent questioning of the "definitive text," displaces Western European and U.S. canons, legitimizes his own writings in Argentina, and opens the way for innovation in the margins and the center alike. To further explore the potential of writing as (mis)translation in the periphery, we turn next to a study of how Borges makes use of displacement and irreverence in his fictions, beginning with *Historia universal de la infamia.*

3

Writing as Translation

INTRODUCTION

To SAY THAT EVERY ACT OF WRITING IS AN ACT OF TRANSLATION MAY seem like an exaggeration. Yet I would like to begin this chapter with that assertion, and with the premise that writing and translation are synonymous acts of creation. In order to maintain such a hypothesis, we must address the following questions: what kind of translation do we mean when we say that translation and writing are one and the same? Similarly, what kind of writing are we referring to with this assertion? And, in particular, what does Borges as a writer from Argentina gain by writing as translation?

In chapter 2, I suggested that Borges's theories on translation—his challenge of the concept of the "definitive text," his formulation of creative infidelities, and his focus on the importance of shifts in readers and context in determining the meaning of a text—were intimately connected to the writing of his own fictions. To further explain what I mean by this, we begin this chapter with a discussion of Borges's process of creating texts in *Historia universal de la infamia* (1935). In composing these stories, some of the earliest of his career, Borges explicitly reveals the sources from which his own versions are derived. But identifying the pre-text does not diminish the value or the legitimacy of Borges's versions. On the contrary: it is the changes that Borges enacts upon them—the infamies against the original—that both connect and separate Borges's texts and his pre-texts. Most often, this mistranslation occurs at a linguistic and cultural level, which allows Borges to appropriate selected fragments from his sources and situate them in an Argentine context.

One of the most striking aspects of the stories in *Historia universal de la infamia* is the similarity between the creative infidelities Borges utilizes to write them, and the mistranslations he valorizes in "Los traductores de *Las 1001 Noches*." This should not be that surprising, however, given what we know about Borges's stories, and the fact that Borges develops his ideas about translation around the same time as when he writes the texts of *Historia universal de la infamia*. This important overlap extends not only to when Borges writes these texts, but also to where he publishes them. In August 1933, after the release of the book *Discusión* the year before (which includes "Las versiones homéricas"), Borges begins editing the *Revista Multicolor de los Sábados* for *Crítica* with Ulyses Petit de Murat. Borges continues to coedit the magazine and publish numerous stories, collaborations, essays, reviews, and translations there until October 1934. It is here that we find early versions of all but one of the texts in *Historia universal de la infamia*, where they already appear under the general title "Historia universal de la infamia." Borges also publishes early versions of the first two parts of "Los traductores de *Las 1001 Noches*" in *Crítica's Revista*.[1] Furthermore, although Borges actively translates throughout his life, he undertakes more translations in the 1930s and into the early 1940s than at any other time of his career.[2]

After discussing the process of writing as translation that Borges inaugurates in *Historia universal de la infamia*, we turn to "Pierre Menard, autor del *Quijote*," Borges's most important text on the topic of translation. This story, written in a style that blurs the line between criticism and fiction, deals with Pierre Menard and his work, which includes, most famously, his absurdist efforts to (re)-write (*not* transcribe) Cervantes's *Don Quijote* word for word. Critics often observe that "Pierre Menard" articulates its own theory of reading and of writing. But what has not been sufficiently explored, and what cannot be emphasized enough, is the interconnectedness between these theories and Borges's theories of translation. Or, better yet, their synonymous nature, the way in which "Pierre Menard" demonstrates that a theory of reading *is* a theory of writing *is* a theory of translation. We begin to see this by noticing that nearly every aspect of the text, including Menard's "visible work" (i.e., his work prior to his rewriting of the *Quijote*), is related to the theorizing of translation.

However, it is in Menard's "invisible work," in the nature and audacity of Menard's main project and in its surprising results, that we find the text's key contributions to the study of translation and literature. For somehow Menard's text turns out to be drastically different from Cervantes's, even though the sections he completes consist of exactly the same words as the original. How is this possible? How can the same exact words, in the same language, have completely different meanings—both the old and the new, without losing either—when they are written by Menard as opposed to Cervantes? We address this paradox by approaching it through Borges's own theories of translation. As we saw in chapter 2, for Borges the merit of a translation depends on its *infidelities*, on the uses that the translator/recreator makes of irreverence and displacement. Similarly, as we will see in this chapter, the success of Menard's version depends on its *incompleteness* and on its recontextualization. Menard's text is drastically different from Cervantes's because of what it omits from the original. This difference, for Borges, represents an irreverent displacement from the whole to the fragment that plays a major role in his practice of writing as translation. The other key consideration is the temporal and spatial displacements that alter the meaning of the sections of the *Quijote* that Menard manages to (re)write; that is, the shifts from early seventeenth-century Golden Age Spain to early twentieth-century Symbolist France framed by a sarcastic Argentine narrator from the late 1930s[3].

These points are made even more poignant by the irony of Menard's choice of the *Quijote* as his pre-text, since Cervantes's novel is one in which issues of originality and authorship are very much put into play. We need only remember, for example, the vertiginous effect created upon the reader in chapter 9 of Part 1, when we learn that the text is actually a fictionalized translation of Cide Hamete Benengeli's "original" Arabic version.[4] Not coincidentally, one of the sections that Menard completes is this very same chapter, thus drawing our attention to this effect, both in Cervantes's novel and in Borges's story. The labyrinthine levels of irony and what they have to teach us, as well as how they amuse us, expand as we delve deeper into various aspects of "Pierre Menard," including the resonance with the "original" *Don Quijote*.

After discussing "Pierre Menard," we turn to "Examen de la obra de Herbert Quain" (1941), a story which also contains a relevant commentary on translation. In particular, we consider how the structure of Quain's novel *April March* illustrates Borges's play with the indeterminacy of the original, which leads to a discussion of the value of difference and variation. We then conclude this chapter by analyzing two essays, included in *Otras inquisiciones* (1952), in which Borges further develops specific aspects of his theories of translation. In "Sobre el *Vathek* de William Beckford"

(1943), Borges returns to the issue of fidelity, but goes much further than before, as he suggests that an original can be unfaithful to the translation. More than a mere play on words, this inversion releases the translation from its dependence on the original, and helps to reveal the power structures that traditionally force translations (and all manner of rewritings) to be predetermined by the so-called original text. In "El enigma de Edward FitzGerald" (1951), Borges reflects on the kind of unexpected crossings that occur between author and translator, between an original and a translation, to produce a new text. By discussing the "mysterious collaboration" of an author and a translator across centuries, continents, cultures, religions, and languages, Borges demonstrates the extent to which writers and translators—and writing and translation in general—mirror and depend on each other and, when successful, are conflated to create the "miracle" of a new version.

A Process Inaugurated: The Infamies of the Writer/Translator

The key to the "ejercicios de prosa narrativa" [exercises of narrative prose], as Borges calls the texts in *Historia universal de la infamia* in his "Prólogo a la primera edición" [Prologue to the First Edition] (*OC* I: 289), is understanding the importance of Borges as a reader who is manipulating a previous text to create a new one. Throughout *Historia universal de la infamia*, from the "Prologue" to the "Índice de las fuentes" [Index of Sources], Borges provides every indication that his texts derive from prior sources. From the "Index," for example, we know that the "biografía infame" [infamous biography] of "El impostor inverosímil Tom Castro" [Tom Castro, The Implausible Impostor] is taken from the Eleventh Edition of *The Encyclopedia Britannica*; that *The History of Piracy* by Philip Gosse is the pre-text for "La viuda Ching, pirata" [Ching, The Pirate Widow]; that "El proveedor de iniquidades Monk Eastman" [Monk Eastman, Provider of Iniquities] comes from *The Gangs of New York* by Herbert Asbury; and so on. As Sylvia Molloy explains, these "protoficciones" [protofictions] consist of a narrator who "relee un texto previo—unidad supuestamente clausurada, significativa en sí . . . —y dialoga con él" [rereads a previous text—a supposedly closed unity, which is meaningful in and of itself . . . —and dialogues with it] (31).

This technique, inaugurated in *Historia universal de la infamia*, actually becomes Borges's *modus operandi* in all his fictions. Borges's texts delight in conflating the acts of writing and reading.[5] But there is another crucial factor that must be incorporated into this formulation: the role of translation in setting the elements of the fictions in motion. Molloy correctly states that "el texto borgeano recurre a la historia previa para organizarla de manera diferente" [the Borgesian text returns to previous stories to organize them in a different manner] (32). The way it does so is through a practice of mistranslation, of writing as (mis)translation.

Borges's fictions work with a certain motion and instability that is the same as the "hecho móvil" [movable event] that Borges describes in his discussion of the *Iliad* in "Las versiones homéricas." Borges's fictions delight in blurring the lines between scribe, reader, and author, between the visible text and the pre-text. Borges's own fictions are perhaps the best example of his postulation, found in his essays on translation, that all texts are "drafts," mistranslations of previous versions. The relationship between reading and translation becomes analogous to the relationship between reading and writing. In this sense, translation is an ideal metaphor for writing. But Borges's texts go beyond this metaphor. The development of Borges's theories of translation is so interwoven with the development of his fiction that translation and writing become nearly interchangeable practices of creation.

Beatriz Sarlo astutely observes that "para Borges . . . el aprendizaje de la literatura se hace a partir de la traducción y la versión, que son modalidades mayores de la producción de textos. Este principio sólo puede autorizarse en otro: la originalidad no es un valor estético" [for Borges . . . learning literature is accomplished through translations and versions, which are major modalities of the production of texts. This principle can only be authorized by another: originality is not an aesthetic value] (*Borges, un escritor,* 118–19). Which is to say, the idea that the "definitive text" is a fallacy opens the way for the valorization of mistranslations—of "versions and perversions," as Sarlo calls them at another point (*Jorge Luis Borges,* 42). This is exactly what we see in the creative infidelities that Borges valorizes in "Los traductores de *Las 1001 Noches*," and it is perfectly synonymous to the process Borges follows in the stories of *Historia universal de la infamia.*

The opening story "El atroz redentor Lazarus Morell" [The Dread Redeemer Lazarus Morell] is an excellent example of this process. Borges himself tells us in the "Índice de las fuentes" that the pre-texts for his story are Mark Twain's *Life on the Mississippi* and Bernard Devoto's *Mark Twain's America*. But another, larger pre-text is history itself, as we see in the beginning of the story, where we find an eclectic enumeration of events that derive from a proposal by Bartolomé de las Casas. The latter thus functions, unexpectedly, as an originating move that leads to all the other items on the list:

En 1517 el Padre Bartolomé de las Casas tuvo mucha lástima de los indios que se extenuaban en los laboriosos infiernos de las minas de oro antillanas, y propuso al emperador Carlos V la importación de negros, que se extenuaran en los laboriosos infiernos de las minas de oro antilla-nas. A esa curiosa variación de un filántropo debemos infinitos hechos: los *blues* de Handy, el éxito logrado en París por el pintor doctor orien-tal don Pedro Figari, la buena prosa cimarrona del también oriental don Vicente Rossi, el tamaño mitológico de Abraham Lincoln, los quinien-tos mil muertos de la Guerra de Secesión, los tres mil tresceintos mil-lones gastados en pensiones militares, la estatua del imaginario Falucho, la admisión del verbo linchar en la decimotercera edición del *Dicciona-rio de la Academia*, el impetuoso film *Aleluya*, la fornida carga a la bayoneta llevada por Soler al frente de sus *Pardos y Morenos* en el Cer-rito, la gracia de la señorita de Tal, el moreno que asesinó Martín Fierro, la deplorable rumba *El Manisero*, el napoleonismo arrestado y encala-bozado de Toussaint Louverture, la cruz y la serpiente en Haití, la san-gre de las cabras degolladas por el machete del *papaloi*, la habanera madre del tango, el candombe. (*OC* I: 295)

[In 1517, the Spanish missionary Bartolomé de las Casas, taking great pity on the Indians who were languishing in the hellish workpits of An-tillean gold mines, suggested to Charles V, king of Spain, a scheme for importing blacks, so that they might languish in the hellish workpits of Antillean gold mines. To this odd philanthropic twist we owe endless things—W. C. Handy's blues; the Parisian success of the Uruguayan lawyer and painter, Don Pedro Figari; the solid native prose of another Uruguayan, Don Vicente Rossi; the mythological dimensions of Abra-ham Lincoln; the 500,000 dead of the Civil War and the $3,300,000 spent in military pensions; the entrance of the verb *to lynch* into the thirteenth edition of the dictionary of the Spanish Academy; King Vi-dor's impetuous film Hallelujah; the lusty bayonet charge led by the Argentine captain Miguel Soler, at the head of his famous regiment of "Mulattoes and Blacks," in the Uruguayan battle of Cerrito; the Negro killed by Martín Fierro; the deplorable Cuban rumba "The Peanut Vendor"; the arrested, dungeon-ridden Napoleonism of Toussaint L'Ouverture; the cross and the snake of Haitian voodoo rites and the blood of goats whose throats were slit by the *papaloi's* machete; the habanera mother of the tango, the *candombe*.][6]

Borges concludes the list by adding one more unpredictable outcome of De las Casas's foundational gesture, the existence of the protagonist of Borges's text: "Además: la culpable y magnífica existencia del atroz redentor Lazarus Morell" (*OC* I: 295) [And, further, the great and blameworthy life of the nefarious redeemer Lazarus Morell (*Borges a Reader,* 42)].

This long, heterogeneous list serves to place the villain of the story within an American historical context. However, because of the incongruous combination of references and allusions, which suggest strange equivalencies between major and minor—and between U. S. and Latin American—historical events and cultural productions, the enumeration creates a rupture within the very historical context that it seeks to delineate. Borges dialogues with the major narrative (the pre-text) of history and rearranges events so as to vary their relative weight.[7] In this manner, the enumeration problematizes our concepts of causality and determinism. Bartolomé de las Casas's move is the originating cause that, in turn, leads to all the effects included in the list. But without such a list, one would probably not associate any of the items with this originating causation, nor with each other. The irony is the idea that there could actually be a single event responsible for the history of black African slavery in the Americas.

But once we have identified a point of departure, once the originating gesture is created, the possibilities expand almost exponentially; there is a sense that the list could go on indefinitely: "A esa curiosa variación [Bartolomé de las Casas' proposal] . . . debemos *infinitos* hechos" [To this odd philanthropic twist we owe *endless* things]. To the degree that it might, it functions as a *mise-en-abyme* of Borges's concept of literature and of the place of history within it: versions of versions, rewritings of previous texts, loosely and fluidly connected. The enumeration is a mistranslation of the pre-text of history, of an unstable (because invented) original. It allows Borges to rewrite the text of American history with regard to our preconceptions of Bartolomé de las Casas and the references associated with him. The text provides us a glimpse into an "other" universal history of the Americas, an infinity enclosed within a hypercondensed narrative structure—much like the description of the narrator's vision in "El Aleph."

Furthermore, Borges shifts the universal—the universal that is the title of the book and the implied universal history that functions as the context of this and the other stories of *Historia universal de la infamia*—from the U. S., out of the pages of Mark Twain's text, to the shores of the Río de la Plata. Borges achieves this displacement through the linguistic specifics of his (re)writing, and through the interpolation of Argentine references and allusions, such as the one to the *Martín Fierro*, here and elsewhere in the text. Similarly important in this move is the affinity that Borges establishes between the Mississippi and South American rivers later in the story: "El Mississippi es río de pecho ancho; es un infinito y oscuro hermano del Paraná, del Uruguay, del Amazonas y del Orinoco" [The Mississippi is a river with a wide chest; it is an infinite and dark brother of the Paraná, the Uruguay, the Amazon, and the Orinoco] (*OC* I: 295).

The transformations that create the displacement toward the margins are a recoding akin to translation. The language that Borges utilizes to retell the stories found in the British and U. S. sources listed in the "Índice de las fuentes," the diction and vocabulary of the texts in *Historia universal de la infamia*, are unquestionably Argentine.[8] Through this kind of acculturation, Borges selectively rewrites the narratives of the pre-texts (both historical and fictional), appropriating and recontextualizing the narratives of the center. In the process, Borges delineates a new space for himself and other Latin American writers in the margins. This appropriation of selected fragments from the center represents an inversion of traditional power relationships and reveals the indispensable potential that mistranslation affords the periphery.

In this sense, although the term "infamia" in *Historia universal de la infamia* refers, at one level, to the place of the characters in the stories with respect to history and fiction, it also refers to the relationship Borges establishes with his pre-texts, whether they be fictional, historical, or a combination of both. Borges treats history and the universal—both of which are traditionally defined by the Metropolis—with equal irreverence. Lazarus Morell, Tom Castro, the Widow Ching, Monk Eastman, and the other villains of *Historia universal de la infamia* are not the only thieving impostors who invert traditional roles and expectations in these texts. It is Borges himself, through the masks of his narrators, who steals and distorts, who misreads and mistranslates, to invert previously accepted North-South and center-periphery mappings.

Borges finds a strategy here to which he returns time and again in his fictions. Through the selective rewriting of previous texts, the original is destabilized, establishing the legitimacy and potential of the version, of the mistranslation. In the process, literary traditions and history itself can be questioned. By shifting the universal toward Argentina and placing it in a specific linguistic and cultural context, all manner of literary, historical, and epistemological issues can be reconsidered. From Argentina, Borges claims both the center and the periphery. Borges discovers that to write in Argentina, or anywhere else in Latin America, involves an act of irreverence. In this sense, the villains in *Historia universal de la infamia*, as well as the long line of traitors that reappear throughout Borges's stories, personify this innovative potential of irreverence and displacement.[9] To betray from the margins—to commit an act of infamy, to mistranslate—is to write.[10]

"Etcétera": Museum of Translated Fragments

Another clear manifestation of the importance of mistranslation as a strategy for the creation of the texts in *Historia universal de la infamia* is found in the final section of the book, entitled "Etcétera" [Etcetera]. This section consists of six brief texts, each of which is a rewriting of a fragment from a veridical pre-text acknowledged at the end of each story in parenthesis.[11] In the "Prólogo a la primera edición," Borges says about these: "En cuanto a los ejemplos de magia que cierran el volumen, no tengo otro derecho sobre ellos que los de traductor y lector" [As far as the examples of magic that close this volume, I have no right over them other than those of a translator and a reader] (*OC* I: 289). But there is actually very little difference between the process that leads to the creation of these texts and to that of the others in *Historia universal de la infamia*. In both, Borges rereads a previous text, chooses the elements he wants to use for his own text, and enacts a series of creative infidelities to form a new version in a linguistically and culturally Argentine context.

The linguistic and cultural recontextualization is especially well demarcated in "El brujo postergado" [The Sorcerer Postponed], one of the stories in "Etcétera." Borges's version is an intralingual translation from fourteenth-century medieval Spanish to twentieth-century *rioplatense castellano* [Río de la Plata Spanish]. The temporal and geographic displacements are foregrounded by Borges's *acriollamiento* of this medieval text. Furthermore, at the end of the story, in the parenthesis in which the source is named, Borges points out that Don Juan Manuel also had a pre-text from which he drew. Borges's story comes "del *Libro de Patronio* del infante don Juan Manuel, que lo derivó de un libro árabe: *Las cuarenta mañanas y las cuarenta noches*" [from the *Book of Patronio* by the Infante don Juan Manuel, who derived it from an Arab book: *The Forty Mornings and the Forty Nights*] (*OC* I: 342). As a mistranslation of a mistranslation, "El brujo postergado" exemplifies Borges's formulation of literature.[12]

In his "Prólogo a la edición de 1954" Borges refers to the stories in *Historia universal de la infamia* as "el irresponsable juego de un tímido que no se animó a escribir cuentos y que se distrajo en falsear y tergiversar (sin justificación estética alguna vez) ajenas historias" [the irresponsible game of a shy man who did not dare write his own stories and amused himself with the falsification and distortion (sometimes without aesthetic justification) of the stories of others] (*OC* I: 291). However, as Sarlo indicates, there is certainly "más insolencia que timidez en la idea de saquear historias ajenas, alterarlas, agregarles detalles, acriollarlas en su vocabulario y confiarlas a la ironía y la parodia" [more insolence than shyness in the idea of pilfering the stories of others, altering them, adding details, Argentinizing them in his own vocabulary, and confiding them to irony and parody] (*Borges, un escritor,* 117). Such falsifications and distortions in fact constitute a key aspect of Borges's aesthetics. In "El escritor argentino y la tradición," some twenty years after *Historia universal de la infamia*, Borges articulates a process of irreverence by which a writer from the periphery can innovate within Occidental traditions, without being paralyzed by their historical weight. We will discuss this essay and its relationship to Borges's theories of translation in detail in chapter 4. For now, I point out that Borges was already practicing such irreverence in his earliest fictions, in the infamy that inaugurates Borges's practice of writing as translation in the 1930s.

"PIERRE MENARD": THEORIES OF READING, WRITING, AND TRANSLATION

Borges time and again identified "Pierre Menard, autor del *Quijote*" (first published in *Sur*, May, 1939) as his first story.[13] Although we need not take Borges at his word here, the fact that Borges himself claims "Pierre Menard" as his foundational fiction is very much relevant, as the story explores so many of the connections among reading, writing, and translation.[14] Of course, this may be precisely why Borges names "Pierre Menard" as the story that inaugurates his career as a fiction writer. Furthermore, it is quite significant that Borges's self-identified first story has so much to do with theorizing translation. As George Steiner has commented: "Arguably, 'Pierre Menard, Author of the *Quixote*' is the most acute, most concentrated commentary anyone has offered on the business of translation" (73). But what exactly is this commentary? How does "Pierre Menard" articulate and put into play Borges's theories of translation?

Pierre Menard is a "textual" character whose distinguishing characteristics are not physical but citational in nature.[15] In the first part of the story, instead of a physical description we are given a citational list of bibliographical information, a composition of a character drawn entirely from textual references. Menard *is* this enumeration; there are no other elements (physical, familial, etc.) to his identity. This construction of a character based entirely on his writings places us fully in the field of textuality. The problematics of intertextuality with which the story deals are introduced to us in this citational character description even before we get to Menard's "invisible work" (i. e., his efforts to rewrite *Don Quijote*). Menard's existence is based on what he has written. But reading creates Menard just as much as writing does since reading and writing are shown to be nearly equivalent activities in this story. "Pierre Menard" creates a web of readers and writers, of rereadings (or misreadings) and rewritings interlayed and interlayered: Menard the reader/rewriter of Cervantes; the narrator who reads Menard's partial texts; and we, readers of an Argentine narrator's sarcastic commentaries about Menard. But what is the difference between a rereading and a misreading? And how is a text altered from one reading to the next? If meaning varies with reader and context, can any reading be assumed to apprehend the "original," intended meaning of a text? Are not *all* readings, "Pierre Menard" suggests, in fact misreadings?

Furthermore, the theory of reading articulated by "Pierre Menard" is also a theory of translation. This begs the question whether *every* theory of reading is not, by implication, also a theory of translation (and vice versa). This follows from the idea that every reading, every interpretation, is a translation, even within the same language. As Roman Jakobson observes: "The cognitive level of language not only admits but directly requires recoding interpretation, i. e., translation" (149). These connections between reading and translation are also discussed by George Steiner, who states:

> When we read or hear any language-statement from the past, be it Leviticus or last year's best-seller, we translate. Reader, actor, editor are translators of language out of time. The schematic model of translation is one in which a message from a source-language passes into a receptor-language via a transformational process. The barrier is the obvious fact that one language differs from the other, that an interpretative transfer, sometimes, albeit misleadingly, described as encoding and decoding, must occur so that the message "gets through." Exactly the same model—and this is what is rarely stressed—is operative within a single language. But here the barrier or distance between source and receptor is time. (28–29)

There is perhaps no better text to illustrate the equivalence between the theorizing of reading and the theorizing of translation than "Pierre Menard."

ISSUES OF TRANSLATION IN MENARD'S "OBRA VISIBLE"

To understand the implications of the interconnections between reading and translating we must examine Menard's *curriculum vitae*, as Balderston calls it (*Out of Context,* 18), as well as his Quixotic efforts to write Cervantes's novel anew. Several critics have noted that the catalogue of Menard's "visible work" in the first half of the story is not at all arbitrary.[16] But what has not been sufficiently studied is the extent to which nearly every aspect of the citations in Menard's "visible work" are explicitly or implicitly related to issues of translation. In this sense, these items perfectly anticipate Menard's masterwork, his partial rewriting of the *Quijote*, and the issues raised by such a task.

The role of translation in Menard's preparation can be seen beginning with item (a) on the list: "Un soneto simbolista que apareció dos veces (con variaciones) en la revista *La conque* . . ." [A symbolist sonnet that appeared twice (with variations) in the journal *La conque*] (*OC* I: 444).[17] The second version of the poem is a rewriting with variations, which makes it a (mis)translation.[18] Menard's very first literary exercise reminds us of Borges's conception of literature as a series of "drafts," of versions of versions.

Several of the next items on the list[19] refer to issues of language and translation as they were treated in the seventeenth century. As George Steiner has observed, these citations "point towards the labours of the seventeenth century to construct an *ars signorum*, a universal ideogrammatic language system" (73). The intertextuality here becomes broader in scope when we realize that Borges, like his character Menard, also wrote monographs about a number of these seventeenth-century thinkers. In a brief piece about Wilkins (published in *El Hogar*, July 7, 1939, soon after the first publication of "Pierre Menard"), which he later expands into "El idioma analítico de John Wilkins" (*La Nación*, February 8, 1942; later included in *Otras inquisiciones*, 1952), Borges states: "El *Ensayo de una escritura real y de un lenguage filosófico* (1668) propone un catálogo razonado del universo y deriva de ese catálogo un riguroso *idioma internacional*" [The *Essay towards a real character and a philosophical language* (1668) proposes a rationalized catalogue of the universe and derives from this catalogue a rigorous *international language*] (*Textos cautivos,* 334; emphasis added). The "international language" that Borges identifies—a single, universal language based on a poetic, utopic construction (i. e., Wilkins's rationalistic catalogue of the universe)—can be seen as an attempt to repair the disaster at Babel.

The linguistic invention that Borges finds in Wilkins's *Essay* is, in turn, very much like another of Menard's texts from his "visible work," item (b): "Una monografía sobre la posibilidad de construir un vocabulario poético de conceptos que no fueran sinónimos o perífrasis de los que informan el lenguaje común, 'sino objetos ideales creados por una convención y esencialmente destinados a las necesidades poéticas . . .'" [A monograph about the possibility of constructing a poetic vocabulary of concepts that are not the synonyms or periphrasis of common language, but ideal objects created through convention and essentially destined for poetic needs . . .] (*OC* I: 444). In essence, this monograph by Menard is a rewriting of Wilkins's *Essay.*[20] Borges's and Menard's interest in efforts to construct universal languages or new linguistic systems is related to the aesthetic potential of these models. Borges sees such systems—precisely because they point at the irresolvable and irreversible condition of the multiplicity of languages—as idealizing language machines, as sources for the poetic production of narrative. The difference created by Babel affords a potential for (mis)translation, which is to say, for writing.

The idea of a language (or translation) machine as a model for literary production is also found in Ramón Lull's *Ars magna generalis*, a numerically based "thinking machine" about which both Menard and Borges wrote monographs. Menard's work on Lull is referred to in item (f): "Una monografía sobre el *Ars Magna Generalis* de Ramón Lull. . . ." [A monograph about Ramón Lull's *Ars Magna Generalis*] (*OC* I: 445). Borges's discussion of this thirteenth-century text is found in his essay "La máquina de pensar de Raimundo Lulio" [Raimundo Lulio's Thinking Machine] (note the translation of Lull's name) (*El Hogar*, October 15, 1937), in which he states:

Como instrumento de investigación filosófica, la máquina de pensar es absurda. No lo sería, en cambio, como instrumento literario y poético. (Agudamente anota Fritz Mauthner . . . que un diccionario de la rima es una especie de máquina de pensar). El poeta que requiere un epíteto para "tigre," procede en absoluto como la máquina. Los va ensayando hasta encontrar uno que sea suficientemente asombroso. "Tigre negro" puede ser el tigre en la noche; "tigre rojo", todos los tigres, por la connotación de la sangre. (*Textos cautivos,* 178)

[As an instrument of philosophic investigation, the thinking machine is absurd. It would not be, instead, as a literary and poetic instrument. (Fritz Mauthner astutely notes . . . that a rhyming dictionary is a kind of thinking machine.) The poet who requires en epithet for "tiger," proceeds absolutely like the machine. He tries them out until he finds one that is sufficiently startling. "Black tiger" could be the tiger at night; "red tiger," all tigers, because of the connotation of blood.]

As with Leibniz's and Wilkins's efforts, Borges again emphasizes the literary and poetic significance in the theorizing of such a machine. Thus, a "thinking machine," conceived as a language/translation machine, serves as a schematic model of the writer's process of outputting text.

The importance of these ideas is also seen in item (h) of Menard's "visible work:" "Los borradores de una monografía sobre la lógica simbólica de George Boole" [The drafts of a monograph about George Boole's symbolic logic] (*OC* I: 445).[21] As in the previous items, we find an allusion to the desire for a *lingua franca*, as well as a connection between mathematical and alphabetical symbolic systems.[22] Something similar is at play in Menard's interest in chess, as demonstrated by two items of his "visible work." The first is (e): "Un artículo técnico sobre la posibilidad de enriquecer el ajedrez eliminando uno de los peones de torre. Menard propone, recomienda, discute y acaba por rechazar esa innovación" [A technical article about the possibility of enriching chess by eliminating one of the pawns of the rook. Menard proposes, recommends, discusses and finally rejects the innovation]. The second is: (g): "Una traducción con prólogo y notas del *Libro de la invención liberal y arte del juego del axedrez* [sic] de Ruy López de Segura . . ." [A translation with a prologue and notes of the *Book of the liberal invention and art of the game of 'axedrez'* (sic) by Ruy López de Segura . . .] (*OC* I: 445). We note at once that the latter of these is a translation, an art which Menard clearly practices throughout his writing career. Also, since Ruy López de Segura founded the modern system of chess around 1560 (Fishburn, 145), translating/rewriting his text is, in a way, analogous to rewriting/translating Cervantes's text, if we think of Cervantes as the founder of the modern system of the novel.

Furthermore, items (e) and (g) are reminiscent of two other experiments relating to the game of chess with which Borges was very much acquainted: one by his friend, the Argentine artist Xul Solar (1887–1963); the other found in Lewis Carroll's *Through the Looking Glass*.[23] There is in all likelihood a wink towards Xul, in fact, in Borges's spelling of chess: "a̲xedrez" (instead of "ajedrez"). Xul, who shared with Borges a concern for issues relating to language, invented a "Pan juego" (a wild, expanded version of chess), as well as two languages, "Neocriollo" and "Pan lengua."[24] In both *Through the Looking Glass* and Xul's inventions, altering the rules of chess functions as a metaphor for questioning the structural and semantic rules of language, thus raising issues of meaning and understanding. These references reveal Menard's and Borges's interest in the arbitrary and constructed aspects of language, especially of literary and poetic language. Lull, Wilkins, Leibniz, Descartes, Boole, Lewis Carroll, and Xul Solar all attempt to design systems to artificially alter the meaning of words. Each and every time, however, these attempts fail.

Borges analyzes such attempts and failures in the aforementioned "El idioma analítico de John Wilkins." Here, Borges eventually uses Humean skepticism to negate the possibility of constructing a universal language. This metaphysical turn can also be understood in terms of the myth of Babel. After describing "las arbitrariedades de Wilkins" [Wilkins's arbitrarinesses] and of the other proposals for artificial languages that he has considered in this essay,[25] Borges states:

> Notoriamente no hay clasificación del universo que no sea arbitraria y conjetural. La razón es muy simple: no sabemos qué cosa es el universo. . . . Cabe sospechar que no hay universo en el sentido orgánico, unificador, que tiene esa ambiciosa palabra. Si lo hay, falta conjeturar su propósito; falta conjeturar las palabras, las definiciones, las etimologías, las sinonimias, del secreto diccionario de Dios. (*OC* II: 86)

> [Obviously there is no classification of the universe that is not arbitrary and conjectural. The reason is very simple: we do not know what the universe is. . . . We must suspect that there is no universe in the organic, unifying sense inherent in that ambitious word. If there is, we must conjecture its purpose; we must conjecture the words, the definitions, the etymologies, the synonymies of God's secret dictionary. (*Borges a Reader,* 141–42)]

The tower of Babel cannot be reconstructed because we do not know what it would look like; we do not have access to "God's secret dictionary." Any attempt to do so remains arbitrary and ineffectual. This applies to the linguistic utopias Borges delineates in "El idioma analítico de John Wilkins," and about which Menard writes in his "visible work."

In Borges, when we reach the conclusion that the disaster at Babel *cannot* be reversed, and that difference and multiplicity of languages and cultures *cannot* be undone, what we find is not a sense of loss (as in most translation theory), or of anxiety (as in Walter Benjamin), or of melancholy (as in José Ortega y Gasset), nor of exhaustion (as in Paul de Man), but rather of potential. For where the thinkers alluded to in "Pierre Menard" fail in their efforts to alter the meaning of words, Menard finds a way to succeed in his version of the *Quijote.* The paradox, of course, is that he will do so without changing languages, without even having to rely on the potential afforded by the distance between distinct linguistic systems. Or rather, what "Pierre Menard" shows is that such distance occurs intralingually as well as interlingually. Temporal and geographic displacements, it turns out, can accomplish Pierre Menard's (or Wilkins's, or Xul Solar's) objectives of constructing a new language—of changing symbolic values and rearranging the connections between signifier and signified—much better than their analytic efforts to do so.

Given the connections between Menard's interest in systems of chess, mathematics, and language, it is not surprising to find him turning next to the rules of French language itself, in the following two items, (i): "Un examen de las leyes métricas esenciales de la prosa francesa, ilustrado con ejemplos de Saint-Simon . . ." [An examination of the essential metric rules of French prose, illustrated with examples from Saint-Simon]; and (j): "Una réplica a Luc Durtain (que había negado la existencia de tales leyes) ilustrada con ejemplos de Luc Durtain . . ." [A reply to Luc Durtain (who had denied the existence of such rules) illustrated with examples from Luc Durtain] (*OC* I: 445).[26] The emphasis in these items is on the formal aspects of prose, on the essential poetic rules that constitute such aspects. The issue is whether such rules can actually be established and, if so, the implications of these for the practice of writing, or of translation. In other words, do such strict rules make interlingual translation that much more difficult, or outright impossible?

This question becomes even more complicated when we look at Menard's next item, a translation of Quevedo, (k): "Una traducción manuscrita de la *Aguja de navegar cultos* de Quevedo, intitulado *La boussole des précieux*" [A manuscript translation of *Compass for Navigating Cultisms* by Quevedo, entitled *La boussole des précieux*] (*OC* I: 445). *Aguja de navegar cultos* is a short satirical work that attacks linguistic preciosity (Fishburn, 7). It is thus extremely ironic that Menard should choose the word "précieux" for his translation of "cultos."[27] For our purposes here, we note that Menard's translation of Quevedo, even before his translation of Cervantes, already problematizes the issue of fidelity by drawing our attention to the similarities and differences between time periods and literary choices.

Also relevant is Menard's item (n): "Un obstinado análisis de las 'costumbres sintácticas' de Toulet . . ." [An obdurate analysis of the 'syntactical habits' of Toulet . . .] (*OC* I: 445). The phrase "costumbres sintácticas" [syntactical habits] resonates with the emphasis Borges places in "Los traductores de *Las 1001 Noches*" on the "hábitos literarios" [literary habits] of the translator and on the "movimiento sintáctico" [syntactical movement] that occurs in the process of translation. Menard's choice of Toulet as an object of study is suggestive because his works include *Le mariage de Don Quichotte* (1902), a rewriting of Cervantes (Fishburn, 244).

Menard follows this up with another translation, (o): "Una trasposición en alejandrinos del *Cimetière marin* de Paul Valéry . . ." [A transposition into alexandrines of Paul Valéry's *Cimetière marin*] (*OC* I: 445). Valéry wrote the *Cimetière marin* in decasyllabic verses to break with the tradition of the French alexandrine poem. As both Olaso (105–6) and Balderston (19) point out, this rewriting of Valéry's poem from one form to another represents a perversion of Valéry's "original" intent. Menard's translation of the form seemingly undoes the poetic objective of the poem itself. However, as Evelyn Fishburn suggests, "Borges may have remembered that Valéry himself was not averse to transposing poems into a different metre" (58). The ambivalent nature of this item is ripe with possibilities: did Menard know what he was doing? On what aspect of Menard's perverse translation does Borges want us to focus? Suffice it to say that Menard's transposition, although intralingual, raises the issue of what happens to a poem once its form is altered. In addition, Menard's production of a new (per)version of Valéry's poem again reminds us of Borges's constant questioning of the "definitive text," and of his concept of literature as a series of "drafts," of versions of versions.

The next item on the list points at the subjective nature of meaning. Menard writes, item (p): "Una invectiva contra Paul Valéry. . . . (Esa invectiva, dicho sea entre paréntesis, es el reverso exacto de su verdadera opinión sobre Valéry. Éste así lo entendió y la amistad antigua de los dos no corrió peligro.)" [An invective against Paul Valéry. . . . (This invective, we note parenthetically, is the exact opposite of his real opinion about Valéry. The latter understood this and the longtime friendship between the two was not damaged)] (*OC* I: 445). In addition to the humor of the parenthetical remark, there is also the idea that the meaning of a text can be the exact opposite of what it appears to be at a literal level, an important concept that is taken up again and amplified in Menard's (re)writing of the *Quijote*.

Menard composes several other poems, listed as item (r): "Un ciclo de admirables sonetos para la baronesa de Bacourt . . ." [A series of admirable sonnets for the Baroness de Bacourt] (*OC* I: 446). Finally, item (s) is a handwritten list ("una lista manuscrita") that Menard has made of "versos que deben su eficacia a la puntuación" [verses that owe their efficiency to their punctuation] (*OC* I:

446). Again we find the importance of syntax in questions of aesthetic value. But the last item of Menard's "visible work" is actually the footnote that accompanies item (s): "Madame Henri Bachelier enumera asimismo una versión literal de la versión literal que hizo Quevedo de la *Introduction à la vie dévote* de San Francisco de Sales. En la biblioteca de Pierre Menard no hay rastros de tal obra. Debe tratarse de una broma de nuestro amigo, mal escuchada" [Madame Henri Bachelier also lists a literal version of the literal version that Quevedo made of the *Introduction à la vie dévote* by San Francisco de Sales. There are no traces of such a work in Pierre Menard's library. This must have been a joke of his that she misunderstood] (*OC* I: 446). But is this really a joke? Is it not possible that Menard has in fact accomplished such a task? If he has, it would not be strange that the narrator could not find it in Menard's library, for there would be no way to distinguish Menard's version from Saint François de Sales' "original," since the two would look exactly the same and would thus fall into the category of Menard's "invisible work." Although the issue remains unresolved, Borges is clearly playing with concepts of authorship and originality. The confusion, the game of reflecting versions, of translations of translations, serves as a perfect transition from Menard's "visible" to his "invisible work." [28]

THE AESTHETICS OF PIERRE MENARD'S "INVISIBLE" MASTERPIECE

Enacting the Fragment: Irreverence in Action

As Borges's readers well know, Menard's main project is his attempt to write Cervantes's *Don Quijote* anew. The effort is Herculean and Quixotic, absurd and impossible. The result is masterful and unbelievable, and points at the core tenets of Borges's aesthetics. When the narrator of the story completes his enumeration of Menard's "visible work" and turns to discuss his "invisible work," he describes the latter in these terms:

Paso ahora a la otra: la subterránea, la interminablemente heróica, la impar. También, ¡ay de las posibilidades del hombre!, la *inconclusa*. Esa obra, tal vez la más significativa de nuestro tiempo, consta de los capítulos noveno y trigésimo octavo de la primera parte del *Don Quijote* y de un fragmento del capítulo veintidós (*OC* I: 446; emphasis added).

[I turn now to that other part, which is subterranean, interminably heroic, and unequaled. It is also—oh, the possibilities inherent in the man—*inconclusive*. This work, perhaps the most significant of our time, consists of the ninth and thirty-eighth chapters of Part One of *Don Quijote* and of a fragment of the twenty-second chapter.]

Menard's work remains unfinished ("inconclusive"). However, not only does this not detract from Menard's results, it actually helps to constitute his success. Paradoxically, much as in "Los traductores de *Las 1001 Noches*" Borges argues that a translation's merits lie precisely in its *infidelities*, here the success of Menard's masterpiece rests in large part on the fact that it remains *incomplete*.

The narrator of "Pierre Menard" declares that despite the obstacles faced by Menard, his fragmented version is ironically more subtle, more refined, than that of Cervantes:

El fragmentario *Quijote* de Menard es más sutil que el de Cervantes. Éste, de un modo burdo, opone a las ficciones caballerescas la pobre realidad provinciana de su país; Menard elige como "realidad" la tierra de Carmen durante el siglo de Lepanto y de Lope. ¡Qué españoladas no habría aconsejado esa elección a Maurice Barrès o al doctor Rodríguez Larreta! Menard, con toda naturalidad, las elude. En su obra no hay gitanerías ni conquistadores, ni místicos, ni Felipe Segundo ni autos de fe. Desatiende o proscribe el color local. Ese desdén indica un sentido nuevo de la novela histórica. Ese desdén condena a *Salammbô*, inapelablemente (*OC* I: 448).

[Menard's fragmentary *Quijote* is more subtle than Cervantes's. The latter, in a coarse manner, opposes the tales of knighthood with the meager, provincial reality of his country; Menard chooses as "reality" the land of Carmen during the century of Lepanto and Lope. What Hispanophile would not have advised Maurice Barrès or Dr. Rodríguez Larreta to make such a choice! Menard, as if it were the most natural thing in the world, eludes them. In his work there are no bands of gypsies, conquistadors, mystics, Philip the Seconds, nor autos-da-fé. He disregards or proscribes local color. This disdain indicates a new approach to the historical novel. This disdain condemns *Salammbô* without appeal.] (*Borges a Reader,* 101)

A fragmentary *Quijote*, as these statements show, eliminates certain elements from Cervantes's version of which Borges seemingly disapproves: namely regionalism and local color (which Barrès and Rodríguez Larreta included in their attempts to write historical novels). Pierre Menard, however, creates his text by using fragments of a text from the past, but in an entirely new time and in a drastically different context. Thus, Menard's move condemns Flaubert's *Salammbô*, a novel "rich in action and 'local color,'" (Fishburn, 211) that epitomizes the kind of historical novel that Borges always criticized.[29]

The incompleteness of Menard's *Quijote* speaks to the impossibility of making a total, perfect translation—either in the same language or from one language to another. If it is impossible to make such an intralingual translation, it is clearly unfeasible to make an interlingual one. Babel cannot be reconstructed: even if there were only one language, changes in time and context constantly alter meaning. The same text, the same utterance, can never have the same meaning twice. Better yet: texts accumulate meaning through changes and shifts in time and space, so that with each displacement their potentiality expands. Even though Menard's version is a word-for-word re-creation, it is still a *mis*translation of Cervantes's novel. This aesthetic of the fragment, the disregard for the intrinsic sacred worth of the original as a whole, is an irreverent position that contributes to creating new meanings and texts.

In effect, Menard chooses and selects ("Menard chooses") what he wants to take from Cervantes, and disregards or eliminates ("disregards or proscribes") what he finds superfluous. Menard's process may look like an act of direct copying; but his theft also consists of important and major omissions. Menard takes several fragments ("out of context," to use Balderston's phrase) and omits everything else. The effect is a thorough disruption of the original text, and a subsequent enacting of new meanings through a displacement of the copied sections. In this sense, Menard's fragmentary *Quijote* is as deformed and altered a rewriting as the translations by Galland, Burton, and Mardrus that Borges valorizes in "Los traductores de *Las 1001 Noches*." Quite clearly, omissions, as much as interpolations or any other kind of changes that the translator/recreator undertakes, are an essential aspect of Borges's theory of translation and, by implication, of Borges's theories of reading and of writing.

The potential of the fragment is released once the fragment is taken from its original site and recontextualized—reinscribed—in the target one.[30] In "Pierre Menard," this occurs not only from Cervantes's (whole) version to Menard's (partial) one, but also into Borges's story itself. There is a series of displacements enacted in the text, each representing an act of irreverence and a shift in meaning and value. Menard's "invisible work" is framed within a narrator's voice, and this narrator, as witnessed by his linguistic and cultural allusions, is very clearly Argentine.[31]

Menard's Hall of Mirrors: Has Anyone Seen the Original?

The success of Menard's project is intensified by the irony and relevance of the specific sections that Menard manages to rewrite from Cervantes's novel. Menard's version consists of "los capítulos noveno y trigésimo octavo de la primera parte del *Don Quijote* y . . . un fragmento del capítulo veintidós" [the ninth and thirty-eighth chapters of Part One of *Don Quijote* and of a fragment of the twenty-second chapter] (*OC* I: 446). There is nothing random about the sections that Borges has Menard complete. In a quintessential Borgesian move, these sections reflect the main points of "Pierre Menard," even as they suggest a rereading of Cervantes's novel.

Chapter XXII of the first part of the *Quijote*, for example, recounts the adventures of the galley slaves and introduces the character Ginés de Pasamonte. In the dialogue between don Quijote and Ginés, the latter makes numerous puns and other plays on words that don Quijote constantly misunderstands. The episode emphasizes a certain arbitrary nature of language and its polysemantic possibilities, even when two interlocutors speak the same language. In this same chapter, Ginés talks about his autobiography, compares it with other picaresque novels, and describes his inability to finish it because his life is not yet complete. Both the misunderstandings of language and the play between reality and fiction in Ginés's *incomplete* autobiography help explain Menard's interest in this chapter, of which he only managed to complete a fragment— just as Ginés has only completed a fragmented version of his autobiography.[32]

The significance of the two chapters that Menard manages to rewrite completely is even greater. Of chapter XXXVIII, the arms and letters debate, the narrator exclaims:

> Es sabido que Don Quijote . . . falla el pleito contra las letras y en favor de las armas. Cervantes era un viejo militar: su fallo se explica. ¡Pero que el Don Quijote de Pierre Menard—hombre contemporáneo de *La trahison des clercs* y de Bertrand Russell—reincida en esas nebulosas sofisterías! (*OC* I: 448–49)

[It is known that Don Quijote . . . passes judgment against letters and in favor of arms. Cervantes was an old soldier, which explains such a judgment. But that the Don Quijote of Pierre Menard—a contemporary of *La trahison des clercs* and Bertrand Russell—should relapse into these nebulous sophistries! (*Borges a Reader,* 101)]

The narrator's outrage at Menard's choice of arms over letters, as Balderston argues in *Out of Context* (18–38), is due to the shift in context between Cervantes's time period and Menard's. As the narrator of "Pierre Menard" himself mentions: "No en vano han transcurrido trescientos años, cargados de complejísimos hechos" [It is not in vain that three hundred years have passed, filled with the most complicated of events] (*OC* I: 448). To choose arms over letters in the socio-historical context in which Menard wrote his version (i. e., between the two world wars) would indeed sound outrageous to most people today.

The epitome of how the meaning of words can change with time comes toward the end of the story, when the narrator quotes both Cervantes and Menard from chapter IX (two quotations that look— and are—identical), and argues that these same exact words have completely different meanings (*OC* I: 449). What we find here is that new meaning is created, and that this new meaning—which appears to be the opposite of the old meaning—paradoxically coexists with the old precisely because the fragment from Cervantes has been reinscribed in "Pierre Menard." In addition, the section alluded to in Cervantes is again in no way arbitrary. At the end of chapter VIII of *Don Quijote*, we suddenly learn that there are apparently two authors of the novel, suggesting that Cervantes's narrator, who had until then carried full authorial weight, actually depends on another author of an unknown pre-text. Chapter IX then begins the story anew, this time incorporating how Cervantes's narrator finds the "*Historia de don Quijote de la Mancha, escrita por Cide Hamete Benengeli*" [*Story of Don Quijote of the Mancha, Written by Cide Hamete Benengeli.*][33] We thus reach the vertiginous moment in which we realize that the text we are reading is itself a translation of Cide Hamete Berengeli's fictional original (Cervantes, 139–44).

Arguably the first modern novel, *Don Quijote* is structured as a story within a story, as a translation of various pre-texts. It is a rewriting of the chivalresque and picaresque novels, but also of an Arabic pre-text that exists only within the confines of the novel itself. From its very origins, the novel seems to function around the paradoxical impossibility of locating a stable original. Cervantes's narrator finds Cide Hamete's manuscript in Toledo, a city that, a few centuries earlier, at the time of Alfonso X, was a kind of Babylon in which Castilians, Moors, and Jews managed to coexist and to thrive, with one of the most active and important schools of translation in Western history. Borges alludes to that Babylon from his own modern one, in Buenos Aires, through Menard's rewriting of chapter IX of the *Quijote*.

The passages that Borges's narrator quotes from chapter IX as an example of the difference between Cervantes and Menard both read as follows: "La verdad, cuya madre es la historia, émula del tiempo, depósito de las acciones, testigo de lo pasado, ejemplo y aviso de lo presente, advertencia de lo por venir" [Truth, whose mother is history, who is the rival of time, depository of deeds, witness of the past, example and lesson for the present, warning for the future] (*OC* I: 449). The narrator argues that in the case of Cervantes, "esa enumeración es un mero elogio retórico de la historia" [this enumeration is a mere rhetorical eulogy of history], but that, in the case of Menard, it is startling, unexpected:

> La historia, *madre* de la verdad; la idea es asombrosa. Menard, contemporáneo de William James, no define la historia como una indagación de la realidad sino como su origen. La verdad histórica, para él, no es lo que sucedió; es lo que juzgamos que sucedió. Las cláusulas finales—*ejemplo y aviso de lo presente, advertencia de lo por venir*—son descaradamente pragmáticas. (*OC* I: 449; emphasis in the original)

> [History, *mother* of truth; the idea is astounding. Menard, a contemporary of William James, does not define history as an investigation of reality, but as its origin. Historical truth, for him, is not what took place; it is what we think took place. The final clauses—*example and lesson for the present, warning for the future*—are shamelessly pragmatic.]

Read through Menard (and through William James), the possibility that history can recount its own "truths" seems highly questionable. Instead, history becomes "what we judge it to have been" ("es lo que juzgamos que sucedió").[34] This section of Cervantes's text also deals with issues of veracity by alluding to the relationship between Spaniards and Moors and how this affects ideas of history and authorial power. Cervantes's originality, built atop the supposed original manuscript of Cide Hamete through an act of translation, inaugurates the modern novel. Menard's version reflects this moment, displaces it temporally and geographically, and, according to his own claims, inaugurates Borges's fiction. The accomplishments of Menard's project confuse any possible definitions of "originality" and "truth." This very confusion (confusion, as in Babel) alters and expands meaning.

The brilliance of Borges's text here resides in that, even as it manipulates the recontextualizations that amplify meanings, the previous ones are *not* lost. In other words, the reader can actually access multiple meanings—Cervantes's and Menard's, the old and the new, the original and the translation—even when these meanings are opposite in nature. The displacements lead to a multiplication of layered meanings, which, even if they contradict each other, remain present for the reader to appreciate. And it is precisely here where we find the potential of writing as (mis)translation from the periphery.

Every text, every citation, points back to a previous original— Menard's works to Cervantes's, Cervantes's to Cide Hamete's— but when we reach the "original" original, so to speak, we discover it to be a fictional creation. Versions of versions, all "drafts," without a "definitive text" anywhere to be found: a thorough, destabilizing, decentering of the concept of originality located at the very core of the creative process. Each translation from one supposed original to the other—from Cide Hamete to Cervantes to Menard to Borges—introduces a distancing from the very text to which this process tries to reach. A distancing encountered the closer we try to get to an illusory original, temporal and spatial displacements that distort the meaning of a text (for the reader, for the translator, for the writer) without even needing to change languages—these are the elements that constitute the importance of translation for Borges, and the elements that constitute his process of writing.

And the role of the fragment here can be understood in terms of the shifts in context from the site from which the fragment is taken (with irreverence, as Borges would say), to where it is inserted (to innovate, to renovate). The unexpected outcome of this move (e. g., from Cervantes's whole novel to Menard's few fragments) is that it creates gain instead of loss. Herein lies the true genius of "Pierre Menard." When Menard carries out his strange project and arrives at his fragmentary, recontextualized version of the *Quijote*, we end up with a situation bursting with new possibilities: "El texto de Cervantes y el de Menard son verbalmente idénticos, pero el segundo es casi infinitamente más rico. (Más ambiguo, dirán sus detractores; pero la ambigüedad es una riqueza.)" [The texts by Cervantes and by Menard are verbally identical, but the latter is almost infinitely richer. (More ambiguous, its detractors might say, but ambiguity is a richness)]. The labyrinthine levels of irony add to the "richness" of Menard's version—or of Borges's story, rather. The space created by the ambiguity referred to in the parenthetical remark expands to create the potential for the production of literature in the margins. Although Menard's project lies in the field of the absurd, the story leads us to reflect upon what such a rewriting of the *Quijote* implies. The humor, the pleasure of the text, is created not just by Menard's project, nor by the narrator's relationship to Menard, but by the reader's recognition that the absurd makes sense, that in a way Menard's version may just be more interesting, less unavoidable, more courageous than Cervantes's. And this occurs, paradoxically, because it is a fragmented, recontextualized version of it—which is to say, a mistranslation.

THE INDETERMINACY OF THE ORIGINAL: HERBERT QUAIN'S *APRIL MARCH*

"Examen de la obra de Herbert Quain" (first published in *Sur*, April 1941, then included in *Ficciones*, 1944) is another fiction from this period that can be read as a commentary on translation.[35] Of particular interest in this regard is one of the novels reviewed in the story, Quain's "novela regresiva, ramificada" [regressive, ramified novel] *April March*. This novel's innovation, what makes it a "game," as the narrator of the story insists (*OC* I: 462), is its structure: the novel begins at the end, is followed by three possible antecedent events that lead to it, each of which has in turn three possible additional antecedent events leading to it. Significantly, Quain does not discard any of his plot lines; he includes them all as a network of potentiality. The first event in chronological terms (i.e., the original) does not necessarily determine how the narrative will follow. The reader is not limited to an individual, correct, predetermined interpretation, but is free to follow his/her own. The multiple and multiplying plot lines, the different possibilities, are like the diverging translations of the *Iliad* that Borges compares in "Las versiones homéricas": they are all "sinceras, genuinas y divergentes" [sincere, genuine and divergent] (*OC* I: 240). In both cases, difference is posited as a privileged site for literary creation, full of aesthetic and narrative potential.

In this sense, "Examen de la obra de Herbert Quain" raises the issue of determinism and reveals an important contrast between Borges and a line of thinking associated with Walter Benjamin. As Ricardo Piglia states in a recent interview:

> Yo creo que la teoría mística de Benjamin apunta a cierta determinación; si el texto determina su lectura pertinente, [eso] implica una teoría de la lectura de la literalidad. . . . El texto tiene algo que es un plan que define cómo debe ser leído y el exegeta lo único que busca es el camino que le permite avanzar en la línea de esa determinación y la lectura correcta es aquella que surge de captar aquello que surge como lectura correcta.
>
> Borges [en cambio] plantea que todas las lecturas son correctas (claro, después [se juzga que] algunas son eficaces o no, pero no es una cuestión de "corrección"). No habría un esquema por el cual esto podría ser definido por el texto como si el texto fuera un programa que define ya cómo será su dirección verdadera. (Piglia interview 8/16/99)

> [I think that Benjamin's mystical theory points toward certain determination; if the text determines its pertinent reading, [this] would imply a theory of reading and of literalness. . . . The text contains something like a plan that defines how it should be read; the only thing that the exegete looks for is the path that allows him to go forward in the line of that determination; the correct reading is the one that appears from capturing what appears to be the correct reading.
>
> Borges [instead] proposes that all readings are correct (of course, afterward [one judges] if a reading is efficient or not, but it is not a question of "correctness"). There would not be a scheme defined by the text as if the text were a program that already carried the definition of what its real direction will be.]

Instead of a predetermined, single line that could be traced from the source to the target text, Borges proposes a broad map of viable options—a "topography," in Deleuze and Guattari's terms[36]—that undermines the supremacy of the original by rupturing its power to determine how it must be read or translated. It is not that the different versions do not have equal aesthetic value, of course, as evidenced by the fact that Borges does not hesitate to express his preferences between the various translations that he compares in "Las versiones homéricas" and "Los traductores de *Las 1001 Noches*." But Borges does present them all as valid and, in the case of Herbert Quain's work, emphasizes the role of the reader in choosing and determining these preferences. This map of potential versions, instead of a single, literal version predetermined by the original, contributes to destabilizing the myth of the original and of its deterministic prepotency.

Borges's challenge to the determinacy of the original begins with some of his earliest essays. In "La fruición literaria" (*La Prensa*, January 23, 1927, then included in *El idioma de los argentinos*, 1928), for example, he takes a verse out of context to demonstrate how meaning is over-determined by the reader's preconceptions of the author, the time period, the place, and everything else that constitutes the context in the reader's mind.[37] Borges's texts constantly make us question our beliefs as readers and force us to face our dependency on the concept of originality. In "Examen de la obra de Herbert Quain," Borges attributes his position to Quain through an ironic narrator:

> Quain solía argumentar que los lectores eran una especie ya extinta. "No hay europeo—razonaba—que no sea un escritor, en potencia o en acto." Afirmaba también que de las diversas felicidades que puede ministrar la literatura, la más alta era la invención. Ya que no todos son capaces de esa felicidad, *muchos habrán de contentarse con simulacros.* (*OC* I: 464; emphasis added)

> [Quain used to argue that readers were already an extinct species. "There is no European," he would reason, "who is not a writer, potentially or in actuality." He also maintained that of the diverse pleasures that literature can administer, the highest was its invention. However, since not everyone is capable of such pleasure, *many must make due with simulacra.*]

The shift from the European who is ironically already a writer (even if only potentially so!), to the others who must remain satisfied with the simulacra, validates the copy, the translation, which is implicitly what is available to the non-Europeans—including to Argentines like Borges himself.

EXAMINING THE *VATHEK* BY WILLIAM BECKFORD:
THE UNCANNY INFIDELITY OF THE ORIGINAL

In "Sobre el *Vathek* de William Beckford" (first published in *La Nación* on April 4, 1943, later included in *Otras inquisiciones*,

1952), Borges returns to a consideration of the basic issue in the theorizing of translation: the question of fidelity. This short essay deals with the relationship between an original event and the recounting of that event, between an original text and its translation. By framing his discussion within a number of comments about biographies, Borges also hints at the close relationship between the problematics of fidelity in translation and that of veracity in narrative itself; in other words, between translation and history. The entire essay builds toward the startling assertion that an original can be unfaithful to its translation. This statement, more than a mere inversion of terms, represents how far Borges goes in his conception of what translation can afford a writer; it also reflects the process Borges utilizes time and again in his fictions.

Inspired by a recent reading of a biography of William Beckford, "Sobre el *Vathek* de William Beckford" begins with a long reflection on the nature of biographies, in which Borges reiterates his lifelong disdain for biographies, especially those that focus on the writer's life while ignoring their works.[38] Borges, instead, is interested in Beckford's *Vathek*, the "novela a cuyas últimas diez páginas William Beckford debe su gloria" [novel to the last ten pages of which William Beckford owes his glory] (*OC* II: 107). Borges recounts the story of the *Vathek* in a hypercondensed version of Beckford's Oriental gothic romance. Beckford's novel is the tale of how the caliph Vathek builds a Babylonian tower that leads to the greatest of splendors, which turn out to be located in a palace that is also the Inferno (*OC* II: 108). The trajectory that the caliph travels in the *Vathek* serves as a moral against building such a tower. Borges observes, however, that as opposed to the story of Doctor Faustus, or the many medieval legends in which Hell functions as the punishment for the sins of those who strike a deal with the forces of evil, in the *Vathek* the Inferno "es el castigo *y* la tentación" [is the punishment *and* the temptation] (*OC* II: 108; emphasis added). The temptation of rebuilding the tower of Babel leads to an Inferno, but not one in which the architect is merely punished. In an unexpected inversion, Borges's reading of the end of the *Vathek* makes the palace of the Inferno a reflection of the tower: both temptation *and* punishment, inseparable, horrible, yet desirable.

Borges then shifts the focus of the essay and discusses other writers, including Stevenson, Chesterton, Poe, and Melville, whose work captures a certain nightmarish horror. Borges suggests that the *Vathek* is a precursor to this branch of nineteenth-century supernatural literature:

> Creo, sin embargo, que *Vathek* pronostica, siquiera de un modo rudimentario, los satánicos esplendores de Thomas de Quincey y de Poe, de Charles Baudelaire y de Huysmans. Hay un intraducible epíteto inglés, el epíteto *uncanny*, para denotar el horror sobrenatural; ese epíteto (*unheimlich* en alemán) es aplicable a ciertas páginas de *Vathek*; que yo recuerde, a ningún otro libro anterior. (*OC* II: 109)

> [I believe, however, that *Vathek* anticipates, at least in a rudimentary fashion, the Satanic splendors of Thomas de Quincey and Poe, of Charles Baudelaire and Huysmans. There is an untranslatable epithet in English, the epithet *uncanny*, to denote the supernatural horror; that epithet (*unheimlich* in German) applies to certain pages of *Vathek*; as far as I can recall, it applies to no other book before it.]

Shortly thereafter, Borges presents the key moment of the essay: "Sólo tres días y dos noches del invierno de 1782 requirió William Beckford para redactar la trágica historia de su califa. La escribió en idioma francés; [Samuel] Henley la tradujo al inglés en 1785. *El original es infiel a la traducción*" [William Beckford required only three days and two night of the winter of 1782 to write the tragic story of his caliph. He wrote it in French; [Samuel] Henley translated it into English in 1785. *The original is unfaithful to the translation*] (*OC* II: 109; emphasis added).

The idea that the original can be unfaithful to its translation goes even further than the challenges to fidelity that Borges expresses in "Los traductores de *Las 1001 Noches*." There, Borges valorizes mistranslations and creative infidelities and suggests that a translation can surpass the original. But here, Borges's move disrupts the very core of the concept of fidelity. The inversion of the two terms thoroughly devalues the original through a paradox that deconstructs any preestablished relationship between translation and original. The mere thought that the original is somehow unfaithful to the translation (and not the other way around, as the phrase is traditionally used) is startling. It takes the ground on which we were just comfortably standing out from under us.

But is Borges merely playing games here, or is it actually possible to imagine that an original might be unfaithful to its translation? What circumstances might lead to such an inversion? After making his unexpected assertion, Borges discusses the relative ability of eighteenth- and nineteenth-century French and English to communicate the supernatural horrors of the *Vathek*: "Saintsbury observa que el francés del siglo XVIII es menos apto que el inglés para comunicar los 'indefinidos horrores' (la frase es de Beckford) de la singularísima historia" [Saintsbury observes that eighteenth-century French is less apt than English to communicate those 'undefined horrors' (the phrase is Beckford's) of this unique story] (*OC* II: 109). In other words, English is found to be better suited for the expression of this particular utterance than eighteenth-century French, despite the fact that it was originally written in French. Fidelity, then—if there is any room left to talk about such a concept after the challenge to it that this essay represents—appears to depend on the relationship between content and language, but not necessarily on the original language in which the text was written.[39]

This explains the long paragraph on the nature of the uncanny prior to the statement about fidelity. Stevenson, Chesterton, De Quincey, Poe, and the other writers whom Borges argues are prefigured by the *Vathek* create a specific historical literary context that reveals what has been accomplished in the genre of the supernatural in English. Seen in this light, read contextually, it is the English version of the *Vathek* (i.e., the translation) that serves as the precursor to nineteenth-century fantastic literature. The original (in French, by Beckford) is thus unfaithful to this translation, for it is the latter that is the prefiguration of future uncanny literature.

If the *Vathek* is a precursor for the nineteenth-century writers Borges mentions in this text, they, in turn, are precursors of Borges himself. This essay thus creates an unexpected literary lineage traced through translation: unexpected in that it finds the *Vathek* to be a major source for fantastic literature, but also because translation is given a decisive creative role in its transmittal. A major element that makes this possible is that translation is ruptured from the determinacy of the original. It is the translation that is the precursor, not the original; translation makes this lineage—now freed from the binds of the original—possible.

In chapter 2 we saw how Borges valorizes creative infidelities to sidestep traditional demands for fidelity. Now, in "Sobre el *Vathek* de William Beckford," we see that a mistranslation (in this case enacted by the different literary and cultural resonances possible when moving a text from one language into another) can become so distanced from the source that every aspect of the relationship between them can be scrutinized. This extends not only to which is "better" (i.e., more efficient, more "correct"), but also to which is more faithful. But faithful to what? The very concept loses meaning as its prejudices are revealed. After Borges's inversion, it becomes as valid to ask if the original is faithful to the translation, as the other way around. The use of paradox serves to empty fidelity of its preconceptions. It shows it to be an unnecessary, biased judgment traditionally used to assert the power of the original over the translation by demanding its loyalty to it.

Furthermore, the validation of translation that accompanies the statement "the original is unfaithful to the translation" is a move of special importance for a writer from the margins. Such an inversion implies that the margins can change (i.e., mistranslate) the center, that the latter can be reread and rewritten by the versions (i.e., the simulacra) of the periphery. In the process, the very structures that stabilize the canons of the Metropolis are undermined. If the original (from the center) is unfaithful to the translation (from the margins), then the center is found to be inadequate to continue exhorting its demands for fidelity. The act of misreading from the periphery is not only validated, it is also strongly favored for its potential for innovation.

"El Enigma de Edward FitzGerald": The Mysterious Collaboration of the Writer and the Translator

"Sobre el *Vathek* de William Beckford" alerts us to the different resonances that source and target texts awake in their respective languages and literatures, and how that difference itself can be a privileged site for the production of narrative, of writing as (mis)-translation. In "El enigma de Edward FitzGerald" (first published in *La Nación* on October 7, 1951, then included in *Otras inquisiciones*, 1952) Borges presents a similar situation, but from an entirely unexpected perspective: one that helps explain his thoughts on the relationship between the writer and the translator and, by implication, between writing and translation in general. In this case, too, the translation supplants the original and transforms it nearly beyond recognition, to the extent that the original might be considered unfaithful to it. Here, though, the translation reaches such a level through an apparent merger, or conjunction, between the writer of the source and that of the target texts. The only difficulty in comprehending how such a joining comes about is that writer and translator are separated by seven centuries, and several languages, cultures, literary traditions, and religions. The text in question is Edward FitzGerald's 1859 English version of Omar Khayyám's eleventh-century Persian *Rubáiyát*.

Borges's familiarity with FitzGerald's *Rubáiyát* goes back to his youth, as his own father translated FitzGerald's English version into Spanish and published it in several issues of *Proa* in 1924 and 1925. Borges wrote a brief introduction to his father's translation, which was published in *Proa* and then included in *Inquisiciones* (1925). That essay already contains some of the core arguments that Borges later expands upon in his main essays on translation, including the idea that mistranslation can aesthetically improve an original through the use of creative infidelities. Borges distinguishes between the translator's "veracidad" [veracity, or fidelity] and its "hermosura" [beauty], and argues that the latter justifies FitzGerald's numerous "licencias" [licenses] (*Inquisiciones* 136–37). Similarly, commenting on his father's version in Spanish, Borges identifies the transformation in form that the poem incurs, namely an alteration in rhyme scheme, and praises this mistranslation as an improvement (*Inquisiciones,* 137).

Borges returns to FitzGerald's *Rubáiyát* in the highly structured essay "El enigma de Edward Fitzgerald." The text consists of two long, parallel paragraphs—the first dealing with Umar ben Ibrahim al Khayyami, the second with Edward FitzGerald—followed by two shorter ones in which the conjunction of the two writers is considered. Each long paragraph contains a summary of that writer's life and work, hypercondensed in typical Borgesian style into a miniature fictional narrative. Although the two men described in each paragraph are radically different, the parallel structure through which they are presented anticipates the move at the end of the essay, where Borges discusses how Omar and FitzGerald merge into one to compose the new version of the *Rubáiyát* in English.

Borges first narrates the story of the Persian mathematician, scholar, and poet Umar ben Ibrahim al Khayyami (b. between 1025 and 1050—d. between 1123 and 1131). The events that Borges recounts sound exotic, but turn out to be factual, similar in tone to some of the (infamous) biographies in *Historia universal de la infamia*.[40] In addition, as if to reinforce the importance of translation, Omar's very name changes throughout the course of the essay. Although this has to do with the different spellings of his name in

Persian, Arabic, Spanish, and English, the effect is to illustrate how his name, as well as his work, is transformed through time.[41]

In the second paragraph Borges summarizes the life and work of the Victorian poet and translator Edward FitzGerald (1809–83), born seven centuries after Omar. The account of FitzGerald's training and literary activities traces how FitzGerald reaches Omar and establishes certain connections between the careers of the two men. FitzGerald reads and rereads the *Quijote*[42] (just as Omar studied and explicated the Koran, perhaps), and falls in love with the dictionary in which he searches for words (whereas Omar studied the "Enciclopedia de los Hermanos de la Pureza" [Encyclopedia of the Brethren of Purity]). From the study of Spanish FitzGerald progresses to that of Persian and begins a translation of the *Mantiq al Tayr* (the *Parliament of Birds*). This latter text, an allegorical representation of pantheism, directly mirrors the reference in the Omar paragraph to the transmigration of souls. In Borges's recounting, FitzGerald approaches Umar not only poetically (which he will need for the translation of the *Rubáiyát*), but also in matters of intellectual interest.

FitzGerald then comes across Omar's poems, devotes himself to translating them, and eventually publishes the first of several editions of Omar's *Rubáiyát* in 1859. Omar's original quatrains are disconnected from each other; they form separate, unrelated four-verse poems. FitzGerald combines the series of quatrains and reorganizes them into a single, coherent text. His translation is known to be a complete rewriting of the original, as he combined some quatrains and omitted many of Omar's specific cultural and Islamic references.[43] The result, as Borges states, is nothing short of miraculous:

> Un milagro acontece: de la fortuita conjunción de un astrónomo persa que condescendió a la poesía, de un inglés excéntrico que recorre, tal vez sin entenderlos del todo, libros orientales e hispánicos, surge un extraordinario poeta, que no se parece a los dos. . . . Algunos críticos entienden que el *Omar* de FitzGerald es, de hecho, un poema inglés con alusiones persas; FitzGerald *interpeló, afinó e inventó*, pero sus *Rubáiyát* parecen exigir de nosotros que las leamos como persas y antiguas. (*OC* II: 67–68; emphasis added)

> [A miracle occurs: from the fortuitous conjunction of a Persian astronomer who condescended to write poetry, from an eccentric Englishman who peruses Oriental and Hispanic books, perhaps without completely

understanding them, emerges an extraordinary poet who does not resemble either of them. . . . Some critics believe that FitzGerald's *Omar*
is, in fact, an English poem with Persian allusions; FitzGerald *interpolated, refined, and invented*, but his *Rubáiyát* seems to demand that we
read them as Persian and ancient.]

FitzGerald's process of translation, his use of paraphrase and adaptation, his interpolations, finishing touches, and inventions, is exactly like the creative infidelities that Borges valorizes in "Los
traductores de *Las 1001 Noches*." Such mistranslation, just as in
the versions Borges compares in that essay, creates an unexpected
effect of hyperfidelity, as FitzGerald's version yields a text that
seems especially "Persian and ancient." Once again, Borges makes
us question our understanding of fidelity in translation: fidelity to
what image of the Orient, in this case, and constructed by whom?

But Borges does not stop there. In the last two paragraphs of the
essay, Borges discusses the "conjeturas de índole metafísica" [con-
jectures of a metaphysical nature] arising from the "fortuita conjunción" [fortuitous conjunction] which leads to the creation not just
of a new literary text, but seemingly of a new poet. Borges first
considers the possibility that there may have been a transmigration
of souls, through the centuries, from Omar (who once professed the
existence of such a doctrine) to FitzGerald (around 1857), and
seemingly suggests that metempsychosis and pantheism are behind
the transformation of Omar's loose verses into FitzGerald's coherent poem (*OC* II: 68). But almost immediately Borges introduces
an element of doubt that undermines both these conjectures: "Más
verosímil y no menos maravillosa que estas conjeturas de tipo so-
brenatural es la suposición de un azar benéfico" [More credible and
no less marvelous than these conjectures of a supernatural sort is
the supposition of a fortuitous chance] (*OC* II: 68). This ambiguity
complicates Borges's position with regards to the esoteric concepts
of metempsychosis and pantheism. Some critics have argued that
pantheism provides the key to unraveling nearly all of Borges's
enigmas.[44] Such a reading, however, is overly simplistic and tends
to erase the specifics of the texts in which Borges refers to pantheism.

It is safe to say, on the other hand, that Borges utilizes metempsychosis as a metaphor to make unexpected connections between dissimilar writers and texts, such as the conjunction between Omar
Khayyám and Edward FitzGerald. In this case, it links the writer

and the translator and emphasizes the process of transformation that occurs from one version to another. But the point is not just that a text (Omar's quatrains) is moved across time, space, cultures, and languages and metamorphosed into a new version (FitzGerald's *Rubáiyát*). Rather, it is the number of alterations that occurs along the way that is of interest to us. It is the fact that FitzGerald mistranslates—"FitzGerald interpeló, afinó e inventó" [FitzGerald interpolated, refined, and invented]—that makes the transmigration a success.

Borges leaves unresolved the issue of exactly how and why Fitz-Gerald was able to recreate Omar's *Rubáiyát* so well. This is perhaps appropriate, given the intrinsic mystery at the core of any creative production, including that of translation. Borges concludes the essay with a reflection on this sense of mystery, specifically that involved in the collaboration between a writer and a translator:

> Toda colaboración es misteriosa. Ésta del inglés y del persa lo fue más que ninguna, porque eran muy distintos los dos y acaso en vida no hubieran trabado amistad y la muerte y las vicisitudes y el tiempo sirvieron para que uno supiera del otro y fueran un solo poeta. (*OC* II: 68)

> [Every collaboration is mysterious. This one between the Englishman and the Persian was more so than any other because the two were very different, and in life they would perhaps not have become friends; death and vicissitudes and time served to make one know of the other and the two to become a single poet.]

Borges significantly expands the idea of collaboration, an activity usually applied to an interaction that occurs at the same time and place. In this sense, "El enigma de Edward FitzGerald" illustrates that all translations are a mysterious collaboration between the writer of the source text and that of the target text. By analogy, it suggests that *all* acts of writing involve a mysterious collaboration between one writer (of a given pre-text) and another (who rewrites/mistranslates fragments of such a pre-text, and recontextualizes it to create new meanings).[45]

In addition, the "conjunction" of Omar and FitzGerald, which leads to the formal "configuration" of the English version of the *Rubáiyát*, presents the idea of writer and translator as doubles. One cannot exist without the other; regardless of how different they are (as is the case with Omar and FitzGerald), they are two faces of the same coin. Taken to its extreme, they appear to merge; at first sight, as readers of FitzGerald's *Rubáiyát*, we see only the final product in its nearly perfect form. The "configuration" hides the fact that behind the "conjunction" there is a tension, an extreme difference between the pre-text and the rewritten new text, between the source and the target languages—as well as between source and target cultures, time periods, religions, and so on—which makes the final product possible. Metempsychosis works well as a metaphor for this process, but it minimizes the differences and suggests a certain determinism that Borges's texts contradict.

Perhaps that is why Borges prefers to call the "conjunction" of Omar and FitzGerald a "fortuitous chance" of literature and history. It is a fortuitous turn of events, but one that is only so in retrospect. The "fortuitous chance" in this essay is carefully and systematically structured by Borges to explore what is behind the mysterious collaboration between writer and translator, between text and pre-text. As doubles, the writer and the translator, the new version and its precursors, mirror and complement each other. However, it is not until this reflection is thoroughly distorted—by FitzGerald's creative infidelities—that the mysterious "miracle" of their "conjunction" can occur.

CONCLUSION: WRITING AS TRANSLATION

In the work he initiates in *Historia universal de la infamia* Borges develops the core aspects of a poetics based on a practice of mistranslation, of an irreverent use of creative infidelities that takes advantage of spatial and temporal displacements to create new texts. Significantly, Borges delineates his main ideas about translation around this same time, in "Las versiones homéricas" (1932) and "Los traductores de *Las 1001 Noches*" (1935), and is himself actively involved in numerous translation projects. This practice of writing as translation reaches a new level with "Pierre Menard, autor del *Quijote*" (1939), a text that both utilizes and illustrates Borges's theories of reading, writing, and translation, as well as the interconnectedness between them. Then, from "Pierre Menard" on, writing as translation becomes Borges's modus operandi, as seen in the narratives of *Ficciones* (1944) and *El Aleph* (1949) through those of *El informe de Brodie* (1970). Throughout these texts Borges illustrates that, in his own phrase, the "indefinite and nearly infinite" spectrum of possible applications of the practice of writing as translation creates new and limitless space for the production of narrative in Argentina and, by extension, throughout Latin America.

A key aspect of the practice of writing as translation is the process of selection involved in how Borges takes from his sources. The very act of selecting a fragment represents an act of irreverence, as it omits the rest of the pre-text and disrupts its prior integrity. Even before these fragments are mistranslated into another context, the process of taking them out of their old context challenges the supposed prepotency of the original, as well as the system in which it was produced. This move, initiated in *Historia universal de la infamia*, is put to use with extreme efficiency in "Pierre Menard, autor del *Quijote*." The brilliance of this story derives from how the fragments from the *Quijote* that Menard manages to rewrite, which have no intrinsic value in and of themselves, gain unexpected aesthetic, semantic, and cultural value once their potential is enacted by being placed in a new context: from Cervantes's early seventeenth-century baroque Spain, to Menard's early twentieth-century symbolist France, to Borges's late 1930s Argentina.

In many of his fictions, Borges takes a fragment with irreverence (whether the fragment be a direct citation, a translation proper, or a historical or literary reference or allusion) and displaces it toward the shores of the Río de la Plata, where it is reinscribed to enact its potential. We can think, for example, of Aureliano and Juan de Panonia, the antagonistic theologians in "Los teólogos" (1947), whom Borges extrapolates from various historical references to develop into a narrative about the relative nature of orthodoxy and heterodoxy, the manners in which these two need each other for their existence, and the dangers involved in any extreme belief system.[46] We also see this practice in "Biografía de Tadeo Isidoro Cruz (1829–74)" (1944) and "El fin" (1953), texts that actively rewrite the *Martín Fierro*.[47] In another sense, it is also used in "La forma de la espada" (1942), in which the 1922 Irish rebellion is recontextualized into a gaucho story of honor and infamy.[48] In the process, Borges suggests that literary texts and traditions, as well as history itself, can be reevaluated and rewritten from the periphery. This is seen in "Historia del guerrero y de la cautiva" (1949), in which the story of the traitor Droctulft, as told by Croce, is translated onto Argentine history, with specific allusions to Borges's own nineteenth-century ancestors. The story can then be read as a reworking of the foundational theme of civilization and barbarism, as well as of Esteban Echeverría's "La cautiva" (1837).[49]

These examples suggest the extent to which Borges utilizes a practice of writing as translation throughout his fictions. At times, this shift, this mistranslation—always complex and full of surprises—can be as subtle and deceiving as a recontextualization of the same exact words (as in "Pierre Menard"). More often than not, it occurs at a linguistic level. Such appropriation is inaugurated by Borges in *Historia universal de la infamia*, in which Borges's acculturation creates an added displacement toward the Río de la Plata at the very level of syntax and diction. This leads to the startling result of locating some of the world's most infamous villains (e.g., Lazarus Morell, Tom Castro, Ching the Pirate Widow, Hákim de Merv) in an unmistakable Río de la Plata version, complete with South American references and colloquialisms.

Borges's irreverent moves are so innovative that questions such as "is the translation faithful to the original?" can be restated as "is the original faithful to the translation?" His texts consistently challenge the "supersticiosa ética del lector" [superstitious ethics of the reader] and reveal the prejudices behind the privileging of the original. Through a constant undermining of the concept of originality, Borges shows that the traditional demand for fidelity is merely another way to express the power and determinacy assigned to the original over the translation—and, by implication, to the canons of the center over the simulacra of the margins. Borges proposes, instead, that we consider all translations and all acts of writing as a mysterious collaboration between multiple versions, which are always available for new readings in new contexts. A collaboration that can seem that much more mysterious when we realize that every act of writing is an act of translation: whether we think of it as a fortuitous twist of fate ("un azar benéfico" [a beneficent chance]), as a miracle we can attribute to a conjunction of dissimilar elements, or as the syntactical conjunction of creative infidelities opening new ground for innovation in the periphery.

The greatest displacement—the greatest miracle, if we wish— that Borges achieves through the practice of writing as translation is to situate "La biblioteca de Babel" (1941) and "La lotería de Babilonia" (1941) in Argentina. The linguistic and cultural shifts that identify Buenos Aires as a twentieth-century Babylon, and Borges's texts as the inside of the Tower of Babel, raise all manner of cultural political questions. What does such irreverence and displacement represent for Argentina, and for Latin American literatures? What implications does it have for writers from marginal literatures (with respect to Western European and U.S. centers) in general? In the next chapter we address these questions in particular, as we continue to explore the consequences of Borges's theories of mistranslation for writers in the periphery.

4

The Aesthetics of Irreverence: Mistranslating From the Margins

INTRODUCTION

IN CHAPTER 3 WE TRACED THE DEVELOPMENT OF BORGES'S PRACTICE of writing as translation as an expansion of his theories of (mis)-translation. In this chapter we further explore the potential of this irreverent position for the periphery. Translation—like any act of reading or of writing—has drastically different cultural political implications for writers in geopolitical margins than it does for those in geopolitical centers. What is Latin American literature, what might Latin American literature be? What is the role of translation in the development of Latin American literatures? How does writing/reading/translating in Latin America affect one's place in Occidental traditions? And how can the margins be theorized to avoid their implied limitations?

Some of the most astute answers ever provided to these questions are found in Borges's seminal 1951 conference, "El escritor argentino y la tradición." In many ways, this text functions as a road map for writers from Argentina—as well as those from Latin America, and perhaps from the periphery at large—to position themselves with respect to Occidental canons without being defined and restricted by them. The key, according to Borges, is to take a stance of irreverence toward the traditions of the center. Borges claims marginality itself as a privileged site for innovation; this sets the stage for a reconsideration of center–periphery dichotomies and preconceptions of influence, value, and canon formation. In addition, there is an important connection to be made between "El escritor argentino y la tradición" and Borges's theories of (mis)translation. As I present in the first part of this chapter, I believe that this connection is crucial to understanding what irreverence, displacement, and marginality mean for Borges, and how he puts these to use in some of his most poignant fictions. Furthermore, the points of contact between "El escritor argentino y la tradición" and Borges's theories of (mis)translation reveal the broader implications of writing as translation for Latin America. Displacement and irreverence, enacted through creative infidelities and recontextualization: herein lies the potential of translation for the periphery.

In "El escritor argentino y la tradición," Borges speaks of the "fortunate consequences" of a position of "taking with irreverence" from existing traditions which is afforded to writers in the periphery by the very virtue of their marginality. As part of his argument Borges mentions one of his own stories in particular, "La muerte y la brújula" (1942), as an example of the "fortunate" results of such irreverence. I thus analyze this story with an eye to the displacements that allow Borges to "capture . . . the flavor of the outskirts of Buenos Aires," as he himself states. The substitutions that create a new version of Buenos Aires, read in connection with several other relevant texts by Borges, suggests a remapping of peripheral literatures that challenges the center and its canons.

Perhaps Borges's most important commentary on difference— cultural, historical, religious, and linguistic—is found in "La busca de Averroes" (1947), which has one of history's most famous translators, the medieval Arab philosopher Averroes, as its protagonist. In a text that raises all manner of questions about the role of translation in hermeneutic processes, Borges narrates a story of defeat, while paradoxically demonstrating the value of otherness itself. Articulated from Borges's periphery, the text seeks to account for the distances between Aristotle, Averroes, and Borges *not* by correcting or denying difference, but by engaging in highly productive processes of rereading/rewriting/mistranslating.

To analyze the extent to which the effects of these processes are significantly different in the periphery than they are in the center, we turn next to a discussion of "El Aleph" (1947). In particular, we contrast Borges's use of Dante as a pre-text with T. S. Eliot's fundamentally different use of the same pre-text in *The Waste Land* (1922). In Borges's story one of the canons of Western literature is displaced to the basement of a house in a Buenos Aires neighborhood. From this irreverent margin, Borges takes on universal issues, including questions of aesthetics and representation.

The potential of the periphery, as we explore it in this chapter, has at its core a conflictive duality between the foreign and the local (between the European and the Argentine, in the case of Borges), which is made explicit in "El Sur" (1953). The story provides us with a textual embodiment of this duality, seen in every feature of the protagonist Juan Dahlmann. The tensions personified by Dahlmann and his mixed ancestry contribute to a remapping of center–periphery/north–south dichotomies. The duality in the story is presented as a source of deep tension, but also of the potential of the periphery to incorporate previous traditions through irreverent rereadings and rewritings. This is brought to the forefront by the appearance of *The Thousand and One Nights*, which functions as a key reference to highlight the role of translation in the problematics of identity and representation in Argentina.

The articulation of an aesthetics of irreverence from the margins, such as that found in Borges, has implications that need to be explored separately for different writers in their particular historic and cultural moments. One of the conclusion of this chapter, then, is that we need many more studies into the various traditions of mistranslation found throughout Latin America. As Borges's texts constantly illustrate, translation—whether we mean translation proper or other processes of writing as translation—need not have the negative connotations of a practice that leads to derivative, inferior versions. Rather, translation can become a process through which innovation is possible. And innovation from the periphery, because of the periphery's condition of marginality, represents a literary and political challenge to the center, to traditional views on influence and originality, and to preestablished determinations of aesthetic value and canon formation.

IRREVERENCE DEFINED:
"EL ESCRITOR ARGENTINO Y LA TRADICIÓN"

Borges's 1951 essay "El escritor argentino y la tradición" establishes what amounts to a program of how literatures can be developed in the periphery.[1] Borges's main argument is that the very fact of writing from the margins provides Argentine writers with a special opportunity to innovate without being bound to the canons of the center. This occurs because South American writers, much like Jewish and Irish writers, are at once apart from and a part of the center, which gives them much potential freedom and mobility.

Marginality itself, Borges suggests, allows Latin American writers to build and renovate their literatures by taking with irreverence from any and all traditions. As we will see, this position of taking with irreverence as a form of innovation for/from the margins is one of the clearest indications of the central role of mistranslation and displacement in Borges's aesthetics, although the topic of translation is never explicitly mentioned in "El escritor argentino y la tradición."

The essay is structured as a critical response to three possible solutions to the "problem" of the Argentine writer and tradition.[2] Borges undermines and demonstrates the historical inaccuracy of the first two positions fairly quickly. The first is the idea that Argentine tradition can be thought of as a continuation or extension of Spanish tradition. To this, Borges responds that Argentina has always defined itself in opposition to Spain, culturally as well as politically, and that Argentina has distanced itself to such a degree from Spain that Spanish literature is actually more foreign to Argentine readers than French or English literature (*OC* I: 271). The second position to which Borges responds is the idea that Argentina is disconnected from its European heritage altogether, that it is a young, primitive place, so that Argentine writers should not try to treat European themes at all. Borges finds this position utterly unfounded; he cites, just as one example, the recent events in Europe, namely the Spanish Civil War and World War II, which had a profound resonance in Argentina (*OC* I: 271). Borges dismisses this ridiculous hypothesis with ease.

The final stance that Borges takes on is the one with which Borges most strongly disagrees: the idea that Argentine tradition, in a cultural nationalistic vein, should abound in local color and deal exclusively with local themes. Borges aims his sharpest rhetorical barbs against cultural nationalism, arguing specifically against writers and intellectuals from the time of the Centenario—principally the figures of Ricardo Rojas (1882–1957) and the Leopoldo Lugones (1874–1938) of *Odas seculares* (1910) and *El payador* (1916). Using the nationalistic celebrations of 1910 as a springboard, Rojas and Lugones, among others, emphasized the local in part to define an Argentine identity and citizenship that excluded the vast number of immigrants entering the country at the turn of the twentieth century.[3] These writers sought to create a very specific image of the Argentine, one that drew on the gauchesque poetry of the nineteenth century, as epitomized by José Hernández's *Martín Fierro*. They thus defined Argentina's national tradition in relation to the symbolic figure of the gaucho, his land (the pampas), and his language.

Borges finds this position extremely limiting and reacts strongly against it and its cultural exclusionism. Besides, as Borges argues, such a constraining definition of Argentine literature is simply inaccurate, as it identifies only one aspect of Argentina's literature: the line that holds that the national literature should be founded through the cipher, the intralingual translation, of the gaucho myth. A more accurate account, as we saw in chapter 1, must include the line that goes back to Sarmiento and the Salón Literario of 1837, which was interested in incorporating French philosophy, literature, and culture—through interlingual translation, displacement, and appropriation—into the foundations of the Argentine nation. In other words, both intralingual and interlingual writing as translation, both the *Facundo* and the *Martín Fierro*.

Borges states: "La idea de que la poesía argentina debe abundar en rasgos diferenciales argentinos y en color local argentino me parece una equivocación" [I believe that the idea that Argentine poetry must abound in particularly Argentine traits and in Argentine local color is a mistake] (*OC* I: 269).[4] Borges equates an emphasis on local color with cultural nationalism. He challenges the legitimacy of such a position, exposing its rigid literary and political divisions and laying bare its fanaticism and shallowness:

Además, no sé si es necesario decir que la idea de que una literatura debe definirse por los rasgos diferenciales del país que la produce es una idea relativamente nueva; también es nueva y arbitraria la idea de que los escritores deben buscar temas de sus países. Sin ir más lejos, creo que Racine ni siquiera hubiera entendido a una persona que le hubiese negado su derecho al título de poeta francés por haber buscado temas griegos y latinos. Creo que Shakespeare se habría asombrado si hubieran pretendido limitarlo a temas ingleses, y si le hubiesen dicho que, como inglés, no tenía derecho a escribir *Hamlet*, de tema escandinavo, o *Macbeth*, de tema escocés. El culto argentino del color local es un reciente culto europeo que los nacionalistas deberían rechazar por foráneo. (*OC* I: 270)[5]

[Furthermore, I do not know if it is necessary to say that the idea that a literature must define itself according to the differentiating traits of the country that produces it is a relatively new idea; also new and arbitrary is the idea that writers must seek themes from their own countries.

Without going any further, I believe that Racine would not have even understood someone who denied his right to the title of the poet of France because he sought out Greek and Latin themes. I believe that Shakespeare would have been amazed if they had pretended to limit him to English themes, and if they had told him that, as an Englishman, he did not have a right to write *Hamlet*, with its Scandinavian theme, or *Macbeth*, with its Scottish theme. The Argentine cult of local color is a recent European cult which the nationalists should reject as foreign.]

Borges's sarcasm speaks to the dangers of self-imposed cultural nationalisms, especially for writers in the periphery. Borges uses European examples (i.e., Racine, Shakespeare), who one would never think of limiting to their countries of origin, to address the question of the Argentine tradition. The displacement establishes an analogy wherein it becomes clear that the limitations of cultural nationalism should not be imposed on anyone, and especially not on Latin American writers. In this formulation, aesthetic value take priority over political national divisions. Borges claims for the margins the same possibility of the highest of aesthetic production—whether that be through intralingual or interlingual writing as translation; or, more likely, through a dialogical combination of both.

But if the three aforementioned positions do not accurately represent Argentine tradition, then "¿Cuál es la tradición argentina?" [What is the Argentine tradition?] (*OC* I: 272). Having rhetorically dismissed the other options, Borges states:

Creo que podemos contestar fácilmente y que no hay problema en esta pregunta. Creo que nuestra tradición es toda la cultura occidental, y creo también que tenemos derecho a esta tradición, mayor que el que pueden tener los habitantes de una u otra nación occidental. (*OC* I: 272)

[I believe that we can answer this question easily and without any problems. I believe that our tradition is the entirety of Western culture; I also believe that we have a right to that tradition, greater than that which the people of any other given Western nation might have.]

Borges then discusses the preeminence of Jews in Western culture and of the Irish in British culture:

Recuerdo aquí un ensayo de Thorstein Veblen, sociólogo norteamericano, sobre la preeminencia de los judíos en la cultura occidental. Se pregunta si esta preeminencia permite conjeturar una superioridad innata de los judíos, y contesta que no; dice que sobresalen en la cultura occidental, porque actúan dentro de esa cultura y al mismo tiempo no se sienten atados a ella por una devoción especial; "por eso—dice—a un judío siempre le será más fácil que a un occidental no judío innovar en la cultura occidental"; y lo mismo podemos decir de los irlandeses en la cultura de Inglaterra. Tratándose de los irlandeses, no tenemos por qué suponer que la profusión de nombres irlandeses en la literatura y la filosofía británicas se deba a una preeminencia racial, porque muchos de esos irlandeses (Shaw, Berkeley, Swift) fueron descendientes de ingleses, fueron personas que no tenían sangre celta; sin embargo, les bastó el hecho de sentirse irlandeses, distintos, para innovar en la cultura inglesa. (*OC* I: 272–73)

[I recall here an essay by the North American sociologist Thorstein Veblen, about the preeminence of Jews in Occidental culture. He asks himself if that preeminence allows the conjecture of an innate superiority of the Jews, and he answers no; he says that they are outstanding in Occidental culture because they act within that culture, but at the same time they do not feel tied to it by any special sense of devotion; "that is why," he says, "it will always be easier for a Jew than for a non-Jewish Occidental to innovate in Occidental culture"; and we can say the same about the Irish in the culture of England. In the case of the Irish, there is no reason for us to suppose that the profusion of Irish names in British literature and philosophy is due to a racial preeminence, because many of those Irish (Shaw, Berkeley, Swift) were descendents of the English, individuals who did not have any Celtic blood; however, it was enough for them to feel Irish, different, to innovate in English culture.]

And Borges claims for Argentine writers the same potential for innovation that he sees in Jewish and Irish writers:

Creo que los argentinos, los sudamericanos en general, estamos en una situación análoga; podemos manejar todos los temas europeos, manejarlos sin supersticiones, con una *irreverencia* que puede tener, y ya tiene, consecuencias afortunadas. (*OC* I: 273; emphasis added)

[I believe that we Argentines, we South Americans in general, are in an analogous situation; we can handle all European themes, handle them without superstitions, with an *irreverence* that can have, and has already had, fortunate consequences.]

This unexpected analogy between Latin American and Jewish and Irish writers has far-reaching implications. Borges astutely perceives that it is their simultaneous status as insiders *and* outsiders which has allowed the Jews and Irish to act—and innovate—within those cultures without feeling bound by any special devotion to it: "They act within that culture, but at the same time they do not feel tied to it by any special sense of devotion." Partial difference, feeling themselves different from ("it was enough for them to feel . . . *different*") and not entirely a part of the center, is precisely what frees Jewish, Irish, and Latin American writers—and perhaps all writers from the periphery—from the weight of the traditions of the center.

While it is true that the Cabalistic tradition, as well as the parody and satire of Irish letters, are important in Borges's work,[6] more relevant here is that Borges consciously aligns himself with two marginal traditions whose history of oppression and colonization is well known. As Sylvia Molloy has said:

> Borges reclama esa marginalidad, justificándola plenamente, para toda la literatura hispanoamericana. Mejor: para toda literatura lateral. . . .
>
> La irreverencia parece consecuencia inevitable de esa marginalidad aceptada y asumida: declararse marginal—es decir excéntrico—equivale a constituir un centro en la misma circunferencia, a reconocer la existencia del centro tradicional y a definirse con respecto a él, pero también a alejarse deliberadamente de ese centro, para verlo mejor y—si fuera necesario—para burlarse de él. (*Las letras de Borges*, 60–61)

> [Borges claims that marginality, fully justifying it, for all of Spanish American literature. Better yet: for all peripheral literature. . . .
>
> Irreverence seems to be an inevitable consequence of that marginality, accepted and assumed: to say one is marginal—which is to say eccentric—is equivalent to constituting a center in the very circumference, to recognizing the existence of the traditional center and to defining oneself with respect to it, but also to purposefully distancing oneself from that center, to see it better and—if necessary—mock it.]

Borges thus suggests an alliance of peripheral traditions whose connections reside precisely in their marginality.

Irreverence puts in motion the displacement that is so important for Borges. This irreverence, as Borges's texts repeatedly illustrate, can be accomplished through a variety of techniques, including blurring the borders between genres as well as cultures and languages, through fragmentation and appropriation and recontextualization, by a combination of apocryphal and veridical citations—in

other words, through variations on processes of writing as translation. Any writer from the periphery, because they are both *a part
of* Occidental culture, yet *apart from* it, can draw from any and all
literatures with irreverence. This opens the way for the kind of innovation Borges identifies in Jewish and Irish writers, and which he
argues is possible for Latin American writers as well. The distance
between center and periphery, the difference created by such a distance, need not be a detriment—it need not relegate the margins to
the production of inferior copies. Difference, realized through displacement and irreverence, is claimed by Borges because of the potential it affords writers from the margins. The simulacra from the
edge, the practice of writing as translation—which Borges begins
with his earliest work in the 1920s and 1930s—becomes the privileged method by which peripheral writers can originate in their own
literatures, and challenge those of the center.

The irreverent position that Borges postulates for the periphery
in "El escritor argentino y la tradición" challenges the major/minor
and center/periphery categories and the distinctions that serve to reinforce canonical traditions.[7] This is in no way to say that Borges is
somehow a marginal or minor writer; on the contrary. Rather, because he works consciously in the periphery, in a geopolitically
"minor" country, Borges sees himself in a privileged position to
innovate, an innovation that becomes a challenge of the center and
so-called "major" traditions. Borges inverses these dichotomies to
transform seeming limitations into potential merit; in other words,
Borges transforms the "margins" and the "minor" into sites of potentiality. As Deleuze and Guattari state: "There is nothing that is
major or revolutionary except the minor" (*Kafka,* 26). On the other
hand, Borges's formulation is not at all a privileging of the margins
to the exclusion of the center. If the center is a "moveable event,"
as Borges says of Homer in "Las veriones homéricas," then it can
be displaced, and the periphery, too, can (re)occupy the center.
Thus, the patrimony of the margins becomes all literature, all
themes and topics, all styles and forms. It is both the universal and
the local, articulated from the point of view—in the languages, in
the irreverent displacements—of the periphery.

DISPLACEMENT IN ACTION:
THE "FORTUNATE CONSEQUENCES" OF IRREVERENCE

But what are, precisely, the consequences afforded by the condition of marginality that Borges claims for himself, for Argentina,

and for all of Latin America in "El escritor argentino y la tradición"? What is Borges referring to when he says that taking with irreverence: "Can have, and has already had, fortunate consequences"? In what manner have Latin American writers been able to draw from different traditions to innovate with irreverence?

As part of his arguments in "El escritor argentino y la tradición," Borges provides several examples from Argentine literature to answer these questions. He takes *Don Segundo Sombra* (1926) by Ricardo Güiraldes (1886–1927) as a case of a novel that one might think of as being especially Argentine because of its setting in the pampas and its gaucho and *criollo* themes.[8] However, Borges argues that stylistically *Don Segundo Sombra* owes more to early twentieth-century French poetry than to anything in the gauchesque tradition, and that the plot is heavily influenced by Rudyard Kipling's *Kim* and Mark Twain's *Huckleberry Finn*. According to Borges, though, this does not reduce the value nor the Argentine nature of the novel; on the contrary. Borges argues that these influences—these mistranslations—were in fact necessary:

> Para que nosotros tuviéramos ese libro fue necesario que Güiraldes recordara la técnica poética de los cenáculos franceses de su tiempo, y la obra de Kipling que había leído hacía muchos años; es decir, Kipling, y Mark Twain, y las metáforas de los poetas franceses fueron necesarios para este libro argentino, para este libro que no es menos argentino, lo repito, por haber aceptado estas influencias. (*OC* I: 271)

> [For us to have that book it was necessary for Güiraldes to remember the poetic techniques of the French circles of his time, and the work of Kipling which he had read many years before; in other words, Kipling, and Mark Twain, and the metaphors of the French poets were necessary for this Argentine book, for this book that is no less Argentine, I repeat, for having accepted these influences.]

Borges's comments are meant to take Güiraldes's novel back from the nationalists who had claimed it as part of a narrowly defined Argentine tradition based on the gauchesque. Borges, instead, describes *Don Segundo Sombra* as a combination of the foreign and the local, functioning together to produce an especially Argentine text. Considered through Borges's own conflation of reading, writing, and translating, this taking from the foreign with irreverence (i.e., from French symbolism, from Kipling and Mark Twain) can be seen as a process of interlingual translation, and the incorporation of local themes, culture, and language as an act of intralingual translation. Thus, it is the irreverent cross of the foreign and the local—of intralingual and interlingual translation—which displaces the center to the margins (i.e., to the Argentine pampas), to create *Don Segundo Sombra*'s aesthetic value as well as its *"argentinidad."*

Borges's moves with *Don Segundo Sombra* is a counterexample to Harold Bloom's theory of an anxiety of influence.[9] What we find in Borges is something akin to a celebration of influence, a delighting in distorted/displaced influence. Borges's challenges to the theorizing of influence and tradition dates to his earliest texts, as evidenced by "Torres Villarroel (1693–1770)" (first published in *Proa*, November 1924, then included in *Inquisiciones*, 1925). Villarroel, a minor Golden Age Spanish poet, is usually held to be minor (in a traditional sense) because his poetry so closely resembles Quevedo, easily succumbing to the influences of the Baroque master. But Borges maintains that Villarroel's value lies precisely in his similarity to Quevedo, thus defying traditional scholarship by inversing the negative connotations associated with direct influence. This is analogous to the move that Borges makes in "Pierre Menard," as we saw in chapter 3, in which influence does not cause anxiety and exhaustion, even when faced with the likes of Cervantes, once we realize that unexpected meanings can result from displacement and recontextualization of selected fragments. Any possible anxiety is mocked and appropriated through Borges's transformative irreverence. Instead of producing anxiety, this position of irreverence—seen as the value of the periphery itself and thought of as the synonymous and interchangeable events of reading, writing, and translation—becomes a site of nearly unlimited potentiality.

THE FOREIGN AND "THE FLAVOR OF THE OUTSKIRTS OF BUENOS AIRES" IN "LA MUERTE Y LA BRÚJULA"

With regard to his own work, Borges refers to one of his stories in "El escritor argentino y la tradición" as an example of the "fortunate consequences" of taking with irreverence: "La muerte y la brújula" (first published in *Sur*, May 1942, then included in *Los mejores cuentos policiales* in 1943, and in *Ficciones* in 1944). Borges states that he finally accomplishes in this story something he had attempted to do in his early work, but which, in his own estimation, he had failed to achieve there: to capture the essence of the outskirts of Buenos Aires:

Durante muchos años, en libros ahora felizmente olvidados, traté de redactar el sabor, la esencia de los barrios extremos de Buenos Aires; naturalmente abundé en palabras locales, no prescindí de palabras como cuchilleros, milonga, tapia, y otras, y escribí así aquellos olvidables y olvidados libros; luego, hará un año, escribí una historia que se llama "La muerte y la brújula" que es una suerte de pesadilla, una pesadilla en que figuran elementos de Buenos Aires deformados por el horror de la pesadilla; pienso allí en El Paseo Colón y lo llamo Rue de Toulon, pienso en las quintas de Adrogué y las llamo Triste-le-Roy; publicada esa historia, mis amigos me dijeron que al fin habían encontrado en lo que yo escribía el sabor de las afueras de Buenos Aires. Precisamente porque no me había propuesto encontrar ese sabor, porque me había abandonado al sueño, pude lograr, al cabo de tantos años, lo que antes busqué en vano. (*OC* I: 270–71)

[For many years, in books now happily forgotten, I tried to write the flavor, the essence of the outer neighborhoods of Buenos Aires; naturally I abounded in local words, I did not omit words like *cuchilleros*, *milonga*, *tapia*, and others, and I wrote those mostly forgettable and forgotten books; then, about a year ago, I wrote a story entitled "Death and the Compass" which is a kind of nightmare, a nightmare in which there are elements of a Buenos Aires deformed by the horror of the nightmare; I think there of the Paseo Colón and call it the Rue de Toulon, I think of the country houses of Adrogué and call them Triste-le-Roy; once the story was published, my friends told me that I had finally captured in my writing the flavor of the outskirts of Buenos Aires. Precisely because I had not pretended to find that flavor, because I had abandoned myself to the dream, I was able to accomplish, after so many years, what I had before sought in vain.]

What he tried to do before through the use of local color—with words such as "cuchilleros, milonga, tapia"—now succeeds because Borges juxtaposes the European onto his South American city. In fact, the entire story can be seen as (re)drawing a map of Buenos Aires where the various crimes occur, but one "artfully disguised by French, German, Jewish, Irish, and Nordic toponyms and surnames" (Bell-Villada, 92).[10]

But "La muerte y la brújula" actually contains a double displacement: of the European toponyms and surnames onto the map of

Buenos Aires, and of Borges's efforts to describe the outskirts of Buenos Aires onto these European toponyms and surnames. The series of substitutions that the text enacts is a technique that Borges uses often in his stories.[11] Such substitutions function at a symbolic and lexical level as a way to reinscribe the European within Borges's Argentine context, but also to juxtapose the Argentine onto the European. These substitutions also illustrate the connections between displacement and translation. Translation always involves substitution, the displacement of toponyms and surnames, from one language into another, from one literary system into another. In translation proper, a text is taken out of its source context, and displaced/rewritten into the target one. As Derrida points out, translation of proper names underscores both the impossibility and the absolute necessity for translation, and points to the untranslatable in the original, as well as translation already in the original.[12] The substitutions that Borges enacts in "La muerte y la brújula"—the irreverent displacement of selected fragments—posits (mis)translation as an agent of transformation, and even resistance, in Latin America.

Borges suggests this position in his 1944 "Prologue" to *Artificios*:

["La muerte y la brújula"], pese a los nombres alemanes o escandinavos, ocurre en un Buenos Aires de sueños. . . . Ya redactada esa ficción, he pensado en la conveniencia de amplificar el tiempo y el espacio que abarca; la venganza podría ser heredada; los plazos podrían computarse por años, tal vez por siglos; la primera letra del Nombre podría articularse en Islandia; la segunda, en Méjico; la tercera, en el Indostán. (*OC* I: 483)

["Death and the Compass," despite the German or Scandinavian names, takes place in a Buenos Aires of dreams. . . . After I had written that fiction, I thought about the desirability of amplifying the time and space that it covers; the vengeance could be inherited; the periods could be computed in years, perhaps centuries; the first letter of the Name could be articulated in Iceland; the second, in Mexico; the third, in Hindustan.]

This hypothetical expansion of the time and the geography of the plot not only extends the labyrinthic narrative reach of the story, but, read through Borges's theories of (mis)translation, it also broadens the potentiality of the text. The irreverent remapping of the center-periphery dichotomy in "La muerte y la brújula" is now expanded through time and space, across temporal, linguistic, and cultural borders, to other marginal sites: Iceland, Mexico, Hindustan. This speaks of the potential to reevaluate historical, political, and cultural maps from the periphery—a productive mis-reading that Borges claims for the margins because of its ability to use its distance and difference from the center.

In his comments about "La muerte y la brújula" in the 1944 "Prologue," Borges suggests parallel dialogues, an alliance of sorts, between marginal literatures: Argentina, Iceland, Mexico, Hindustan. In "El escritor argentino y la tradición," Borges draws a broader net, one which connects South American, Jewish, and Irish writers through analogy. In "Alfonso Reyes," a 1959 text written on the occasion of the death of the Mexican writer and intellectual, Borges reiterates the central argument from "El escritor argentino y la tradición," but this time makes clear that the potential of taking with irreverence associated with the condition of marginality applies to all of the Americas:

Hacia 1919, Thorstein Veblen se preguntó por qué los judíos, pese a los muchos y notorios obstáculos que deben superar, sobresalen intelectualmente en Europa. Si no me engaña la memoria, acabó por atribuir esa primacía a la paradójica circunstancia de que el judío, en tierras occidentales, maneja una cultura que le es ajena y en la que no le cuesta innovar, con buen escepticismo y sin supersticioso temor. Es posible que mi resumen mutile o simplifique su tesis; tal como la dejo enunciada, *se aplicaría singularmente bien a los irlandeses en el orbe sajón o a nosotros, americanos del Norte o del Sur. . . .*

El uso [del inglés, el portugués y el español en América] no significa que nos sintamos ingleses, portugueses o españoles; la historia atestigua nuestra voluntad de dejar de serlo. Esa voluntad no es una renuncia; quiere decir que somos herederos de todo el pasado y no de los hábitos o pasiones de tal o cual estirpe. *Como el judío de la tesis de Veblen, manejamos la cultura de Europa sin exceso de reverencia. (Borges en Sur,* 60; emphasis added)

[Around 1919, Thorstein Veblen asked himself why the Jews, despite the many notorious obstacles that they had to overcome, stood out intellectually in Europe. If memory does not betray me, he finally attributed that supremacy to the paradoxical circumstance that the Jew, in Occidental lands, deals with a culture that is foreign to him and in which it does not cost him anything to innovate, with good skepticism and without superstitious fear. My summary might be mutilating or simplifying his thesis; such as I have stated it, it would be *especially applicable to the Irish in the Saxon world, or to us, Americans from the North or the South.* . . .

The use of [English, Portuguese and Spanish in the Americas] does not mean that we feel English, Portuguese or Spanish; our history is evidence of our willingness to cease being so. That willingness is not a rejection; it means that we are the inheritors of the entire past and not of the habits or the passions of this or that ancestry. *Like the Jew in Veblen's thesis, we handle European culture without an excess of reverence.*]

Although this passage repeats many of the arguments of "El escritor argentino y la tradición," it is significant in that Borges extends the mapping of the potentiality of the periphery to the entire American continent.

The claiming and privileging of peripheral spaces and identities resurfaces frequently in Borges's texts. This is the case with the protagonist of "Las ruinas circulares" (first published in *Sur* in 1940, then included in *El jardín de senderos que se bifurcan* in 1941 and in *Ficciones* in 1944), who, as we learn in the opening of the story, comes from an enigmatic country in the "South" which is peripheral to the center of Western civilization:

Nadie lo vio desembarcar en la unánime noche, nadie vio la canoa de bambú sumiéndose en el fango sagrado, pero a los pocos días nadie ignoraba que el hombre taciturno venía del Sur y que su patria era una de las infinitas aldeas que están aguas arriba, en el flanco violento de la montaña, donde el idioma zend no está contaminado de griego y donde es infrecuente la lepra. (*OC* I: 451)

[No one saw him disembark in the unanimous night, no one saw the bamboo canoe sinking into the sacred mud, but within a few days no one was unaware that the silent man came from the South and that his home was one of the infinite villages upstream, on the violent mountainside, where the Zend tongue is not contaminated with Greek and where leprosy is infrequent. (*Labyrinths*, 45)]

In what country is "Zend" spoken? The references here and elsewhere in the text suggest that the action unfolds in the ancient Middle East/Mediterranean region, not far from the origins of Occidental civilization. But the reference to the "South" also resonates with the Río de la Plata region. In any case, although the protagonist's place of origin remains unresolved, it is clearly one that is peripheral to Greece ("where the Zend tongue is not contaminated with Greek"); furthermore, the man travels from the periphery to try his hand at a universal dream: inventing a man from imagination, making a golem come to life.

Still another story in which peripheries are named and connected in a map of displacements and potentiality is "Tema del traidor y del héroe" (first published in *Sur* in 1944, then included in *Ficciones* that same year). The paradoxical tale narrated in this text, of a character who is at once his country's traitor and hero, of a series of events in which history and literature imitate each other to a dizzying degree, takes place in Ireland. But the narrator states that the story could have occurred in other places as well, all of them, significantly, marginal: "La acción transcurre en un país oprimido y tenaz: Polonia, Irlanda, la república de Venecia, algún estado sudamericano o balcánico . . ." [The action takes place in an oppressed and tenacious country: Poland, Ireland, the Republic of Venice, some South American or Balkan state . . .] (*OC* I: 496). Here South America is figuratively paralleled with a handful of peripheral European countries. The fact that it is in the periphery where this story could have, and has, occurred is poignant: it is here that history and literature are displaced, mistranslated, rewritten with irreverence; where oppression meets tenacity. It is here that mistranslation functions as a site of innovation, seen as the potential for literary and historical renovation.

The peripheral literatures that Borges connects in these texts represent a mapping of displacement, enacted through processes of writing as translation. These margins occupy and take from the universal, from the center, with irreverence, but without abandoning their marginality. In the case of Borges and "La muerte y la brújula," this amounts to finally "capturing . . . the flavor of the outskirts of Buenos Aires" through an innovative displacement of the European onto the Argentine and of the Argentine onto the European. Borges's practice of writing as (mis)translation creates a cartography in which margins can innovate precisely because of their difference.

REMAPPING DIFFERENCE:
THE SEARCH IN "LA BUSCA DE AVERROES"

"La busca de Averroes" (first published in *Sur* in June 1947, then included in *El Aleph* in 1949) contains some of Borges's most interesting and complex insights into cultural and linguistic difference and its potential for writers in the periphery. The story recounts a day in the work of the Arab philosopher known as "The Commentator," who lived in Al-Andalusia in the twelfth century (1126 to 1198) and dedicated his greatest efforts to translating and commentating the works of Aristotle. Western civilization as we know it today owes a tremendous debt to Averroes for the inheritance of Aristotle, and with him the core of Greek thought.[13] But "La busca de Averroes" is the story of the failure of Averroes: in particular of Averroes's inability to accurately translate into Arabic two words, "tragedy" and "comedy," which he finds from the beginning and throughout Aristotle's *Poetics*. Furthermore, as it turns out, this is not the only failure in the story, as Borges's text explores the limits of narrative and translation, and perhaps of language itself, in any act of reading and/or imagining an other.

"La busca de Averroes" forces us to consider apparently unbridgeable distances between languages, cultures, religions, and historic periods. But the text also begs the question of how Averroes, despite the linguistic and conceptual constraints of his worldview, manages to be the primary agent in the transmittal of the Greek Aristotle. The text introduces mappings of difference into questions of hermeneutics, demonstrating that such considerations are always mediated through processes of (mis)translation. Once again reworking the origins of Occidental traditions, here in the form of the foundational *Poetics* of the unreachable Aristotle, Borges approaches the search from the margins, while reminding us of the central role of Arabic and Islam in any articulation of the Western canon. Borges's search, from a South American periphery, broadens our cartography, synchronically and diachronically, as difference and otherness are treated as irrefutable and problematic, but also as unexpectedly and undeniably rich in potential.

The story recounts a day in the life of Averroes, as he seeks to resolve "un problema de índole filológica" [a problem of philological nature] (*OC* 1: 582): the translation of the words "tragedy" and "comedy" into Arabic. The irony of the story, as has been pointed out,[14] is that—as he ponders how to translate the words "tragedy" and "comedy" into Arabic—Averroes actually encounters several examples of these very same dramatic concepts, but does not recognize them as the solution he seeks. Early in the story, Averroes observes a group of children playing outside his balcony and fails to realize that their game is precisely the kind of playacting involved in "drama." Then, later that evening, Averroes fails to recognize, like everyone else at a dinner party, that the story that the traveler Abulcásim recounts of an event that he witnessed in China is precisely a form of the "tragedy" discussed in Aristotle's *Poetics*. (The event that Abulcásim witnessed turns out to be a Chinese version of a tragedy, of course.) Averroes cannot read these examples as "tragedy" or "comedy" because his context (his worldview, his paradigm) does not include a conceptual framework that would allow him to interpret them as such.[15] The words "tragedy" and "comedy," for Averroes, are signs devoid of meaning; they are mere signifiers to which Averroes, at the end of Borges's story, finally attaches incorrect significations.

Averroes's failed search suggests that there are some fundamental differences between languages and cultures that are too large to overcome. Borges's text thus underlines the definitive role of cultural and sociohistorical contexts in producing and determining meaning. As Jon Stewart has observed:

> The point is not that a correct definition of tragedy and comedy are in principle impossible but rather that the possibility of the very understanding of the concepts of tragedy and comedy is culturally conditioned. . . . Borges's story . . . tries to portray . . . the necessary connections between language and culture. . . . [Averroes] is ultimately limited to the epistemological categories of his culture. (325–27)

But Averroes's failed search for Aristotle is only part of the story. In the last paragraph of "La busca de Averroes," Borges makes an overt entrance onto the stage of the text as the narrator to tell us of his inability to imagine and recreate Averroes. This limitation, the narrator tells us, is analogous to Averroes's inability to translate Aristotle:

> En la historia anterior quise narrar el proceso de una derrota. . . . Recordé a Averroes, que encerrado en el ámbito del Islam, nunca pudo saber el significado de las voces tragedia y comedia. . . . Sentí que la obra se burlaba de mí. Sentí que Averroes, queriendo imaginar lo que es un drama sin haber sospechado lo que es un teatro, no era más absurdo que yo, queriendo imaginar a Averroes, sin otro material que unos adarmes de Renan, de Lane y de Asín Palacios. (*OC* I: 587–88)

> [In the foregoing story, I tried to narrate the process of a defeat. . . . I remembered Averroes who, closed within the orb of Islam, could never

know the meaning of the terms *tragedy* and *comedy*. . . . I felt that the
work was mocking me. I felt that Averroes, wanting to imagine what a
drama is without ever having suspected what a theater is, was no more
absurd than I, wanting to imagine Averroes with no other sources than a
few fragments from Renan, Lane and Asín Palacios. (*Labyrinths*, 155)]

The story, we realize, actually involves two searches and their parallel failures. The title of the story captures this ambiguity in Spanish, as "La busca *de* Averroes" denotes both Averroes's search for
Aristotle *and* the narrator's search for Averroes. An accurate,
though awkward translation of the title in English might be: "The
Search of/for Averroes".[16]

The appearance of the narrator, in which he admits the failure of
his search, brings to the forefront the multiple levels of mediation
involved in processes of literary imagination. Throughout the story
the narrator self-consciously points to the processes of translation
involved in Averroes's search for Aristotle, and in his own search
for Averroes. In the opening of the story, we see that Averroes's
very name undergoes translation: "Abulgualid Muhámmad Ibn-
Ahmad ibn-Muhámmad ibn-Rushd (un siglo tardaría ese largo
nombre en llegar a Averroes, pasando por Benraist y por Avenryz,
y aun por Aben-Rassad y Filius Rosadis) . . ." [Abulgualid Muhámmad Ibn-Ahmad ibn-Muhámmad ibn-Rushd (a century this long
name would take to become Averroes, first becoming Benraist and
Avenryz and even Aben-Rassad and Filius Rosadis] (*OC* I: 582;
Labyrinths, 148). Averroes embodies the process of translation
through changes and displacements in history, language, and culture. The foreignness of these names highlights Averroes's otherness,
a difference that separates Borges—and us as readers—from him.
By implication, it also points at Aristotle's foreignness, not only for
Averroes, but also for us. Likewise, the proper names in the story,
as well as some cultural specific nouns, are presented with translations in parentheses: "Ocurrió en Sin Kalán (Cantón) . . .";
"Iskandar Zul Qarnain (Alejandro Bicorne de Macedonia)"; "una
cáfila (caravana)"; "Aristú" (Aristóteles)" [It happened in Sin
Kalan (Canton) . . . ; Iskandar Zul Qarnain (Alexander the Great of
Macedonia); a *cafila* (caravan); Aristu (Aristotle)] (*OC* I: 585–87;
Labyrinths, 151–53). The confusion in naming known individuals
and regions in Borges's story reminds us that our conceptions of
geographic and political territories, and their relationship to the
construction of identity, are always mediated through translation.

The entire story, in fact, is structured as a series of searches for and of a text/writer by a reader/translator whose only access is through other texts: all subjective mediations worked through translations of translations. Averroes searches for Aristotle, but he is forced to work: "Sobre la traducción de una traducción" [With the translation of a translation] (*OC* I: 582). Similarly, Borges searches for Averroes, but, as the narrator acknowledges, the only material available to him is: "Unos adarmes de Renan, de Lane y de Asín Palacios" [A few fragments from Renan, Lane and Asín Palacios] (*OC* I: 588; *Labyrinths*, 155). Of these, the main source for Borges is Ernest Renan's 1861 *Averroès et l'Averroïsme*, as suggested by the epigraph of the story.[17] Renan, however, was also very far from Averroes; and he too worked on translations of translations. As Daniel Balderston points out:

Renan knew the work [Averroes's *Middle Commentary on Aristotle's Poetics*, translated into English in 1986 by Charles E. Butterworth] through translations of translations of the original, remarking at one point that the works of Averroes that were available to him were Latin translations of Hebrew translations of a commentary made upon Arabic translations of Syriac translations of Greek originals . . . ; Averroes's inability to read Aristotle directly is more than compensated by his readers' inability (from Thomas Aquinas to Borges) to read him directly. ("Borges, Averroes, Aristotle," 204)

Renan's distance from his subject reminds us that every search in "La busca de Averroes" is displaced. The distance between each reader/writer/text/context must be traversed by a process of translation that seems defined by its inevitable failure: Aristotle ↔ Averroes ↔ Renan ↔ Borges ↔ us. But the process of translation between each of these simultaneously fails *and* succeeds; it succeeds to the extent that it is undertaken knowing that it will fail. Like Sheherazade in *The Thousand and One Nights*, the reader/writer/translator performs his/her task to postpone failure, cognizant of its inevitability: to live is to write is to translate.

Averroes exists in (is constituted by) the process of searching for/translating Aristotle; the narrator exists in (is constituted by) the process of imagining/recreating Averroes; the reader exists in (is constituted by) the process of reading Borges. This emphasis on process makes the reader a protagonist in any construction of meaning. But meaning is culturally and linguistically determined, where

languages are always posited in and by difference. The value is not
in the meaning inherent to the text, but in the search for that meaning, for an interpretation that cannot be closed because it exists in
difference. The potential lies in the very processes of rereading/re-
writing/mistranslating, a statement of especial significance for the
periphery.

The searcher—the reader/translator/writer—only exists in the
process of searching for an other. His/her identity is constituted of
the search itself, shown in Borges to be a process of writing as
translation. This search, the desire for other, leads one to confront,
and to reside, in difference. As Deleuze and Guattari suggest: "Desire is not form, but a procedure, a process" (*Kafka*, 8). Desire,
search, process, difference, identity: these are the elements at play
in Borges's text. The levels of mediation, from Aristotle to Averroes
to Renan to Borges to us, suggest a vertiginous circulation of texts,
a confusion that is only temporarily resolved during the process of
reading/writing/translating (seen as interchangeable operations),
but which deteriorates once that process is abandoned. In the story,
this deterioration is figured by the literal disappearance of Averroes
in front of the mirror right after he has reached his incorrect interpretation of the words tragedy and comedy; and by the disappearance of the narrator once he ceases to think about Averroes:

> Sentí, en la última página, que mi narración era un símbolo del hombre
> que yo fui, mientras la escribía y que, para redactar esa narración, yo
> tuve que ser aquel hombre y que, para ser aquel hombre, yo tuve que
> redactar esa narración, y así hasta lo infinito. (En el instante en que yo
> dejo de creer en él, "Averroes" desaparece.) (*OC* I: 588)

> [I felt, on the last page, that my narration was a symbol of the man I
> was as I wrote it and that, in order to compose that narration, I had to
> be that man and, in order to be that man, I had to compose that narration,
> and so on to infinity. (The moment I cease to believe in him, "Averroes"
> disappears.) (*Labyrinths,* 155)]

The foundational text of literary theory, the *Poetics*, is thus deterri-
torialized; it can only be reached through (mis)translation. Meanwhile, it is the process itself that produces meaning and allows
Borges to recreate Averroes from Argentina, just as Averroes recreated Aristotle from Arabic Al-Andalusia, through (mis)translations
of (mis)translations.

Borges's text points at an aesthetics of mistranslation when the narrator refers to the beauty of Averroes's failed search:

Pocas cosas más bellas y más patéticas registrará la historia que esa consagración de un médico árabe a los pensamientos de un hombre de quien lo separaban catorce siglos; a las dificultades intrínsecas debemos añadir que Averroes, ignorante del siríaco y del griego, trabajaba sobre la traducción de una traducción. (*OC* I: 582).

[Few things more beautiful and more pathetic are recorded in history than this Arab physician's dedication to the thoughts of a man separated from him by fourteen centuries; to the intrinsic difficulties we should add that Averroes, ignorant of Syriac and of Greek, was working with the translation of a translation. (*Labyrinths*, 149)]

Pathos yes, but also beauty, as in the beauty of processes of mistranslation that put texts in motion and delight in difference and displacement.[18] This valorization of mistranslation, of writing as (mis)translation, can also be thought of as an aesthetics of the limits—which is to say, an aesthetics of the margins. Translation, in Borges's texts, forces us to confront difference, the constitutive difference of Latin American identity. The passage from one text and context to the other creates as much distance as it does proximity. The effect is of a hall of distorting mirrors, of refractions enacted through mistranslation, in which what one repeatedly encounters, from one (per)version to the next, is otherness itself—one's own otherness.

We read Aristotle today and believe that we read him correctly. But by displaying Averroes's cultural, linguistic, and historic constraints, Borges also implies the limitations of our worldview. This move destabilizes the notion of Western philosophy, or of the Modern Occident, as a fixed center. To the extent that "La busca de Averroes" is about the search for the origins of literary theory, of Aristotle's *Poetics*, it is about the impossibility of fixing such an origin. Our attempts at recovering, at imagining/rewriting the *Poetics*, Borges shows us, can only be done through a series of translations of translations, replete with equivocation and misinterpretation.

The dizzying reproduction of texts and pre-texts in Borges's story distorts and transforms. It leads to failure, but also to the potential to recreate new meanings and interpretations, in the very search, in the very process of rereading/mistranslating/rewriting.

Borges the narrator tells us that he has sought to tell "the process of a failure"; that process is the process of the reproduction of culture itself. It is a hermeneutic process whose literary and political value resides in it being an event as a process in motion, and not in reaching this or that specific conclusion or interpretation. It is a process of failure, but also a process of opening, through rereading and mistranslation, which resists closure. Motion, circulation, displacement, reading through misunderstanding, recreating through/ in difference and otherness: this is the beauty and the pathos in Averroes's search for Aristotle *and* in Borges's search for Averroes.

Contrasting Effects of Translation in Borges and T. S. Eliot

To further understand the specific role of translation in Latin America, it is useful to ask if Borges's practice of writing as translation is really that different from other practices of intertextuality developed by avant-garde writers in Europe or the U.S. in the first half of the twentieth century. For example, do Borges's rereadings and rewritings of displaced, translated fragments differ from that of European or U.S. modernists? Does modernism itself, with its multiple modes of citation and innovation, not imply a position of taking with irreverence to create ruptures with the traditions that proceeded it?

Borges's formulation of taking with irreverence, as presented in "El escritor argentino y la tradición" and enacted in many of his texts, is, at first sight, reminiscent of T. S. Eliot's famous statement that:

> Immature poets imitate, mature poets steal; bad poets deface what they take, and good poets make it into something better, or at least something different. The good poet welds his theft into a whole of feeling which is unique, utterly different from that from which it was torn. (Bush, 58)

However, despite the apparent similarities in the two positions, the "something" that Eliot refers to, that into which the translated (cited, alluded, or rewritten) fragment is transformed, varies greatly for Anglo-American and for Latin American writers. In fact, there is a major and significant difference between the effects that Eliot achieves through his use of translation and that achieved by Borges and other Latin American writers.[19]

This is perhaps best illustrated with an example in which Borges and Eliot use the same pre-text, but for completely different ends. The pre-text in question is Dante Alighieri's *Divina Commedia*, which is reworked by Eliot in *The Waste Land* (1922) and by Borges in "El Aleph" (first published in *Sur* in 1945, then included in *El Aleph* in 1949). Eliot's use of literary borrowing in *The Waste Land* is a case in which translation, conceived of in a broad sense, is clearly synonymous with poetic creation. Thinking of literary borrowing and citation as processes of translation assures that we do not ignore the cultural political repercussions of taking a fragment out of one context and inserting it into another. When we speak of translation we cannot help but consider the importance of temporal and spatial displacements, of changes in readers and their context, of the fundamental differences between cultures and languages, and of how these affect meaning and interpretation.

The approach Eliot takes in *The Waste Land* stands as the epitome of his efforts to present himself as the inheritor of the canonical center of Western tradition. The tension between fragmentation and unification created by the numerous insertions of translations, citations, references, and allusions in *The Waste Land*—from Homer to Virgil, from the Grail Legend to Baudelaire and Verlaine, from St. Augustine and Dante to Shakespeare—serve to fortify the place of London as a political and cultural center (albeit a destroyed one with a need for reconstruction). Eliot's London is a modern-day Rome, Athens, or Carthage; the entirety of Occidental tradition is conciliated at the site of the text and, ultimately, himself.

In his groundbreaking poem, Eliot transforms London into a modern Purgatory after the Inferno of War World I, which, among other things, functions as a rewriting of Dante's odyssey as led by Virgil. But consider what Borges does with Dante in "El Aleph." Here, Dante is awoken into resonance by the pathetic figure of Carlos Argentino Daneri and the narrator's nostalgic love for the deceased Beatriz Viterbo. The descent into Hades is a climb down a few steps into the basement of an ordinary house (except for the existence of the Aleph), soon to be destroyed, in a neighborhood of Buenos Aires.

Every allusion to Dante in Borges's story is a mistranslation of the original, at once reminding us of the *Commedia*, yet showing us a perverted version of it in mid-twentieth-century Buenos Aires.

Carlos Argentino Daneri is a parodic permutation of Dante's characters: a combination of Dante the poet and Virgil the guide, in both cases a creative infidelity of the original. Similarly, although the narrator's vision of the Aleph, the ultimate moment of epiphany, overwhelms him as much as the total vision of God does Dante in *Paradiso*, the results are quite different. Instead of a total vision of God, the experience blurs the narrator's idealized image of Beatriz Viterbo when it reveals a previous incestuous relationship between her and her cousin Carlos Daneri.

Whereas Eliot's use of Dante seeks a resolution to the Purgatory created by the condition of Modernity and the weight of tradition in England, and keeps London as the seat of cultural power, Borges's reworkings of the *Commedia* becomes a parody set in a specific Buenos Aires context. This recontextualization, this ironic and irreverent use of Dante, creates the opposite effect than that achieved by Eliot. The latter reinforces Western canonical traditions and places himself as their primary successor. Borges's move, on the other hand, displaces one of the fathers of the Western canon (Dante) onto the shores of the Río de la Plata. In the process, Borges's text questions preestablished views on literary influence and transmission, as well as the role of translation in these processes, especially in the periphery.

The combination of displacement and irreverence in "El Aleph" allows Borges to take on the universal—the questions of influence, the narrative issues associated with the possibility (or impossibility) of representing the infinite in a condensed, finite text—within an Argentine context. Borges's mistranslation, his cultural appropriation, validates the margins' capability for participating and contributing to Western traditions, while simultaneously establishing the Argentine tradition itself.[20]

"EL SUR": TEXTUAL EMBODIMENT OF THE NORTH–SOUTH DICHOTOMY

Another key text in considerations of translation and issues of center–periphery dichotomies is "El Sur," written around the same time as "El escritor argentino y la tradición" ("El Sur" was first published in *La Nación* on February 8, 1953, then included in *Ficciones*, beginning with the 1956 edition). The story is notable for the ways it explores what is at stake for the periphery in its incorporation of previous traditions through irreverent rereadings and rewritings. This is brought to the forefront by the protagonist's mixed and conflictive ancestry, and by the appearance of *The Thousand and One Nights*, which functions as a key reference to highlight the role of translation in the problematics of identity and representation in Argentina.

The protagonist of the story, Juan Dahlmann, embodies a duo-ancestry—both European and Argentine—which becomes representative of the duo-origin of the Argentine condition itself.[21] As Beatriz Sarlo has said: "The tension created by this double origin is at the heart of Argentine literature" (*Jorge Luis Borges*, 47). Throughout the story, Dahlmann—who carries his double origin even in his name—experiences his mixed heritage as a source of conflict; of the two, he seems to choose his Argentine destiny. But does Dahlmann really have as much choice as he believes? In other words, does Dahlmann choose the South, or does the South choose him? Can we say for sure what is Argentine and what is European about his choice, about his personal South?

Near the beginning of the story, we are told that the protagonist, "Se sentía hondamente argentino" [he felt profoundly Argentine], and that: "En la discordia de su dos linajes, Juan Dahlmann (tal vez a impulso de la sangre germánica) eligió el de ese antepasado romántico, o de muerte romántica" [In the discord of his two ancestries, Juan Dahlmann (perhaps driven to it by his Germanic blood) chose the one of his Romantic ancestor, or of Romantic death] (*OC* I: 524). Dahlmann feels Argentine, but the choice he makes toward the end of the story may very well have been influenced by his European side ("perhaps driven to it by his Germanic blood"). The tensions and contradictions that Dahlmann enacts in the text suggests that the local and the foreign are in fact inseparable; that it is not North versus South, but rather North *and* South, which defines the Argentine. But this is established only through a reconsideration of what North and South represent, including a remapping in which the Orient—in the form of the references to *The Thousand and One Nights*—plays a significant role. The tension between the foreign and the local serves as a point of departure for the story; it is an intersection that drives the production of narrative in this text and, arguably, in Argentine literature at large.

In the first part of "El Sur," Dahlmann is injured while reading Gustave Weil's German translation of the *Arabian Nights*, even as he expresses that he always felt more Argentine than European.[22]

The very manner in which Dahlmann's injury takes place hints at the main themes of the text: the tension between action (climbing the stairs) and reading, as well as the tension between the Argentine and the European (figured in the German translation that Dahlmann reads). The reference to the German version of the *Nights* appears to be situated in contrast to the other main literary reference in the story, José Hernández's *Martín Fierro*. However, the fact that the German text is a translation of a translation confounds our attempts at direct symbolic assignations.[23] Instead, the presence of a German *The Thousand and One Nights* in Argentina introduces an East-West coordinate to what is otherwise strictly a North–South cartography—even as it foregrounds the importance of translation in such dichotomies.

After Dahlmann is injured, he is taken to a sanitarium on Ecuador Street. The location where he is taken functions as a pivotal hinge in the story. Will Dahlmann go North or South from the Equator ("Ecuador")? Will he die in the modern clinic, imagining a death in a *pulpería* in the Pampas, or will he actually leave the clinic, and travel South to die in a *pulpería* in the Pampas? While in the hospital room, Dahlmann's internal identity conflict becomes overwhelming: "En esos días, Dahlmann minuciosamente se odió; odió su identidad, sus necesidades corporales, su humillación, la barba que le erizaba la cara" [During these days Dahlmann hated himself in minute detail; he hated his identity, his physical needs, his humiliation, the beard that bristled on his face] (*OC* I: 525). In this, the only physical description we get of the protagonist in the entire story, we see a literal embodiment of the North–South dichotomy ("his identity"), as it inhabits Dahlmann's very body ("his physical needs"). The wound Dahlmann suffered as he tried to simultaneously climb stairs and read Weil's German translation of the *Nights* in Buenos Aires, now extends to a physical self-hatred associated with his heavily conflictive heritage. The tension between the foreign and the local holds very real dangers: denying either the European or the Argentine has, apparently, the potential to destroy the body of the text and its protagonist.

The real danger Borges presents in the story, therefore, is not Dahlmann's inevitable, Romanticized death at the end. Rather, it is allowing the tension of his—and Argentina's—double origin to lead to self-hatred. Dahlmann's escape to the South, whether real or imagined, represents the other side of this danger: its potential not for self-destruction, but for self-discovery, for the production of

literature in the periphery. As Dahlmann travels South, what he—
and other Argentines with him—recover is a space that is not only
geographic, but also literary and historical. As he travels South on
the train, Dahlmann stops reading the *Nights* in translation long
enough to look out the window and compare what he sees in the
countryside with his memories of what he has read about the countryside:

> También creyó reconocer árboles y sembrados que no hubiera podido
> nombrar, porque su directo conocimiento de la campaña era harto infe-
> rior a su conocimiento nostálgico y literario. . . . La soledad era perfecta
> y tal vez hostil, y Dahlmann pudo sospechar que viajaba al pasado y no
> sólo al Sur. (*OC* I: 526–27)

> [He also thought he recognized trees and fields that he would not have
> been able to name, as his direct knowledge of the countryside was quite
> inferior to his nostalgic and literary knowledge of it. . . . The solitude
> was perfect and perhaps hostile; Dahlmann was able to suspect that he
> was traveling into the past and not only to the South.]

This intralingual mediation of the South is combined with an interlingual translation of the North—Dahlmann's European heritage,
his reading of the *Arabian Nights* in a German translation, the modern medical facilities of the sanitarium—as Dahlmann seeks to resolve his identity crisis.

When he reaches the *almacén* where he will meet his end, Dahlmann sees, off to a corner, the old gaucho who will provide him
with the knife for the first and last act of physical bravado of his
life. But this gaucho is very much a symbolic figure, a faded literary creation from the past: "En el suelo, apoyado en el mostrador,
se acurrucaba, inmóvil como una cosa, un hombre muy viejo. Los
muchos años lo habían reducido y pulido como las aguas a una pie-
dra o las generaciones de los hombres a una sentencia" [On the
floor, leaning against the bar, squatted a very old man, immobile as
an object. The long years had reduced and polished him as water
does a stone or generations of men do a sentence] (*OC* I: 527). The
possibility of a knife fight, a major theme from the gauchesque tradition, resurrects the old man, and he comes alive to provide Dahlmann with a *daga* to fight the *compadrito*. When this occurs,
reading and action—which had been separated throughout the
story, as illustrated by the librarian who reads the *The Thousand
and One Nights* in translation and can only dream of the kind of

adventure in which he now finds himself—momentarily unite to create the epiphany of the story. As the old gaucho acts, Dahlmann reads not just his gesture, but the gaucho himself as a cipher of the South, as a figure that returns his Argentine heritage to him: "En ese punto, algo imprevisible ocurrió. Desde un rincón, el viejo gaucho extáctico, en el que Dahlmann vio una cifra del Sur (del Sur que era suyo), le tiró una daga desnuda que vino a caer a sus pies" [At this point, something unforeseeable happened. From a corner of the bar, the old ecstatic gaucho, in whom Dahlmann saw a cipher of the South (of his South), threw him a bare dagger that landed at his feet] (*OC* I: 528).

Paradoxically, this recovery of Argentine tradition leads to Dahlmann's romanticized death. From Borges's point of view, this paradox, much like the displacement of European toponyms and surnames onto a map of Buenos Aires in "La muerte y la brújula," functions as a metaphor of the condition, as well as the potential, of Latin American literature. Identity and representation are sites of conflict that the Latin American writer must face. The best way to do this, as "El Sur" elegantly demonstrates, is not to turn back either on the European or the local, but rather to use the tension between them to carve out new spaces—geographic, historical, and literary—where innovation can proceed.

In prologues and interviews, Borges often identified "El Sur" as his best story.[24] In *Respiración artificial*, Ricardo Piglia argues, through the voice of his character Emilio Renzi, that this is due to the successful cross of Borges's "cuentos de cuchilleros" [stories of knife fighters] (e.g., "Hombre de la esquina rosada" [1935]) with his "cuentos eruditos" [stories of erudition] (e.g., "Pierre Menard: autor del *Quijote*" or "Tlön, Uqbar, Orbius Tertius"). "El Sur" thus merges the two lines of literature that originate in Argentina's nineteenth-century (*Respiración artificial*, 127–30): on the one hand a certain Europeism, the attempt to translate and appropriate French political philosophy and Romanticism that begins with the Salón Literario of 1837, and reaches an apex with Sarmiento's *Facundo*; on the other, the gauchesque tradition as epitomized by Hernández's *Martín Fierro*. The tension embodied by Juan Dahlmann in "El Sur" represents a cross between two kinds of translation, intralingual and interlingual, displaced onto a symbolic South which, in turn, becomes a privileged site for the production of literature in the margins.

CONCLUSIONS: THE VALUE OF THE MARGINS,
THE VALUE OF MISTRANSLATION

To theorize translation is to theorize one's relationship with language, ones own as well as that of others. This activity cannot but differ for writers in the center and in the periphery. The difference between centers and peripheries, in this respect, can be better understood if we consider the role of displacement in translation. Every translated text, whole or part, becomes an object separated from its source context—culturally and historically as well as linguistically. In this, translation and reading are perfectly interchangeable operations: differentiated from its source context, the text is displaced and reinscribed in the target context. This is true regardless of where the reader/translator/writer is situated. But spatial, temporal, and linguistic distances between source and target texts take on a magnified significance in the periphery. When those in the margins read, translate, or rewrite texts belonging to traditions of the center, they often experience an especially acute sense of displacement, of their own otherness, as the geographic and political space between themselves and the center is underscored by the cultural object before them. Thus, an important defining aspect of center–periphery dichotomies is the distance between the two poles: a distance that comes to represent economic and political disparities, even as it establishes and maintains relationships of (inter)-dependency having to do with power and subjectivity. How, then, can a translator—a reader, a writer—from the margins utilize this distance and difference without being burdened by a sense of anxiety or inferiority? How to write an original literature in the margins? Borges's work, as we have seen, provides an invaluable answer to these crucial questions.

In a text entitled "El oficio de traducir" [The Task of Translating] (1975), written a number of years after the ones that we examined in this chapter,[25] in which he is asked to address the issue of translation in Argentina, Borges states: "Para nosotros la traducción al español hecha en la Argentina tiene la ventaja de que está hecha en un español que es el nuestro y no un español de España" [For us, translation into Spanish done in Argentina has the advantage that it is done in a Spanish that is ours and not a Spanish from Spain] (*Problemas de la traducción*, 119). The advantage of translating in Argentina is that one translates into the language of Argentina, of the periphery, and not into the language of Spain, of Europe.²⁶ The distinction between the two Spanishes is important, as it separates and values the Argentine for its implied linguistic, cultural, and historic distinctiveness. Naming the difference between the Spanishes claims difference itself, in the periphery, as a privileged site for innovation. It is precisely this distinction that Borges delineates in "El escritor argentino y la tradición" when he speaks of a potential of the margins, which resides in the very condition of marginality. Innovation from the periphery is never mere literary technique, just as mistranslation from the periphery is never only playful equivocation. Innovation and mistranslation, creative infidelities and recontextualization of displaced fragments: laughter and play, yes, but in the margins these actions also challenge the values of originality and the traditions of the center. To innovate from the margins—to reread, to rewrite, to mistranslate—is to challenge center-periphery dichotomies by remapping accepted cultural and political relationships.

The potential of the margins to take with irreverence, as Borges suggests in "El escritor argentino y la tradición" and in the displaced cartography of "La muerte y la brújula," among other texts, can be extended to the potential of the periphery at large. This potential can be, and already has been, realized through processes of mistranslation, through practices of writing as translation. In Chapter I, we considered Argentina' tradition of mistranslation, as read through Borges's texts on the topic. But this perspective should be expanded to include other traditions of mistranslation throughout Latin America. We could then speak of the importance of equivocation as a means of transforming major discourses and legitimizing the emerging literatures of the periphery. In this sense, my book is part of a what needs to be a much greater inquiry into the constitutive role of mistranslation in the development of Latin American literatures, and the cultural political effects of this mistranslation for the North and South alike. And we say *mis*translation because translation in Latin America, like every act of reading and writing in the margins, has the potential to be a transformative event that includes an account of the distances and differences between centers and peripheries. Translation in Latin America is irreverence as innovation—and can become innovation as resistance; as in the case of "La busca de Averroes," it is both pathos and beauty: acknowledgment of difference and loss; transformation into potentiality and gain.

Several important studies on the role of translation in Latin America have been written, but much more remains to be done in this field.[27] Studying translation in Latin America can contribute key elements to transnational considerations, as it provides a further understanding of how the South reads and constructs the North. Such analyses can help explore when the North is able to export cultural and economic models wholesale, and when the South is able to transform such models, through appropriation and recontextualization, into something different. In this regard, studying translation in Latin America adds another perspective to how discourses and counterdiscourses flow and interact in cultural, economic, and political marketplaces. What needs to be explored, and what this book on Borges hopes to contribute, is how processes of mistranslation—how the displacement of texts and their circulation in new contexts with unexpected meanings—help form and transform the literary systems of both source and target cultures.

In the aforementioned "El oficio de traducir" Borges points to some of these implications when he discusses the differences between cultures and languages for writers in the margins:

> De acuerdo a los diccionarios, los idiomas son repertorios de sinónimos, pero no lo son. Los diccionarios bilingües, por otra parte, hacen creer que cada palabra de un idioma puede ser reemplazada por otra de otro idioma. El error consiste en que no se tiene en cuenta que cada idioma es un modo de sentir el universo, o de percibir el universo. (*Problemas de la traducción*, 120)

> [According to dictionaries, languages are repertories of synonyms, but in fact they are not. Bilingual dictionaries, for their part, would have us believe that every word from a language can be replaced by another from another language. The error resides in that they do not take into account that each language is a way to feel the universe, to perceive the universe.]

Every language represents a distinct worldview, where the language of Argentina, for example, is seen as different from that of Spain. As "La busca de Averroes" illustrates, difference in language is inherently linked to difference in culture, religion, historic time period, and thus to ones interpretation of the world. These distinctions might be limiting, but in the search for the distance between them, when texts and differences are placed in motion, as in

Averroes's search for Aristotle, or Borges's search for Averroes, they are also be full of potential.

This acknowledgment of otherness assures that the margins are not subsumed by the center. The distinction to which Borges refers in "El oficio de traducir" is the very difference that allows him to "capture . . . the flavor of the outskirts of Buenos Aires" in "La muerte y la brújula." It is also the constitutive elements of the specific context of "El Aleph," with its irreverent rewriting of Dante in the basement of an old house in a neighborhood of a Río de la Plata capital. The distinction that differentiates Argentina's language and history is also the conflictive potential embodied in the protagonist of "El Sur," in which mixed ancestry is shown to be problematic but essential in issues of identity and representation.

As Borges implies, to translate in Argentina is to write Argentina. The condition of Babel, the multiplicity of languages in the world, is not to be feared; rather, it should be seen as a limitless source of potential. It is this attitude, this aesthetics of irreverence constituted of the condition of marginality itself, that turns translation into a privileged site of innovation, cultural and political, in Borges, in Argentina, in Latin America, and, arguably, in the periphery at large.

5

Borges Reads Joyce:
A Meeting at the Limits of Translation

INTRODUCTION

THROUGHOUT THIS STUDY, WE HAVE EXPLORED HOW BORGES'S theorizing of translation functions to expand the potential of (mis)-translation for the margins, to innovate and create new texts and unexpected meanings. As we have seen, an aesthetics of irreverence, combined with a practice of writing as translation, is especially significant for writers from the periphery. As we have found, and as a number of other critics have pointed out, the act of reading, for Borges, is intimately connected to that of writing. His texts constantly blur and contaminate the distinctions between writer, reader, and text. By extension, whom Borges chooses to read and how is always relevant to what Borges writes. With this in mind, we turn now to a study of how Borges reads Joyce, in the widest sense of the term "to read." Joyce is an especially apt case to analyze for a number of reasons, including the fact that Borges's textual dialogue with Joyce includes translation, numerous readings, and several re-writings. Since it is a dialogue that involves all three, it will help us see how Borges's theories of reading, of writing, and of translation work together in response to a single writer.

Borges maintained a complicated, lifelong dialogue with Joyce, which began with a review and one-page translation of *Ulysses* in 1925 and extended all the way to his attendance at the Centenary celebration of Joyce's birth in Dublin in 1982. This fact will allow us to consider how Borges's reactions to Joyce developed with time, in parallel with the development of his writings. Using Borges's own theories of (mis)translation as a frame, we will examine how Borges puts his ideas into practice in his 1925 translation. We will then consider a number of ways in which Borges responds to

Joyce, all of which represent potential meeting points. These responses include several articles and reviews that Borges wrote about Joyce, a comparison of their treatment of metempsychosis (in *Ulysses* and in "El acercamiento a Almotásim"), an unexpected intersection between Funes and Joyce, and a shared precursor in Richard F. Burton's *The Thousand and One Nights*.

Throughout this dialogue, Borges presents a carefully chosen image of Joyce, emphasizing what he admires, and strongly criticizing what he does not. In the process, Borges skillfully exploits his similarities and differences with this Irish writer to "create" a specific version of Joyce, as a precursor:[1] the Joyce who innovated in language to constantly challenge the Metropolis. In addition, the extent to which translation and polyglottism are crucial aspects of Joyce's work makes a study of Borges's textual dialogue with Joyce that much more complex. We will therefore look briefly at the role that translation plays in Joyce to better understand Borges's responses to Joyce and to compare the importance of translation in both. This will raise issues regarding the relationships between translation, influence, reading, and writing.

In *The Cyclical Night*, L. A. Murillo theorizes an imaginary meeting between Borges and Joyce. By studying side by side how these two writers work with irony, he begins to lay the groundwork for such a meeting. In this chapter, I propose to go one step further to make such a meeting possible. The site of this meeting occurs at a number of intersections, of convergences and divergences, of texts and writers and aesthetic postulations. The site of the theoretical encounter between Borges and Joyce also occurs between two parallel margins: Buenos Aires and Dublin. By looking at how Borges reads, translates, and rewrites Joyce, as well as the role of translation in both, we will explore what such a meeting reveals about Borges and about the possibilities and limits, if any, of translation.

FIRST CONTACT: A (MIS)READING BEGINS

In the January, 1925 issue of *Proa*, calling himself the first "aventurero hispánico" [Hispanic adventurer] to arrive at Joyce's *Ulysses*, Borges provides a brief commentary of the novel followed by a translation of its last page.[2] Despite its brevity (or perhaps: with characteristic brevity), the article manages to introduce Joyce to Argentine readers and to make a number of insightful comments about *Ulysses*—which turn out to be telling about Borges himself—in the space of four quick pages before going on to the by-now celebrated translation of the last page of *Ulysses*. The translation becomes a key part of Borges's reading of Joyce; and the decisions that Borges makes in it are interesting in how they illustrate Borges's theories of (mis)translation.

Borges begins his essay, entitled "El *Ulises* de Joyce" [Joyce's *Ulysses*], in a humble tone, stating that he will not attempt to describe the entirety of the text; however, this tone should be seen as a warning sign, since Borges's humility can never be read literally, but should be seen instead as a rhetorical tool. Borges leaves a comprehensive description to Valéry Larbaud, who had already prepared one by then, as Borges informs us, in issue #18 of the *Nouvelle Revue Française*.[3] Borges also makes another disclaimer of sorts about *Ulysses*, as he confesses not to have "desbrozado las setecientas páginas que lo integran" [made his way through the seven hundred pages that compose it], and instead to "haberlo practicado solamente a retazos" [have practiced it only in fragments] (3). This comment suggests a fragmentary reading of Joyce and expresses an ambivalent sentiment about *Ulysses* that Borges would repeat, in one form or another, throughout his life.

However, despite the previous assertions, Borges says that he knows the text with the "aventurera y legítima certidumbre que hay en nosotros, al afirmar nuestro conocimiento de la ciudad, sin adjudicarnos por ello la intimidad de cuantas calles incluye ni aun de todos sus barrios" [adventurous and legitimate certainty that we have when we affirm our knowledge of the city, without claiming, because of this, the intimacy of how many streets it has, nor even of all its neighborhoods] (3). This establishes a certain affinity regarding the importance of the city in both writers, presenting the idea of the geography of the text, a concept that both writers would explore throughout their writings. This is especially evident in Borges's poetry of the time—*Fervor de Buenos Aires* (1923), *Luna de enfrente* (1925), and *Cuaderno San Martín* (1929)—all of which contain the careful working of the text as a map of the city. This affinity does not end with Borges's early poetry, of course, but also extends to many of Borges's fictions, in which the role of the labyrinthine city, as a literal or a figurative construction, is often crucial.[4]

Independent of his efforts to distance himself from Joyce by stating that he had not read *Ulysses* in its entirety, Borges's essay reveals the extent to which Borges very quickly grasped some of the key facets of *Ulysses*. Borges discusses the importance of Joyce's Irishness, stating "siempre los irlandeses fueron agitadores famosos de la literatura de Inglaterra" [the Irish were always famous agitators in England] (3), and declaring that Joyce emerges directly from this "costumbre de osadía" [practice of audacity] (4). Irish literature, particularly in relation to English language and tradition, will continue to be important to Borges throughout his career. One of the main reasons for this, as Borges already suggests in this early text, is the special place of Irish writers (like Jewish, like Latin American writers) in relation to the Metropolis. As we saw in chapter 4, Borges expounds this idea most clearly in "El escritor argentino y la tradición" (1951), in which he reveals how being *a part of*—yet *apart from*—the center affords writers from the margins with the opportunity to use any and all traditions, selectively and with irreverence, without feeling bound by the weight of Occidental canons.

Borges also discusses *Ulysses* in highly metaphoric language, with the occasional use of neologisms, both elements typical of his early writings. His commentary includes an analysis of subjectivity and perspective in Joyce's novel:

> El *Ulises* es variamente ilustre. Su vivir parece situado en un solo plano, sin esos escalones ideales que van de cada mundo subjetivo a la objetividad, del antojadizo ensueño del yo al transitado ensueño de todos. La conjetura, la sospecha, el pensamiento volandero, gozan de iguales privilegios en él y la perspectiva es ausencia. (4)

> [*Ulysses* is variously illustrious. It seems to live on only one plane, without those idealistic steps that go from each subjective world to an objective one, from the whimsical illusion of the I to the traveled illusion of everyone. Conjecture, suspicion, wandering thoughts, all are equally privileged in it; and the perspective is one of absence.]

These observations echo the considerations of subjectivity that Borges's essays and poetry of the time often raised.[5]

Noteworthy, too, are Borges's comments about Joyce's study of human consciousness with relation to time, although they do end with an ironic joke, representative of the humorous and ambivalent tone underlying much of Borges's discussion. In this case, the humor serves to undermine the verisimilitude of Borges's humble stance at the beginning of the article:

> Su tesonero examen de las minucias más irreducibles que forman la conciencia, obliga a Joyce a restañar la fugacidad temporal y a diferir el movimiento del tiempo con un gesto apaciguador, adverso a la impaciencia de picana que hubo en el drama inglés y que encerró la vida de sus héroes en la atropellada estrechura de algunas horas populosas. Si Shakespear [*sic*]—según su propia metáfora—puso en la vuelta de un reloj de arena las proezas de los años, Joyce invierte el procedimiento y despliega la única jornada de su héroe sobre muchas jornadas de lector. (No he dicho muchas siestas.) (5)

> [His tenacious study of the most irreducible trifles that make up consciousness, force Joyce to stop the flow of temporal evanescence and differ the movement of time with a soothing gesture, contrary to the goading impatience that existed in English drama, and which enclosed the life of its heroes in the rushed strait of a few populated hours. If Shakespeare—according to his own metaphor—placed in the turning of an hour glass the feats of the years, Joyce inverts the process and unfolds his hero's single day across the many days of the reader's. (I did not say many *siestas*.)]

With these parenthetical asides Borges throws in underhanded barbs even as he praises Joyce. This highlights Borges's own wit, and also seems quite appropriate in a discussion of Joyce, a writer for whom humor and parody are such basic staples.

The most sincere appreciation of Joyce in the article, on the other hand, refers to the use of multiple styles and rhetorical figures within one text, as well as the polyglot aspects of *Ulysses*:

> Es millonario de vocablos y estilos. En su comercio, junto al erario prodigioso de voces que suman el idioma inglés y le conceden cesaridad en el mundo, corren doblones castellanos y siclos de Judá y denarios latinos y monedas antiguas, donde crece el trébol de Irlanda. Su pluma innumerable ejerce todas las figuras retóricas. (6)

> [He is a millionaire of word plays and styles. In his trade, along with the prodigious treasury of voices that the English language amasses, and which bestow to it Caesarity in the world, flow Spanish doubloons and Jewish shekels and Latin denaries and ancient coins, where the Irish clover grows. His innumerable quill practices every rhetorical figure.]

Note the metaphoric language with which Borges states that the language of *Ulysses* includes Latin ("denaries"), Greek ("ancient coins"), Spanish ("doubloons"), and Old Testament references ("Jewish shekels"), all of which add up to compose Joyce's Irish tongue ("Irish clover"). The coin images, for their part, contribute to an implication of the flow and interchange of languages, of a marketplace of languages at the site of the text. Borges's observations make it difficult to believe that Borges did not read the entire novel, as he states earlier. But the issue is not how many pages Borges actually read; rather, it is the position that Borges delineates for himself. "El *Ulises* de Joyce" shows Borges to be a highly selective, irreverent, and creative reader of Joyce.

Borges returns to his mask of humility in the conclusions of his essay, in a tone of apparent unequivocal homage:

> Joyce es audaz como una proa[6] y universal como la rosa de los vientos. De aquí a diez años—ya facilitado su libro por comentadores más tercos y más piadosos que yo—disfrutaremos de él. Mientras, en la imposibilidad de llevarme el *Ulises* al Neuquén y de estudiarlo en su pausada quietud, quiero hacer mías las decentes palabras que confesó Lope de Vega acerca de Góngora: "Sea lo que fuere, yo he de estimar y amar el divino ingenio deste Cavallero, tomando del lo que entendiere con humildad y admirando con veneración lo que no alcanzare a entender". (6)

> [Joyce is audacious as a prow and universal as the rose of the winds. Ten years from now—once his book is facilitated by more intractable and more devout commentators than I—we will enjoy it. Meanwhile, in the impossibility of taking *Ulysses* with me to Neuquén,[7] and of studying it in its deliberate quietness, I wish to make use of the honorable words that Lope de Vega confessed regarding Góngora: "Whatever it may be, I shall esteem and love the divine ingenuity of this Gentleman, humbly taking from him what I might understand, and venerably admiring that which I am unable to understand."]

But the quotation from Lope de Vega is really a double-edged sword. Although it sounds extremely laudatory, it can be read ironically. Disguised as praise, it is also a move that equates Joyce with Góngora—and we know Borges had about as much sympathy for Góngora as Quevedo did. We thus note that even in this first essay, which is generally interpreted as the one place where Borges demonstrates his greatest admiration for Joyce,[8] Borges's reading of Joyce is already ambivalent. The praise is not unequivocal, but reveals a certain reserve, expressed through humor and irony, which will only grow as Borges continues to dialogue with Joyce, as Borges oscillates between recognizing some affinities with Joyce, but also distancing himself from other aspects of the Irish modernist.

In any case, the depth of Borges's insights into *Ulysses* at such an early date is quite astonishing. "El *Ulises* de Joyce" shows Borges at the avant-garde of Joycean reception, even four years before the publication of the French translation of *Ulysses*. His remark about the need for commentaries and guides anticipates Gilbert's *James Joyce's Ulysses, A Study* (1930). Well ahead of his time in Argentina and internationally, Borges realizes not only the importance of Joyce's work, but also provides an insightful reading of Joyce's project based on what is supposedly a partial read of *Ulysses*. In the process, he begins to shape—to misread, to mistranslate—which Joyce he wishes to present to his Argentine readers.[9]

"NOTA SOBRE EL *ULISES* EN ESPAÑOL": THE TASK OF THE BORGESIAN TRANSLATOR

In 1945, Salas Subirat published a complete translation of *Ulysses* in Argentina. Borges reviews Subirat's translation in "Nota sobre el *Ulises* en español" [A Note About *Ulysses* in Spanish] (*Los Anales de Buenos Aires*, January, 1946); this text is relevant for us because of the specific connections between Borges's theories of (mis)translation and Joyce. Borges opens his review with the following assertion: "No soy de aquellos que místicamente prejuzgan que toda traducción es inferior al original. Muchas veces he comprobado, o he podido sospechar, lo contrario" [I am not one of those who mystically prejudges all translations to be inferior to the original. Many times I have confirmed, or suspected, the opposite] ("Nota," 49). Consistent with his other writings on translation, Borges clearly states that a translation need not be inferior to the original. After providing several examples of this position, Borges repeats, almost verbatim, his challenge of the concept of a "definitive text" from "Las versiones homéricas."[10] Borges's defiance of traditional conceptions of originality is specifically useful in its relation to Joyce. I would argue, in fact, that the suggestion that the "definitive text" is a fallacy is one of the strongest affinities between these two very different writers.[11]

In his review, Borges acknowledges the verbal accomplishments of *Ulysses*, even as he underlines what he sees as the novel's chaos: "El *Ulises*, tal vez, incluye las páginas más caóticas y tediosas que registra la historia, pero también incluye las más perfectas. Lo repito, esa perfección es verbal" [*Ulysses* might just contain the most chaotic and tedious pages that history has ever recorded, but it also contains some of the most perfect ones. I repeat, that perfection is verbal] ("Nota," 49). Next, Borges states: "En esta primera versión hispánica del *Ulises*, Salas Subirat suele fracasar cuando se limita a traducir el sentido" [In this, the first Spanish version of *Ulysses*, Salas Subirat tends to fail when he limits himself to translating the meaning] ("Nota," 49). In trying to translate the meaning, Subirat misses what Borges considers the most important aspect of the text: its verbal ingenuities. The instances that do succeed, on the other hand, are: "Aquellos pasajes en que el texto español es no menos neológico que el original" [Those sections in which the Spanish text is no less neologistic than the original] ("Nota," 49).

This sets up Borges's conclusion, which can be read as a specific guideline of how one might approach translating Joyce: "Joyce dilata y reforma el idioma inglés; su traductor tiene el deber de ensayar libertades congéneres" [Joyce expands and reforms the English language; his translator must try to undertake liberties of a similar kind] ("Nota," 49). Borges identifies what Joyce does with English, then states that the translator must undertake an analogous operation with Spanish. The translator must seek to establish the same relationship with the target language as the writer does with the source language.[12] The task of the Borgesian translator is thus to establish a position with respect to his own tongue that is the same as that which the writer has with his. In this sense, the responsibilities of a Borgesian translator become nearly synonymous with those of the writer of the source text, but enacted in, and on, a different language.[13]

Is such a task possible? In Borges's own judgment, the job of translating *Ulysses* is: "Muy ardua, casi imposible. . . . *A priori*, una versión cabal del *Ulises* me parece imposible" [Very arduous, nearly impossible. . . . *A priori*, I believe that an exact/complete version of *Ulises* is impossible] ("Nota," 49). But it is not surprising for Borges to state so emphatically that a complete and exact version—"una versión cabal"—of *Ulysses* is not possible. We know from "Las versiones homéricas" and "Los traductores de *Las 1001 Noches*," as we saw in chapter 2, that Borges does not believe that a complete and literal version of any text is possible, and that the translations that Borges most values are those that make the best use of creative infidelities. By the time Borges had written this review, he had already produced, some twenty years before, not a complete, but a reduced, one-page fragment of *Ulysses*. One of the most important creative infidelities that Borges takes in his version is his decision to do a very partial translation of *Ulysses*. Just as his readings of Joyce are fragmentary, so is his rewriting of *Ulysses*.

As we turn now to an analysis of Borges's 1925 translation of the last page of *Ulysses*, we will keep in mind Borges's comments from "Nota sobre el *Ulises* en español." We will want to recall, as well, what Borges says about a translator's "literary habits" in "Los traductores de *Las 1001 Noches*." There, referring to the Newman–Arnold debate (i.e., the argument over whether literal or paraphrastic translations can most faithfully convey the spirit of the original), Borges argues that neither approach, exclusively, is feasible, and that both are impossible if taken to their extremes. Instead, Borges places the emphasis on the literary habits of the translator, on the way he/she is able to manipulate the language, on the "syntactic movement" from one text to the next. Let us examine, then, the syntactic movement and the literary habits as we go from Joyce's text to Borges's.

A Partial Río de la Plata *Ulises*

Borges's 1925 partial translation of Joyce's *Ulysses* is an excellent illustration of Borges's "literary habits" as a translator—which is to say, of Borges's habits in general at this stage in his career. In his version, Borges finds inventive and convincing ways to translate the orality of Molly's monologue, as well as her many idiomatic expressions.[14] Borges has a wonderful knack for translating literally when it helps to capture Molly's personal idiosyncratic modalities. For example, "pinky sugar" becomes "azúcar rosadita," and "my mountain flower" is turned into "mi flor serrana." But Borges also translates freely expressions built into the language, which Molly herself incorporates into her monologue unconsciously. Here are some examples of idiomatic expressions that Borges translates into a very colloquial and appropriate Río de la Plata Spanish that fits in the flow of the monologue:

Joyce	Borges
I love flowers Id love to have the whole place swimming in roses	soy loca por las flores yo tendría nadando en rosas toda la casa
that would do your heart good to see	te alegraría el corazón ver ríos y bañados
rivers and lakes and flowers all sorts of shapes	y flores con cuanta forma Dios creó
wouldnt give a snap of my two fingers	me importa un pito
and why why	y a qué santos
so there you are	están embromados

And here is an example in which Borges manages to translate an idiomatic expression in English into a poetic one in Spanish that does not feel forced:

Joyce	Borges
they might as well try to stop the sun from rising tomorrow	éso es como atajarlo al sol de salir

In this phrase, Borges also displaces the alliteration in s ("*s*ol de *s*alir"), which in the English version comes in conjunction with the next phrase: "the *s*un *s*hines for you he said."

An immediately noticeable aspect of the translation is that Borges is never reluctant to make alterations as he finds necessary. The most important of these is the complete erasure or rewriting of proper names that localize Joyce's text in Dublin in 1904. These omissions contribute to making the fragment function as an autonomous piece, as a (co)creation by the translator. Furthermore, they represent an irreverent recontextualizing of the text from a Joycean Dublin to a Borgesian Buenos Aires. Examples of these omissions and alterations include:

Joyce	Borges
the sun shines for you he said the day we were lying among the rhododendrons on Howth head in the grey tweed suit	Para vos brilla el sol me dijo el día que estabamos tirados en el pasto de traje gris

thinking of so many things he didnt	pensando en tantas cosas que él no
know of Mulvey and Mr	sabía de fulano y zutano y
Stanhope and Hester and	papá y de Ester y del capitan
father and old captain Groves	

In the first of these, the important geographic reference of "Howth head" is eliminated, and "rhododendrons" is changed to "pasto." Leaving out a flower may be important for Molly, the "flower of the mountain," but "pasto" fits better in the flow of Borges's version, and there are plenty of other flowers in the text so that the theme is not lost.

More important, as one of the above quoted examples illustrates ("Para *vos* brilla el sol . . ."), Borges transposes Molly's voice onto an Argentine voice, as he has her speak in the *voseo*, the second person singular conjugation used in the Río de la Plata region. This, then, becomes a key element in Borges's irreverent rewriting of the text, as the fragment is displaced toward, and appropriated from, a specifically Río de la Plata context. In addition, as we see in the second of the above quoted examples, Borges captures the oral rhythm of Molly's speech, while rewriting specific proper names with the Argentine colloquial "fulano y zutano," and changing Hester to a more archetypal, Biblical name Ester. This use of Argentine colloquialisms, combined with the use of the *voseo*, strongly marks the text linguistically and culturally. These alterations—Borges's most blatant and most playful creative infidelities—not only serve to displace the text toward an Argentine context, they also recreate Molly's voice surprisingly and incredibly well. This paradoxical sense of hyperfidelity confirms, in this case, Borges's provocative suggestions that creative infidelities and recontextualizations in fact lead to the most interesting and worthwhile of translations.

In addition, some of Borges's slight alterations are wonderful in how they fit with the overall tone and register of Molly's internal monologue. In the following example, Borges's version is shorter but perhaps more elegant than Joyce's; it makes use of a clever neologism, turning "pasto" into a verb:

Joyce   *Borges*

and all the fine cattle going about   y el ganado pastando

And here are some other choices that Borges makes in which he avoids being too literal:

Joyce	*Borges*
atheist	libre-pensadores
he understood or felt	él comprendía
I could always get around him	lograría engatusarlo siempre

Another innovative moment occurs when Borges translates, "the watchman going about serene with his lamp," as "el sereno pasando quietamente con su farol." By choosing "sereno" instead of, say, "vigilante," Borges transposes the Latinate root, but displaces it unto "the watchman." This elegantly conveys the serenity of the watchman, allowing Borges to improvise with "quietamente."

There is also an unexpected set of decisions that Borges makes toward the end of the fragment. They begin with the phrase "the sea the sea," near the conclusion of Molly's monologue, which reads: "and O that awful deepdown torrent O and the sea the sea crimson sometimes like fire and the glorious sunsets. . . ." The language here becomes more and more sexually charged, the phrases swaying with growing desire, as they build toward the climactic last "yes I will Yes." Borges's version does not lose any of the passion or rhythm of the original: "y Oh ese torrente atroz y de golpe Oh y el mar carmesí a veces como fuego y los ocasos brillantes. . . ." In fact, although Borges does not repeat "el mar" (which might not have the same romantic effect in Spanish as it does in English), and although he says "ese torrente atroz y de golpe Oh" (instead of "that awful deepdown torrent"), the "y de golpe" can actually refer to the "torrente" or to the exclamation "Oh" that comes immediately afterwards, which lends the "Oh" an extra erotic emphasis.[15]

In addition to displacing the Irish idiomatic expressions onto Argentine phrases, to making choices that correspond to the poetic and emotional mood of the text, and to capturing the rhythm of Molly's sensual stream of consciousness, Borges also captures the sexual desire that builds toward the end of the monologue.[16] I also agree with Jorge Schwartz's observation of a very erotic instance in which Borges's solution might be an improvement on the original. Joyce's version says: "and first I put my arms around him yes and drew him down to me"; whereas Borges writes: "y primero lo abracé sí y encima mío lo agaché." And I would add that the conclusion, "yes I will Yes" sounds even more sexually explicit in Borges's Spanish: "sí quiero Sí."[17]

But the point is not to compare the merits of the translation with those of the original. Rather, it is to show that Borges was already practicing in 1925, from the beginning of his writing/translating/reading career, the kinds of irreverent displacements that would mark so much of his work. The examples quoted above reveal that, especially in the area of syntactic decisions, Borges never feels that he has to be literal, but is willing to omit and change and exercise his preferences as needed. By executing these creative infidelities, he is able to be both literal and free, as he reads and captures the spirit of the text and recreates it in an Argentine context. His attention to the details and subtleties of language and his ability to distinguish between what might be an idiosyncratic character trait and a cultural linguistic one is exquisite. And his literary habits reveal a surprising capability to capture the full erotic expression of Molly's speech.

The greatest overall rewriting that occurs in Borges's version, though, is the rendering of the entirety of Joyce's novel into a one-page fragment that uses the Río de la Plata *voseo*. Borges's enactment of the potential of the fragment derives from his deep-rooted irreverence toward all originals and traditions; this is not to say that he rejects source texts, but that he rewrites—mistranslates—them in an Argentine context. This position, as we have seen, creates, through irreverent innovation, a crucial site of potentiality for writers/translators in the periphery.[18] Borges's deletions of most proper nouns and references to previous parts of *Ulysses* transforms his fragment into an autonomous version, thus creating an even greater distance from the source text than that usually associated with translation proper. The omissions and alterations rupture important links with the original, transforming Borges's version into an independent text. This, combined with the use of the *voseo* and the Río de la Plata idioms and colloquialisms, leads to an appropriation that is both textual and contextual. Borges perceives the relationship between the content and the context in Joyce's version (the context being everything that has to do with the language and the setting of Dublin on June 16, 1904), and recreates it in his own image (which includes an analogous context: Borges's Buenos Aires of the mid-1920s). Paradoxically, not only do Borges's creative infidelities lead to a new version, they also produce an unexpected sense of hyperfidelity to the source text. Through his manipulation of language (his "syntactic movement") and the decisions he takes (his "literary habits"), Borges manages to transpose the relationship between text and context from the source to the target language. In his 1946 review, Borges advises translators of Joyce that: "Joyce expands and reforms the English language; his translator must try to undertake congenerous liberties" (49). In 1925, in one page of Argentine Spanish, Borges already accomplishes this task.

METEMPSYCHOSIS: A SHARED METAPHOR FOR (RE)WRITING

In the 1930s, Joyce begins to form part of Borges's vocabulary of literary references and allusions, as evidenced by several mentions of Joyce in *Discusión* (1932) and *Historia de la eternidad* (1936).[19] The most relevant of these from this period is the reference to Joyce in "El acercamiento a Almotásim" (first published in the collections of essays *Historia de la eternidad* in 1936, then included in *El jardín de senderos que se bifurcan* in 1941, and in *Ficciones* in 1944). The intertextuality between "Almotásim" and Joyce is particularly interesting for what it suggests about both writers' use of metempsychosis as a metaphor for the rewriting/mistranslating of previous texts.

"El acercamiento a Almotásim," written under the guise of a review, is one of the first texts in which Borges thoroughly blurs the line between criticism and fiction. But this is not the only distinction blurred in the story. The text presents us with various levels of mediation, beginning with the narrator/critic who introduces the novel that he will review for us: *The Approach to Al-Mu'tasim* by Mir Bahadur Alí. Throughout the story, the narrator refers to the novel and its (fictional) author as if they were real. This effect is magnified by the fact that the narrator substantiates his review with references to other reviews, which turn out to be apocryphal, but which the narrator attributes to real critics/writers (e.g., Phillip Guedalla, Cecil Roberts, etc.). The narrator also tells us about the publishing history of the novel. Significantly, the narrator is only able to get a hold of the second edition of the (fictive) text in question: *The Conversation with the Man Called Al-Mu'tasim*, "beautifully subtitled" by the "author" (the fictional Bahadur) "*A Game with Shifting Mirrors* (Un juego con espejos que se desplazan)." Regarding this second edition, the narrator states: "No he logrado juntarme con la primera, que presiento muy superior. A ello me autoriza un apéndice, que resume la diferencia fundamental entre la versión primitiva de 1932 y la de 1934" [I have not been able to get a hold of the first one, which I presume to be much better. This

I am able to judge thanks to an appendix, which summarizes the fundamental difference between the primitive version of 1932 and the one of 1934] (*OC* I: 414). These apparently innocent comments announce the importance of displacement and reflections/refractions, of reproductions and translations, in the story. The first edition, the original, is unobtainable, unreachable; its supposed superiority eludes us from the start. The irony is the fictional nature of both.[20]

After this introduction, the narrator summarizes Bahadur's novel for us. This condensation of a nonexistent pre-text mirrors the kind of writing as translation that Borges inaugurates in *Historia universal de la infamia*, and points the way to a technique to which he returns throughout his fictions. The plot is the story of a law student in Bombay who one day finds himself in the middle of a battle between Muslims and Hindus, and kills, or thinks he has killed, a Hindu infidel. Running away, he meets a defiler of corpses who tells him about a caste of thieves and a woman who belongs to this caste. The student decides to find her and sets off on a long pilgrimage to this end. Living among the vilest of people, he catches a glimpse of an inconsistency, an alteration, in the infamy surrounding him. This sets him off on a search for the individual who is the source of this implied clarity, as reflected in those whom that person has somehow touched. At the end, it is understood that the ascending progression will lead to Almotásim to himself. The narrator follows this with brief comments on the plot of the novel and concludes with a discussion of its possible sources.

Near the beginning of the story, the narrator explains that *The Approach to Al-Mu'tasim* is a cross, a hybrid, between an allegorical Islamic poem and a detective novel; more specifically, that it is the conjunction of the twelfth-century Persian Ferid Eddin Attar and Wilkie Collins (1824–89), one of the pioneers of the detective genre. Then, in the conclusion of his "review," the narrator returns to Ferid Eddin Attar, to tell us that this Persian was the author of the *Mantiq al-Tayr*, the *Parliament of the Birds*. This poem is in turn summarized in a long footnote at the end of the text, as part of a discussion on pantheism and metempsychosis. Along the way, one of the transmutations that occurs throughout the story is of the name of this Persian poet itself: from Ferid Eddin Attar at the beginning of the text (in the apocryphal quotation attributed to Cecil Roberts), to Farid ud-din Attar in the conclusion, to Farid al-Din Abú Talib Muhámmad ben Ibrahim Attar in the footnote. As we saw in the case of Omar Khayyám in "El enigma de Edward FitzGerald" (in chapter 3), and of Averroes in "La busca de Averroes" (in chapter 4), Ferid Eddin Attar's name itself undergoes a process of (mis)translation, highlighting the differences between the different languages and historic periods, between East and West, and suggesting that even proper names, and everything they imply about identity, alter with changes in context.

The emphasis on the concept of metempsychosis, both in the plot of Bahadur's novel (the transmigration of clarity through the souls of those the student meets in his search), and in the narrator's discussion at the end of the text, strongly suggest that it is the key to the interpretation of "Almotásim."[21] I propose that we look at metempsychosis in this text as a literary recourse, as a form of transformation, of the metamorphosis of previous texts rewritten/ mistranslated in an new context. In this sense, metempsychosis would function as a metaphor for some of the processes of writing as translation that we have discussed in previous chapters.

The crux of the story lies in the narrator's conclusion, which is an apocryphal polemical discussion about the possible precursors of *The Approach to Al-Mu'tasim*. Here, Borges plays a two-faced game, simultaneously leading us to the uses of the concept of metempsychosis in his text, yet warning us against an excessive dependency on such a reading. The clearest example of this is found, significantly, where Borges establishes a connection with Joyce:

Los repetidos pero insignificantes contactos del *Ulises* de Joyce con la *Odisea* homérica, siguen escuchando—nunca sabré por qué—la atolondrada admiración de la crítica; los de la novela de Bahadur con el venerado *Coloquio de los pájaros* . . . conocen el no menos misterioso aplauso de Londres, y aun de Alahabad y Calcuta. (*OC* I: 417)

[The repeated but insignificant points of contact between Joyce's *Ulysses* and Homer's *Odyssey* continue to receive—I shall never know why—the rash admiration of the critics; those of Bahadur's novel with the venerated *Parliament of the Birds* . . . have received a no-less mysterious applause from London, and even from Alahabad and Calcutta.]

Here and elsewhere Borges criticizes the emphasis of scholarship on the parallels between Joyce's *Ulysses* and Homer's *Odyssey*. For Borges is not nearly as interested in the parallels that a text draws with its sources, as he is in the differences and the distances between them. Borges's comments call attention to the importance of metempsychosis in *Ulysses*, as well as in "Almotásim," even as they warn us about the limitations of such reductive readings.

In a complex game of reflections and refractions that draws us back to the subtitle of Bahadur's novel ("*A Game with Shifting Mirrors*")—a game that is also mirrored in the plot of the apocryphal *The Approach to Al-Mu'tasim*—the discussion in the conclusion is not only a consideration of sources and influences, but also a game involving the relationship of these to the writing subject. The series of multiplications and displacements of the subject include the narrator/critic, the apocryphal novelist, and the real critics to which Borges attributes the various apocryphal opinions. These are all contrasted with the appearance of the single "I" of the narrator, who appears toward the end of the conclusion, but is in turn modified by the footnote. Thus, the writing subject, too, undergoes a series of metempsychotic transformations like those of Ferid Eddin Attar's name: a series of illusive translations, underneath which we are left with a "nadería de la personalidad" [nothingness of self], to use Borges's own phrase.

Although Borges acknowledges a certain affinity with Joyce's use of metempsychosis, he also establishes a different use for it in his text. The parallels between *The Approach to Al-Mu'tasim* and its precursors are important, but this would not interest Borges if it were not for the dissimilarities between them as well. None of the precursors referred to in the conclusion or in the footnote, for instance, acknowledge that *The Approach to Al-Mu'tasim* is also a detective novel. Borges is not nearly as interested in identifying direct influences (e.g., Homer for *Ulysses*, the *Parliament of the Birds* for *The Approach to Al-Mu'tasim*), as he is in inventing texts with situations that also *diverge* from their precursors. Such a disruption creates a new relationship with tradition, allowing Borges to use precursors without being bound to them. This leads to the blurring of the distinctions between genres and to the creation of unexpected meanings in new contexts. This is seen in the startling hybrid at the core of *The Approach to Al-Mu'tasim* (i.e., a mystical Persian poem crossed with a detective novel), or in the subtle conjunction of fiction and criticism found in "El acercamiento a Almotásim" itself.

Whenever he criticizes the overly simplistic parallels between Homer's *Odyssey* and Joyce's *Ulysses*, Borges refers to the praise that critics confer upon such parallels. In the process, Borges establishes himself as a different kind of reader of Joyce. In addition, despite some similarities in their use of metempsychosis, Borges in fact proposes an entirely different paradigm of literature than Joyce. The theory of writing that Borges proposes in "Almotásim" is almost diametrically opposed to Joyce's. Borges's text suggests that paraphrasing a novel—rereading it, mistranslating it—can be preferable to writing one, whether that novel is veridical or apocryphal. Why write *The Approach to Al-Mu'tasim*, when Borges can condense it into a few pages, while raising crucial questions about genre, tradition, influence, and writing? This reduction in form, and the contrast between *The Approach to Al-Mu'tasim* and *Ulysses*, is analogous to the idea that Joyce's *Ulysses* can be (mis)translated into one page of Río de la Plata Spanish, as Borges did in 1925.

 Still, although their aesthetics differ so widely with regards to form, metempsychosis does function in similar ways for Borges and Joyce. For both, it is a metaphor for rewriting/mistranslating previous texts and traditions, an irreverent displacement that destabilizes the canons of the center and leads to innovation in new forms and contexts. The approach may differ—it functions primarily through parody for Joyce, through reduction for Borges, with extreme irony in both—as does, quite clearly, the end result, but the process is more similar than Borges ever acknowledged.

(Mis)reading in an Argentine Context: Joyce in *El Hogar*

"Biografía sintéctica: James Joyce"

 From 1936 to 1939, Borges published a bimonthly page in the popular magazine *El Hogar*. Entitled "Libros y autores extranjeros. Guía de lecturas" [Foreign books and authors. A reading guide], it included a vast a array of reviews, articles, and fragmentary translations of foreign literature[22]. In this forum Borges dedicates two articles to James Joyce. In these, he continues his practice of reading Joyce very selectively to construct a partial image of the Irish writer for his Argentine readers.

 The "Biografía sintéctica: James Joyce" [A Synthesized Biography: James Joyce], published on February 5, 1937, is written in a light, conversational tone, more reminiscent of a magazine feature than one of Borges's typical essays. It provides some basic biographical information on Joyce, some of which Borges had already presented in "El *Ulises* de Joyce" in 1925, and states that Joyce has always been attracted by: "Las obras vastas, las que abarcan un mundo: Dante, Shakespeare, Homero, Tomás de Aquino, Aristóteles, el Zohar" [Vast works, those that encompass an entire world: Dante, Shakespeare, Homer, Thomas Aquinas, Aristotle, the *Zohar*][23] (*Textos cautivos*, 83). In his assessment of Joyce's work, Borges all but disregards everything except *Ulysses*, for which he expresses measured praise. Borges irreverently dismisses the work prior to *Ulysses*: "Los primeros libros de Joyce no son importantes. Mejor dicho, únicamente lo son como anticipaciones del *Ulises* o en cuanto pueden ayudar a su inteligencia" [Joyce's first books are not important. Better yet: they are only so as an anticipation of *Ulysses*, or to the extent that they can help decipher it] (*Textos cautivos*, 83). Although many would disagree with this judgment, Borges's comments are accurate in identifying the importance of earlier Joycean texts on later ones.

Borges then recounts the history of the writing of *Ulysses*, both in terms of Joyce's life and of what was happening around him in Europe, namely World War I: "Más que la obra de un solo hombre, el *Ulises* parece la labor de muchas generaciones. A primera vista es caótico; el libro expositivo de Gilbert—*James Joyce's Ulysses*, 1930—declara sus estrictas y ocultas leyes. La delicada música de su prosa es incomparable" [More than the work of a single man, *Ulysses* seems to be the labor of many generations. At first sight it is chaotic; Gilbert's expository book—*James Joyce's Ulysses*, 1930—explains its strict and hidden rules. The delicate music of its prose is incomparable] (*Textos cautivos*, 84). Borges, as we see here, consistently categorizes *Ulysses* as chaotic.[24] Also consistent is what Borges seems to most admire about Joyce: the multiplicity of styles and languages in his work. As in his 1925 essay, Borges emphasizes Joyce's ability to write in multiple styles, which makes his work seem as if it were written by a number of writers instead of just one.

Borges then makes a disparaging reference to *Work in Progress*, which he describes as being merely a polyglot weaving of puns and word plays: "El libro subsiguiente de Joyce, *Obra en Gestación*, es, a juzgar por los capítulos publicados, un tejido de lánguidos retruécanos en un inglés veteado de alemán, de italiano y de latín" [Joyce's next book, *Work in Progress*, judging from the chapters published to date, is a weave of word games in an English streaked with German, Italian and Latin] (*Textos cautivos*, 84). This marks the beginning of Borges's mostly negative reactions to *Finnegans Wake*.[25]

"El último libro de Joyce": Bloomsday, 1939

Borges's second piece about Joyce in *El Hogar*, a review entitled "El último libro de Joyce" [Joyce's Latest Book], appears on June 16, 1939, shortly after the publication of *Finnegans Wake*.[26] It continues Borges's categorization of the *Wake* as being primarily a text of puns and wordplays. As if to emphasize his preference of *Ulysses* over *Finnegans Wake*, Borges publishes his review on Bloomsday, a detail Joyceans would surely not miss. The article is easily Borges's most negative commentary about Joyce's work, presented in a dismissive and condescending tone, irreverent with regard to the "atemorizados elogios" [fearful praise] Borges tells us the *Wake* has received so far in the *NRF* and the *London Times*.

The review begins with an expression of perplexity, a feeling Borges believes other critics must share due to the lack of any explanation whatsoever in their articles praising the *Wake*. Borges states: "Sospecho que comparten mi perplejidad esencial y mis vislumbres inservibles, parciales. Sospecho que están clandestinamente a la espera (yo publicamente lo estoy) de un tratado exegético de Stuart Gilbert, intérprete oficial de James Joyce" [I suspect that they share my essential bewilderment and my useless, partial glimpses. I suspect that they are secretively waiting (I am publicly so) for an exegetic study by Stuart Gilbert, James Joyce's official interpreter] (*Textos cautivos*, 328). As much as anything this apparent bafflement is a critique of the shallowness of critics who praise what they do not understand. For in his next essay about Joyce, "Joyce y los neologismos," Borges will carry out, on a partial scale, the kind of exegesis that he ask for here. In both texts, Borges again treats *Finnegans Wake* with ambivalence, and at times with disdain, as he takes fragments which he can then (mis)read from an Argentine margin.

Borges does make several laudatory comments about Joyce in this review, centered around Joyce's skills with language: "Es indiscutible que Joyce es uno de los primeros escritores de nuestro tiempo. Verbalmente, es quizá el primero" [Without a doubt, Joyce is one of the foremost writers of our time. Verbally, he is perhaps the best] (*Textos cautivos*, 328). Speaking about *Ulysses*, he states: "Hay sentencias, hay párrafos, que no son inferiores a los más ilustres de Shakespeare o de Sir Thomas Browne" [There are sentences, there are paragraphs, that are not inferior to the most illustrious ones by Shakespeare or by Sir Thomas Browne] (*Textos cautivos*, 328). Even within this high praise, though, we see Borges pointing at sections that he likes, not at the entirety of the novel. Borges finds a fragment, in the form of a very brief phrase from the *Wake* that he admires. But his manner makes clear his distaste for the overall project: "En el mismo *Finnegans Wake* hay alguna frase memorable. (Por ejemplo, ésta, que no intentaré traducir: *Beside the rivering waters of, hither and thithering waters of, night.*) En este amplio volumen, sin embargo, la eficacia es una excepción" [Even in *Finnegans Wake* there are some memorable phrases. (This one, for example, which I shall not attempt to translate: *Beside the rivering waters of, hither and thithering waters of, night.*) In this vast volume, however, efficiency is the exception] (*Textos cautivos*, 328). Overall, the article dismisses the *Wake* as a failure: "*Finnegans Wake* es una concatenación de retruécanos cometidos en un inglés onírico y que es difícil no calificar de frustrados e incompetentes. No creo exagerar" [*Finnegans Wake* is a concatenation of puns perpetrated in an oneiric English; it is difficult not to qualify them as frustrated and incompetent. I do not believe that I exaggerate] (*Textos cautivos*, 328). Borges concludes by suggesting that Joyce borrows from Jules Laforgue and Lewis Carroll in his verbal experiments, making his barb doubly sharp by asserting that Joyce's precursors obtained better results than he did (*Textos cautivos*, 329).

On the other hand, we should note that the negative comments that Borges makes in "El último libro de Joyce" contrast with at least one, much more positive assessment that he makes of Joyce in another article in *El Hogar*. This other reference to Joyce is found in the essay "Cuando la ficción vive en la ficción" [When fiction resides within fiction] (*El Hogar*, June 2, 1939), in which Borges discusses a series of *mise-en-abymes* in which he has always been interested, such as the play within the play in Act III of *Hamlet* (*Textos cautivos*, 325–26). One of the last examples of the "laberintos verbales" [verbal labyrinths] that Borges lists, and the one that he considers the most complex, is found in the recently published work by Flann O'Brien (1911–66), *At Swim-Two-Birds*. Borges's praise of this novel is relevant because of its relationship to a certain tradition of Irish literature, and to Joyce in particular; his comments are astute and once again ahead of his time. They also represent a certain appreciation of Joyce and his potential for influence, which suggest how Borges might be thinking of Joyce as a precursor of his own:

At Swim-Two-Birds no sólo es un laberinto: es una discusión de las muchas maneras de concebir la novela irlandesa y un repertorio de ejercicios en verso y prosa, que ilustran o parodian todos los estilos de Irlanda. La influencia magistral de Joyce (arquitecto de laberintos, también; Proteo literario, también) es innegable, pero no abrumadora, en este libro múltiple. (*Textos cautivos*, 327)

[*At Swim-Two-Birds* is not just a labyrinth: it is a discussion of the many ways to conceive the Irish novel, and a repertory of exercises in verse and prose that illustrate or parody all Irish styles. The masterly influence of Joyce (also an architect of labyrinths; also a literary Proteus) is undeniable, but not overwhelming, in this manifold book.]

Influence that is "undeniable, but not overwhelming": this is an accurate statement about the relationship between O'Brien and Joyce in Ireland, and also about Borges and his precursors, including Joyce, in Argentina. Influence that is "undeniable, but not overwhelming": pre-texts that are reworked, but which do not cause exhaustion or paralysis. Not an anxiety of influence, but a playfulness with sources which can always be irreverently displaced and reread/rewritten/mistranslated from Borges's Argentine periphery.

"Joyce y los neologismos": A Borgesian Wakean Reading

Borges's next text about Joyce, entitled "Joyce y los neologismos" [Joyce and his Neologisms] (*Sur 62*, November 1939), is arguably the first important reading of *Finnegans Wake* in Spanish, and certainly the first in Argentina. The brief article begins and ends with a "catálogo de precursores" [catalogue of precursors], all of whom, in one way or another, made use of "portmanteau words." The list, despite its erudite composition, is so incongruent that it comes off as comical. It includes Jules Laforgue (1860–87) and Paul Groussac (1848–1929), both in 1883; Algernon Charles Swinburne (1837–1909) in 1887; "algún porteño (creo que Marcelino del Mazo)" [some *porteño* (I think Marcelino del Mazo)] around 1900; Mariano Brull (1891–1956); Edward Lear (1812–88); and Johann Fischart (1546–90) in 1575. Borges also mentions the presence of compound words in English—"El ingenioso idioma inglés . . . ensambla *whirl* y *twist* y produce *twirl*; *blush* y *flash* y produce *flush*" [The ingenious English language . . . combines *whirl and twist* and produces *twirl*; *blush and flash* and produces *flush*] (*Sur 62*, 59)—to indicate that the evolution of the English language produces portmanteau words of its own accord.

The effect of the "catalogue of precursors" that Borges lists for Joyce is twofold. On the one hand, it seems designed to undermine Joyce's verbal accomplishments in *Finnegans Wake* by demonstrating not only that he is not the first to practice this technique, but that the history of the English language itself produces neologisms and portmanteau words. On the other, the heterogeneous list illustrates how a writer can be said to create his own precursors by influencing, in retrospect, how we read previous texts through the writer in question (again, in terms of "Kafka y sus precursores"). In the case of "Joyce y los neologismos," it is clear that not all the writers that Borges's enumerates can possibly be said to have influenced Joyce in any traditional sense of the term, especially in the case of writers like Groussac or the *porteño* whose name Borges does not recall. The list also retroactively locates something "Joycean" (or "Wakean") in these writers, as "created" by Borges's reading of Joyce itself. This play with preconceptions of influence and precursors is especially interesting as Borges himself defines his relationship with Joyce.

In the second paragraph of the essay Borges identifies two further important precursors of *Finnegans Wake* and moves into a more probing commentary of Joyce's text:

Es sabido que el rasgo más evidente de *Work in Progress* (que ahora se titula *Finnegans Wake*) es la metódica profusión de *portmanteau words*—para usar el término técnico de otro precursor: Humpty Dumpty*. En esa profusión reside la novedad de James Joyce. Tan poderosa y general es la pasión jurídica (o tan débil la estética) que los mil y un comentadores de Joyce casi no examinan los neologismos inventados por él y se limitan a probar, o a negar, que el idioma requiere palabras nuevas. (*Sur 62*, 59–60)

[It is well known that the most evident feature of *Work in Progress* (which is now entitled *Finnegans Wake*) is the methodical profusion of *portmanteau words*—to use the technical term of another precursor: Humpty Dumpty*. It is in that profusion that James Joyce's novelty resides. So powerful and general is juridical passion (or so weak the aesthetic one) that the thousand and one commentators of Joyce hardly ever examine the neologisms invented by him; they limit themselves, instead, to prove, or to negate, that language needs new words.]

Borges alludes to the *Arabian Nights* by mentioning the "the thousand and one commentators" and refers to Lewis Carroll through Humpty Dumpty; both are important sources for Joyce and Borges alike.[27] The reference to Humpty Dumpty is especially relevant, as this character and his fall—a fall into sleep and unconsciousness, into death and night, but also a fall in a Biblical sense, from Eden, and of the utopia of the Tower of Babel—enter the *Wake* from the very first page of the text.[28] Furthermore, locating an aspect of Joyce's verbal manipulation in Carroll's playful, nonsensical word games, at this early date in Wakean reception, is certainly sharp.[29] We should also not forget that it is the character Humpty Dumpty, in *Through the Looking Glass*, who coins the term "portmanteau words."[30]

The paragraph quoted above from Borges's essay is accompanied by a highly creative footnote immediately following the reference to Humpty Dumpty, in which Borges experiments with some of the potentials of translation that abound in *Finnegans Wake*:

> *Cierto lector de Carroll tradujo la balada de *Jabberwocky* al latín macarrónico. El primer verso reza: *Coesper erat: Tunc lubriciles ultravia circum . . .*
>
> En *coesper* se amalgama *vesper* y *coena*; *lubricus* y *graciles*, en *lubriciles*. (*Sur* 62, 60)

> [*A certain reader of Carroll translated the *Jabberwocky* ballad into a macaronic Latin. The first verse reads: *Coesper erat: Tunc lubriciles ultravia circum . . .*
>
> In *coesper* we have the amalgamation of *vesper* y *coena*; of *lubricus* and *graciles*, in *lubriciles*.]

Who can this "certain reader of Carroll [who] translated the *Jabberwocky* ballad into a macaronic Latin" be other than Borges himself? This burlesque imitation in Latin simultaneously echoes Carroll's text and Joyce's experimentation with languages in *Finnegans Wake*. Borges explains the portmanteau words of his Latin translation just like Humpty Dumpty interprets the meaning of the poem for Alice in *Through the Looking Glass*.[31] The footnote is a playful imitation of the process of writing as translation in *Finnegans Wake*, as Borges reproduces Carroll's word games, mistranslated into Latin. Borges demonstrates, in this parodic aside, that he, too, can play at creating polyglot portmanteau words.

Borges goes on to criticize Joyce's commentators for not truly examining the neologisms in *Finnegans Wake* and for being unable or afraid to penetrate the obscurity of Joyce's language. As an example of what he means by this, and almost as if he were calling for the kind of glossing of the *Wake* that readers would undertake over the next sixty plus years, Borges proceeds to unravel a list of about twenty portmanteau words from *Finnegans Wake*. After presenting this list, he refers to the compound words as "monsters,"[32] and comments on a few of them. The tone is less than enthusiastic.

Of these portmanteau words, Borges states that "secular phoenish" is "quizá el más memorable de todos" [perhaps the most memorable of them all], suggesting that it alludes to "cierto verso final de *Samson Agonistes*, en que se llama *secular bird* al fénix de periódicas muertes" [a certain final verse of *Samson Agonistes*, in which the phoenix of periodic deaths is named *secular bird*] (*Sur* 62, 60–61). Borges finds a Miltonesque resonance in a passage of the *Wake* where one would not usually think of Milton. The "secular phoenish" appears very early on in *Finnegans Wake*, in the following sentence: "Phall if you but will, rise you must: and none so soon either shall the pharce for the nunce come to a setdown secular phoenish" (4.15–17). In its context, the line alludes to some of the central themes of *Finnegans Wake*: the fall into sleep or death, and the eventual rebirth at the end of the novel. The "phoenish" (the rising from the dead, as suggested by "Phoenix") will occur in the morning, when the "pharce for the nunce" comes to a "phoenish" ("finish").

On the other hand, "Secular phoenish" also refers to the crime at Phoenix Park, the nature of which is indeed secular: of this world, sexual, sinful, secretive, shameful. But "secular" also means once in an age, especially once in a century, so that the "phoenish" ("finish," or "Phoenix") will arrive after one hundred years, it will be "secular." Phonetically, "secular" also resonates with "circular," so that this process, of death and rebirth, of falling and rising, like the rising and "setdown" ("setting") of the sun, is seen to be a circular event that repeats every night.

In Milton's *Samson Agonistes*, the Phoenix is referred to as a "secular bird," as Borges says. Interestingly enough, it refers to the classical rebirth from the ashes, but also to a rebirth from fame, even though the subject's body is dead.[33] In the *Wake*, such a pattern of fall and rebirth is deeply related to the functions of language, to the collapse of the Tower of Babel and the attempts to rebuild it—all of which points to the potential and the need for translation, for writing as translation. The resonance that Borges has found with the condition of HCE (Here Comes Everybody—all of us and all our languages, in "the confusioning of human races" [35.5]) is unexpected and insightful.

Borges also states: "Otro monstruo de Joyce, hecho de locuciones esta vez, no de palabras sueltas: *el animal que tiene dos espaldas a medianoche.* Shakespeare y la esfinge de Tebas allegaron los materiales" [Another of Joyce's monsters, this one made up of idiomatic expressions, not of loose words: *the animal that has two backs at midnight.* Shakespeare and the Sphinx of Thebes contributed the material] (*Sur 62,* 61). By mentioning the euphemistic expression "the beast with two backs at midnight," which refers to two people engaged in the sexual act, Borges could be thinking of the attachment between HCE and ALP, or of any of the many fantasized couplings in *Finnegans Wake.* He could also be referring to the fact that HCE is asleep and dead to the world, where midnight would signify both the literal night and a figurative death: the subject buried and dead, asleep and dreaming, having a "Miss Somer's nice dream" ["Midsummer's Night Dream" (502.29)]. By referring to Shakespeare and Thebes, Borges also appears to be thinking of Iago in *Othello,* of the riddle of the Sphinx, and possibly even making an allusion to the Egyptian Book of the Dead.[34]

Finally, Borges provides an example of a "retruécano" [pun] that he finds "terrible y majestuoso" [terrible and majestic], and which he states is like "una sentencia de *Urn Burial,* arduamente alcanzada a través de un siglo o de un sueño" [a sentence from *Urn Burial,* arduously reached through a century or a dream]: "*Countlessness of livestories have netherfallen by this plage, flick as flowflakes, litters from aloft, like a waast wizzard all of whirlworlds . . . Pride, O pride, thy prize!*" (*Sur 62,* 61). Borges's choice of this particular line, and his association of it with Browne's text, represents yet another unusual but fascinating reading of a small fragment of *Finnegans Wake.* If we look briefly at the passage that Borges cites (17.26–30), we see that it refers to the "countless" number of "life-stories" told in the pages of the *Wake,* where the "liv" in "livestories" implies that we are dealing with the stories of ALP. These have "fallen" down ("netherfallen" implying that they fall below land, since HCE is buried, and below his consciousness, as he is unconscious), onto this "plage" (page, or place). From the Tower to the "plague," the confusion of Babel on the page. Being "flick as flowflakes" ("thick as snowflakes," where the snow is reminiscent of the end of "The Dead" from *Dubliners*, and of a whiting out that represents either a falling into sleep and unconsciousness, or into death, throughout the *Wake*), the "litters from aloft" ("letters" buried in "litters," which fall from high above, "aloft," in the Daily World), are "like a waast wizzard all of whirlworlds" ("like a vast or hazy [Du. waas = haze, mist] blizzard of whirling worlds or words or winds"). "Whirling" on the "page" are a series of ephemeral objects, including "snow," words, and "livestories." They are the matter from which one might begin to rebuild Babel, by rewriting, by mistranslating.

The sentence that Borges omits in the ellipsis also adds to the meanings of these lines: "Now are all tombed to the mound, isges to isges, erde from erde" (17.28–29). We are dealing precisely with a description of a "seemetery" (a "seeming cemetery" [17.36]), of the subject dead to the world, "tombed to the mound," and returned to the ground, as suggested by the Order for the Burial of the Dead ("ashes to ashes, dust to dust"; G. erde = earth).[35] Borges's association with Sir Thomas Browne's *Urn Burial* is therefore quite relevant,[36] as is the fact that this "sentence," as Borges calls it (both a linguistic sentence and a moral judgment), is reached arduously (after the fall), through a century (remember, it is a "*secular* phoenish"), or a "seemetery," or a dream. The possibilities are nearly endless. And these are created as the result of a fall (including of the Tower of Babel), which incites necessity, but even more important, potential—the polysemantic potential of difference and translation.

ON THE NATURE OF NARRATIVE: FUNES READS JOYCE

Two years later, in a text entitled "Fragmento sobre Joyce" [A Fragment on Joyce] (*Sur 77*, February, 1941), Borges finds a completely different way to dialogue with Joyce. The first part of the piece is an early, abbreviated version of the story "Funes el memorioso" (first published in *La Nación* on June 7, 1942, then included in *Ficciones* in 1944), with the identical plot of a protagonist with perfect and total memory that completely paralyzes him: "Su percepción y su memoria eran infalibles" [His perception and his memory were infallible] (*Sur 77*, 60). The description of Ireneo Funes in this essay is not far from the "Funes" of the final version of the story at all:

Sabía las formas de las nubes australes del amanecer del treinta de abril de mil ochocientos ochenta y dos y podía compararlas en el recuerdo con las vetas de un libro en pasta española que manejó una vez en la infancia. Podía reconstruir todos los sueños, todos los entresueños. Murió de una congestión pulmonar y su vida incomunicable ha sido la más rica del universo. (*Sur* 77, 60)

[He knew the shape of the Southern clouds at dawn of the thirtieth of April of nineteen hundred and eighty-two, and could compare them in his memory with the streaks of a stiff marbled binding of a book that he once held in his childhood. He could reconstruct every dream, every half-dream. He died of a pulmonary congestion; his incommunicable life was the richest in the universe.]

Albeit a draft, Borges's depiction of Funes already represents the creation of a literary monster.

Borges then makes an abrupt shift: "Lo he recordado porque la consecutiva y recta lectura de las cuatrocientas mil palabras de *Ulises* exigiría monstruos análogos. (Nada aventuraré sobre los que e-xigiría *Finnegans Wake* . . .)" [I have remembered him because the consecutive, straight reading of the four hundred thousand words of *Ulysses* would require analogous monsters. (I will not adventure at all about those that *Finnegans Wake* would demand . . .)] (*Sur* 77, 61). Borges seems to be asking how one can read *Ulysses*, from beginning to end, and remember all the details that appear along the way, or if it is even possible to read *Ulysses* in a complete and exact manner. Borges's answer is that only someone like Funes would be capable of such a feat. Through its humor, Borges's text suggests a specific connection between Funes "the monster," and a hypothetical, perfect reader of *Ulysses*. But why does Borges postulate Funes as the ideal reader of *Ulysses*? And how exactly would Funes read *Ulysses*?

Although Borges creates a character who is the ideal reader of Joyce, he himself is apparently opposed to such a complete reading of *Ulysses*—or to such a reading of any text at all. Borges seems to be as opposed to complete, totalizing readings (which would only lead to monsters like Funes), as he is to complete, literal translations—which he has always maintained are impossible, preferring instead mistranslations, creative infidelities, and the recontextualization of selected fragments. Borges refers to this preference, specifically in relation to Joyce, when he states: "A priori, I believe that an exact/complete version of *Ulises* is impossible" ("Nota," 49).

This stance represents one of the major disjunctions between Borges and Joyce, and the idea of Funes reading Joyce reveals how Borges works with this disjunction. Borges sees Joyce as being extremely dedicated to a totalizing mimetic representation of reality. Borges therefore parodies aspects of Joyce's project so as to define an opposing mimetic position. These two opposing positions are dramatized in the story "Funes el memorioso." In the article "Fragmento sobre Joyce," Borges denounces any attempts at an exact or complete reading of *Ulysses*, which would include the readings that seek to organize the text by emphasizing the parallels with Homer. Then he undertakes the kind of reading that he himself favors—a partial, fragmented one that includes a displacement into a new context (Argentina, in his case).

This recontextualization is seen in the many cultural and geographic details of the final version of "Funes el memorioso." The hypothetical, ideal reader of Joyce who Borges postulates turns out to be a "compadrito de Fray Bentos" [*compadrito* from Fray Bentos] who lives with his mother in a "decente rancho" [decent shack] in Uruguay (*OC* I: 485–87). The geographic and historical markers in "Funes," some of which resonate with Borges's own life,[37] displaces the discussion about representation and narrative to the shores of the Río de la Plata. The fragmented reading, for its part, is made explicit in "Fragmento sobre Joyce." Borges states: "Yo (como el resto del universo) no he leído el *Ulises*, pero leo y releo con felicidad algunas escenas" [I (like the rest of the universe) have not read *Ulysses*, but I happily read and reread certain scenes] (*Sur* 77, 61). As in his 1925 translation, which offered a one-page Borgesian sampling of Joyce's vast novel, Borges once again seems to reduce *Ulysses* down to a fragment, in this case a handful of scenes and lines which he admires and cites in the article.[38] In addition, "Funes el memorioso" is an especially apt text with which to consider Borges's dialogue with Joyce, as it deals with some of the main issues of representation in narrative that we find in both writers.

Opposing Mimetic Positions in "Funes el memorioso"

"Funes el memorioso" presents two opposing positions regarding the representation of memory and reality: Funes's and the narrator's. Funes's position, with his perfect and absolute memory, favors a one-to-one, continuous mimetic mapping of reality. The narrator, on the other hand, believes that such mimesis is impossible; he stands instead for a discontinuous version of reality. The verisimilitude of the narrator's position, paradoxically, lies in the incorporation of doubt and ruptures into the narrative flow, of summarizing and selective omissions, of mistranslation, always with a nod toward efficacy. Although it is Funes's position that the story recounts in detail, this position is eventually rejected by the narrator; its possibilities are shown to completely paralyze Funes and to literally fail when the protagonist dies at the end of the story. The narrator—whose position I would like to suggest is an extension of Borges's theories of (mis)translation—puts his stance into practice in the narrating of the story itself, which allows him to defeat Funes's theoretical position, as if the two were engaged in a metaphysical duel.

Two important details draw our attention in the beginning of the story: the emphasis placed on the verb "recordar" [to remember, to recall], and the rivalrous tone that the narrator takes toward the subject remembered, Ireneo Funes. The first of these points directly at the relationship between memory and reality, and their representation in narrative. The second item suggests that the story is not only an anecdote about a strange character with an extraordinary gift, but that it is also about a challenge, a duel, between two ways of looking at the world. Throughout the story, the relationship between the narrator and Funes is like that of two *compadritos* about to engage in a knife fight. This is seen, for example, in the rivalry between the Argentine and the Uruguayan references in the text, in which the narrator is associated with the former, and Funes with the latter. The duel itself turns out to be a talking match, with Funes doing most of the talking. However, his dialogue is not presented directly, but rather through indirect narration, mediated by the narrator. It is always the narrator's account, his representation of reality, which ultimately reaches us.

The story begins with the narrator recalling Funes and simultaneously questioning the veracity of his own memory. This doubt is established from the very first sentence in the story, immediately problematizing the issues of memory and of the narrator's reliability: "Lo recuerdo (yo no tengo derecho a pronunciar ese verbo sagrado, sólo un hombre en la tierra tuvo derecho y ese hombre ha muerto)" [I remember him (I have no right to pronounce that sacred verb, only one man on earth had that right, and that man is now dead)] (*OC* I: 485). However, despite this assertion about not having a right to use the verb "to remember," the narrator goes on to use it six times in the first five sentences alone. There is a startling juxtaposition between the specific details that the narrator provides when he describes Funes and the doubt the narrator introduces regarding the veracity of his memory of such details: "Recuerdo (creo) sus manos afiladas de trenzador" [I remember (I think) his angular, leather-braiding hands] (*OC* I: 485). We see this precise detail, but at the same time the narrator underscores the fact that the detail is remembered, and thus perhaps misremembered.

This inconsistency, like the many contradictions in the narrator's account of the events, reveals the failings of the narrator and the limitations of his memory. This is not accidental, however, as it turns out to be the very kind of narrative (mis)representation that the text privileges. Funes's memory, as we know, is absolute, it is intensely perfect; but (or perhaps: due to) this perfection, he is completely incapacitated. Although he has the capacity to remember every aspect of any day, or the entirety of *Ulysses*, as Borges suggests in "Fragmento sobre Joyce," it would take him exactly the length of that entire day to recall it. He is able to recreate his memory—to represent his remembered reality—in a kind of one-to-one mapping, with total continuity, as if it were a perfect mimesis. But this very capability is overwhelming; it does not allow him to live in the "real" world at all.

To further explore the dichotomy of the two opposing mimetic positions posited in "Funes el memorioso," I would like to briefly examine a scene in Cervantes's *Don Quijote*, in which two very similar opposing positions are presented. Funes's one-to-one mimetic mapping resonates strongly with the story that Sancho narrates in part I, chapter XX of the *Quijote*.[39] In this scene, Sancho becomes a kind of Sheherezade figure as he attempts to save his own life (he is afraid of proceeding into the dark, scary woods) by entertaining Don Quijote through the night with his storytelling. Sancho tells the story of Lope Ruiz, a "pastor cabredizo" [goat herder]. Don Quijote is completely drawn in. Eventually, we reach a point in the story in which, while fleeing from the shepherdess Torralba, Lope Ruiz's way is blocked by a flooded river. There are no boats around and he starts to panic, for he can see Torralba catching up to him. Then he spots a fisherman with a boat, but one so small that only one person and one goat can fit in it. Lope Ruiz

convinces the fisherman to get his three hundred goats across, one
at a time:

> "Entró el pescador en el barco, y pasó una cabra; volvió y pasó otra;
> tornó a volver, y tornó a pasar otra." Tenga vuestra merced cuenta en
> las cabras que el pescador va pasando [Sancho le dice parentéticamente
> a Don Quijote], porque si se pierde una de la memoria, se acabará el
> cuento, y no será posible contar más palabra dél. "Sigo, pues, y digo
> que el desembarcadero de la otra parte estaba lleno de cieno y resbaloso,
> y tardaba el pescador mucho tiempo en ir y volver. Con todo esto, volvió
> por otra cabra, y otra, y otra. . . ." (Cervantes, 243–44)

> ["The fisherman got into the boat and took one goat over, came back
> and fetched another, and came back once more and took another." Keep
> a count of the goats which the fisherman is taking over [Sancho tells
> don Quijote as an aside], for if you lose count of one the story will end,
> and it won't be possible for me to tell you another word of it. "I'll con-
> tinue now and mention that the landing-place on the other side was very
> muddy and slippery, which delayed the fisherman a good deal in his
> journeys backwards and forwards. But, all the same, he came back for
> another goat, and another, and another. . . ."]

But, sure enough, Don Quijote interrupts:

> —Haz cuenta que las pasó todas—dijo Don Quijote—; no andes yendo
> y viniendo desa manera, que no acabarás de pasarlas en un año.
> —¿Cuántas han pasado hasta agora?—dijo Sancho.
> —Yo ¿qué diablos sé?—respondió Don Quijote.
> —He ahí lo que yo dije; que tuviese buena cuenta. Pues por Dios que
> se ha acabado el cuento, que no hay pasar adelante.
> —¿Cómo puede ser eso?—respondió Don Quijote—. ¿Tan de esencia
> de la historia es saber las cabras que han pasado, por estenso, que si
> se yerra una del número no puedes seguir adelante con la historia?
> —No, señor, en ninguna manera—respondió Sancho—; porque así
> como yo pregunté a vuestra merced que me dijese cuántas cabras
> habían pasado, y me respondió que no sabía, en aquel mesmo instante
> se me fue a mí de la memoria cuanto me quedaba por decir, y a fe
> que era de mucha virtud y contento. (Cervantes, 244)

> ["Pretend that he got them all across," Don Quijote said, "and do not
> go on coming and going like that, or you will never get them all over
> in a year."
> "How many have got over so far?" Sancho asked.
> "How the devil should I know?" Don Quijote replied.

"There now, didn't I tell you to keep a good count? Well, there's the
end of the story, God knows there's no going on with it now."
"How can that be?" Don Quijote replied. "Is it so essential to the tale
to know exactly how many goats have crossed that if you are one out
in the number you cannot go on?"
"No, sir, not at all," Sancho answered. "But, when I asked your worship
to tell me how many goats had got across and you replied that you
didn't know, at that very moment everything I had left to say went
clean out of my head, though there were some good and amusing
things coming, I promise you."]

In addition to the hilarity of the moment, Don Quijote's interrup-
tion raises important questions associated with the nature of narrative. What are the assumptions that underlie Sancho's conception
of narrative, as opposed to Don Quijote's? What issues around the
temporality and verisimilitude of narrative must be considered in
order to understand these two conceptions? And how are these issues related to the continuity and discontinuity of narrative?

These two distinct and opposing ways of telling a story resonate
immediately with the positions that the narrator and Ireneo take in
"Funes." Sancho seems to believe that the telling of a story, at least
in this case, should have a one-to-one correspondence between the
events narrated by the story and the telling of the story itself, as if
the time that it takes to tell the story should be parallel to the time
of the events in the story. It is not enough to say that three hundred
goats make it across; he has to name each one, individually, for
them to get across. Don Quijote's way of telling a story, on the
other hand, would admit to an inherent distortion in story telling.
From his point of view, the fact that a mediation must exist between
the content and the form, between the events of the story and the
narrative, is accepted and much preferred, especially if that mediation condenses the plot and makes it more efficient.

In "Funes el memorioso," the narrator declares his strategy,
which the text comes to privilege, in a highly ironic statement:

No trataré de reproducir sus palabras, irrecuperables ahora. Prefiero *re-
sumir con veracidad* las muchas cosas que me dijo Ireneo. El estilo indi-
recto es remoto y débil; yo sé que sacrifico la eficacia de mi relato; que
mis lectores se imaginen los entrecortados períodos que me abrumaron
esa noche. (*OC* I: 487; emphasis added)

[I will not try to reproduce his words, which are now irretrievable. I
prefer to *summarize with veracity* the many things that Ireneo told me.

The indirect style is remote and weak; I know I am sacrificing the efficacy of my story; my readers should imagine for themselves the intermittent periods that overwhelmed me that night.]

The narrator's position favors a discontinuous summarizing, which, paradoxically, utilizes doubt and unreliability to create a more realistic illusion of verisimilitude. Meanwhile, its opposite—perfect and absolute mimesis, as practiced by Funes, by Sancho in the Lope Ruiz anecdote, or by Joyce in *Ulysses* and *Finnegans Wake* (according to Borges)—is shown to be impossible and monstrous.

To "summarize with veracity" might sound like an oxymoron, especially compared to Funes's position of not summarizing at all. However, as these examples illustrate, Funes's position is an impossibility; it leads only to mental and physical paralysis, in the case of Funes, to ridicule and humor, in the case of Sancho Panza, to monstrous, unreadable novels, in the case of Joyce. The sacrifice of efficacy to which the narrator admits is no sacrifice at all: there is much more efficacy in his strategy than in Funes's. In fact, by omitting the overwhelming periods of his encounter with Funes, the narrator's account turns out to be much more efficient than if he were to leave them in. He avoids undertaking a narration that would last an entire night, a reproduction that would be overwhelming to the reader as well as the narrator and would leave us and him as paralyzed as Ireneo Funes. This position helps to explain Borges's repeated statements that he has never read *Ulysses* or *Finnegans Wake* in their entirety, as well as his later assertions that they are simply illegible.

By emphasizing the unreliable elements of his own text, the narrator suggests that narrative is always unreliable and that absolute mimesis is impossible. The most a text can aspire to is what the narrator himself does (and what Don Quijote urges Sancho to do, and what Borges does with Joyce): to "summarize with veracity." "Funes el memorioso" questions the capacity of narrative to represent reality at the most profound of levels; that is, it highlights the fact that reality is always constructed by narrative. Every recounting of reality, according to "Funes el memorioso," is fictional. Ireneo Funes, as a theoretical position of mimesis, is shown to be completely disabilitating.

But "Funes el memorioso" is not a nihilistic parable. The alternative to Funes's position, the narrator's decision to "summarize with veracity," despite (or due to) its omissions and alterations, is full of potential. The narrator's position breaks with the exhaustion implied by the kind of mimesis that Funes—or Joyce, as Borges summarizes him in "Fragmento sobre Joyce"—stands for. In fact, to "summarize with veracity" speaks directly to the core of Borges's aesthetics, to his practice of writing as translation. This applies equally to Borges's theories of reading (as Borges summarizes what he selectively reads, condensing the texts of others into recontextualized fragments), of writing (as seen in "Funes el memorioso" itself), and of translation (as seen in Borges's many fragmentary translations, including that of the last page of *Ulysses*). Thus, the narrative techniques of the narrator in "Funes el memorioso" are analogous to the mistranslations—to the creative infidelities—that Borges valorizes in "Las versiones homéricas" and "Los traductores de *Las 1001 Noches*." Similarly, the impossibility of achieving reliability in narrative, as demonstrated by the narration of "Funes," is analogous to the impossibility of achieving fidelity in translation, in the traditional sense of the term (with its implied privileging of the original). To "summarize with veracity" is to displace fragments, to recontextualize, to seek efficacy as needed, irreverently, from the periphery.

An additional comment about the binary nature (narrator v. Funes, Don Quijote v. Sancho, Borges v. Joyce) of this reading of "Funes el memorioso": Borges and the narrator are of course not one and the same. Borges creates both the narrator and Funes, and he is clearly attracted to his creation of the latter, even if he is a "monstrous hyperbole of the totalizing faculty," as Robin Fiddian has called him.[40] In this sense, the narrator and Funes function as doubles of each other. Albeit true that they participate in a Borgesian duel of *compadritos* which the narrator wins, it must also be noted that they depend on each other—and on the dialogue between them—for their textual identity. Funes and his views on mimesis allow the narrator and his position to exist in contrast to it. It is precisely the tension between the two that opens the way for the kind of discussion that we have explored here.

Likewise, when Borges says that it would require "monsters" like Funes to read *Ulysses* or *Finnegans Wake*, he is not suggesting an all-out negation of Joyce; rather, he creates a dialogue, a theoretical duel, perhaps, with the Irish modernist. This positions Joyce as a certain kind of precursor, as a double who allows Borges to articulate his own ideas in contrasting terms. This irreverent reading of Joyce through Funes creates a very specific version of Joyce. By inventing a fictional projection to read Joyce, Borges sets the terms for the relationship between the two writers. This relationship gains an especially ironic level as Borges's minuscule version of Joyce seeks to express the same literary possibility: to capture every moment, thought, and emotion of a single day. Joyce asks what a novel would look like that tried to account for every aspect of every single moment of a single day. The answer he gives is *Ulysses* for the day, and *Finnegans Wake* for the night. Borges takes this same question, in response to Joyce, and answers with Funes: a short and concise story ("summarized with veracity") that contains a character able to do (because of his perfect memory) what Joyce tried to do. By criticizing Joyce's ideas about representation and mimesis, Borges creates Joyce as a precursor of his own opposing position. In this light, we can look at Borges's conclusions at the end of "Fragmento sobre Joyce" as a judgment that applies to both writers, momentarily seen as doubles of each other:

> El *Ulises* (nadie lo ignora) es la historia de un solo día, en el perímetro de una sola ciudad. En esa voluntaria limitación es lícito percibir algo más que una elegancia aristotélica; es lícito inferir que para Joyce, todos los días fueron de algún modo secreto el día irreparable del Juicio; todos los sitios, el Infierno o el Purgatorio. (*Sur 77*, 61–62)

> [*Ulysses* (everyone knows) is the story of a single day, within the perimeter of a single city. Within that voluntary limitation, it is fair to perceive something more than an Aristotelian elegance; it is fair to infer that for Joyce, every day was in some secret fashion the irreparable Day of Judgment; every place, Hell or Purgatory.]

ULYSSES, FINNEGANS WAKE AND TRANSLATABILITY: FACING THE LIMITS OF TRANSLATION

A misreading that is also an appropriation, Borges's textual dialogue with Joyce creates Joyce as a Borgesian precursor, but a very selective and partial one. But what are the implications of Borges's criticisms of Joyce for issues of translatability? In his reading of Joyce, Borges consistently emphasizes the chaotic nature of *Ulysses* and even more so of *Finnegans Wake*. In his 1925 essay, for example, Borges states: "El *Ulises*, tal vez, incluye las páginas más caóticas y tediosas que registra la historia" [*Ulysses* includes what are, perhaps, the most chaotic and tedious pages that history has recorded]. In the 1941 *Sur* article "Fragmento sobre Joyce," this becomes: "Nadie ignora que para los lectores desprevenidos, la vasta novela de Joyce es indescifrablemente caótica" [No one ignores that for unsuspecting readers, Joyce's vast novel is indecipherably chaotic] (*Sur* 77, 61). And in his 1946 review "Nota sobre el *Ulises* en español": "A priori, I believe that an exact/complete version of *Ulises* is impossible." And as the years went by, we see an increasing tendency in Borges to become more rigid and to describe *Ulysses* and *Finnegans Wake* as untranslatable, or even illegible. In his 1965 *Introducción a la literatura inglesa* [Introduction to English Literature], referring to *Ulysses* and *Finnegans Wake*, he says: "Los libros que hemos enumerado son intraducibles" [The aforementioned books are untranslatable] (*OCC*, 854). In the conference "La ceguera" [Blindness] (first published in *La Opinión* on August 31, 1977, then in *Siete noches* in 1980), he adds: "Tenemos esas dos vastas y por qué no decirlo ilegibles novelas que son *Ulises* y *Finnegans Wake*" [We have those vast and, why not say it, illegible novels: *Ulysses* and *Finnegans Wake*] (*OC* III: 284).

To confuse matters even further, around the time that he makes these later comments, Borges also writes two quite elegiacal poems, "James Joyce" and "Invocación a Joyce," both included in the 1969 collection *Elogio de la sombra*. But even before this, in his texts from the 1940s and early 1950s, "Joyce" had become a part of Borges's vocabulary, almost always alluded to as an important literary reference.[41] The contradictions in Borges's dialogue with Joyce are significant in and of themselves,[42] as they take us toward a consideration of the limits of translation, which is to say to the very limits of reading and of writing.

The entire entry for Joyce in Borges's *Introducción a la literatura inglesa*, mostly of a descriptive nature, oscillates between high praise and underhanded witticisms, as we see from the opening of the text: "El irlandés James Joyce (1882–1941) es, literalmente, uno de los escritores más extraordinarios de nuestro siglo. Su obra capital, *Ulises*, trata de reemplazar la unidad que le falta por un sistema de laboriosas e inútiles simetrías" [The Irishman James Joyce (1882–1941) is literally one of the most extraordinary writers of our century. His major work, *Ulysses*, tries to replace the unity that it is lacking with a laborious, useless system of symmetries] (*OCC*, 853). As he does elsewhere, Borges privileges *Ulysses* over *Finnegans Wake*, but his description of the *Wake* is succinct and to the point. Especially astute is Borges's observation, with its Vichian undertones, about all the hero's forebears being part of HCE in his sleep:[43]

> Aun más extraño es *Finnegan's Wake* [*sic*], que podría traducirse por 'el Velorio de Finnegan', pero que sugiere las ideas de fin, de repetición (*again*) y de despertar. Así como *Ulises* es un libro de la vigilia, *Finnegan's Wake* [*sic*] lo es de los sueños. El héroe es un tabernero de Dublín; nacido en esa ciudad, lleva en sus venas sangre celta, escandinava, sajona y normanda y, mientras sueña, es cada uno de sus antepasados y todas las personas del mundo. El vocabulario de esta novela consta, fuera de las preposiciones y de los artículos, de palabras compuestas, tomadas de los más diversos idiomas, incluso el islandés y el sánscrito. (*OCC*, 854)[44]

> [Even stranger is *Finnegans Wake*, which could be translated as "Finnegan's Wake," but which suggests the ideas of an end, of repetition (*again*) and of an awakening. Just as *Ulysses* is a book of wakefulness, *Finnegans Wake* is one of dreams. The hero is a tavern keeper in Dublin; born in that city, his veins carry Celtic, Scandinavian, Saxon and Norman blood; and while he sleeps, he is each of his ancestors and everyone in the world. The vocabulary of this novel consists of, other than the prepositions and the articles, compound words taken from the most diverse languages, including Icelandic and Sanskrit.]

Also, even Borges's aforementioned comments regarding the illegibility of *Ulysses* and *Finnegans Wake*, in "La ceguera," are supplemented by a measured positive appraisal of Joyce's accomplishments. What Borges finds most redeemable about Joyce's work is his appropriation and manipulation of the English language:

> Ese idioma que estadísticamente supera a todos los demás y que ofrece tantas posibilidades para el escritor, sobre todo de verbos muy concretos, no fue bastante para él. Joyce, el irlandés, recordó que Dublín había sido fundado por los vikingos daneses. Estudió noruego, le escribió una carata en noruego a Ibsen, y luego estudió griego, latín. . . . Supo todos los idiomas y escribió en un idioma inventado por él, un idioma que es difícilmente comprensible pero que se distingue por una música extraña. Joyce trajo una música nueva al inglés. (*OC*: III: 284)

> [That language which statistically surpasses all the others, and which offers so many possibilities for the writer, especially with very specific verbs, was not enough for him. Joyce, the Irishman, remembered that Dublin had been founded by Danish Vikings. He studied Norwegian, he

wrote a letter to the Norwegian Ibsen, then he studied Greek, Latin. . . .
He knew all the languages and he wrote in a language that he invented,
a language that is very difficult to comprehend, but one that is distin-
guished by a strange music. Joyce brought a new music to English.]

It is almost as if its very illegibility, its untranslatability, were what
Borges most admired about Joyce. The issue that surfaces repeatedly in Borges's comments, regardless of their degree of hostility
or of sarcastic wit, is the limits of legibility and translation as they
are problematized by Joyce's verbal experiments. In this way,
Borges directs our attention to a key aspect of Joyce's work, one to
which anyone dialoguing with Joyce must respond.

In 1924, Joyce states that he thinks that *Ulysses* is untranslatable
(Ellmann 561). Borges eventually says the same thing, and repeats
it on a number of occasions. Both writers, however, belie their
statements. As Richard Ellmann details, encouraged by the first
French translations organized by Valéry Larbaud, Joyce decides
that *Ulysses* should be translated into French, and then participates
actively in this production (Ellmann 521–24; 600–602). Joyce
eventually comes full circle, as he states in 1930, now fully immersed in the polyglot *Finnegans Wake*, that: "There is nothing that
cannot be translated" (Ellmann 632).[45] Borges, for his part, had in
a way already translated *Ulysses*—from its entirety in Joycean Irish
English to a one-page Borgesian fragmentary sample in Argentine
Spanish in 1925. The use of translatability is slippery, in this regard, which may just be exactly the point for both Borges and
Joyce.

To further analyze Borges's contradictory comments, it is important to consider how Joyce problematizes translation and whether
translation plays the same role for Joyce as it does for Borges. The
question of translation *in* Joyce's work itself is clearly worthy of its
own study; whereas by looking at translations *of* Joyce's work, one
can find new readings of his texts, as Fritz Senn does in *Joyce's
Dislocutions*. Translation of and in Joyce has immediate implications for considerations of influence and tradition. The fact that
Joyce titles his novel *Ulysses*, for example, already highlights the
fact that the process of translation is at work in the process of writing: "Ulysses," not "Odysseus," to indicate that there is already
one major displacement/mistranslation of the text (from Greek to
Latin), and that Joyce is now presenting another one, in the form of
a modern analogue (from Latin, but also through the entire Euro-

pean tradition since then). As Senn states: "In a [large] sense, everything Joyce wrote has to do with translation, [it] is transferential" (39).

The various roles that translation plays in *Ulysses* and *Finnegans Wake* thoroughly complicates any attempts to translate them into other languages.[46] Senn, for example, identifies three main categories of challenges that a translator of *Ulysses* must face: 1) the polyglot nature of Joyce's text, which requires an interlingual translation of the "foreign" languages in the text; 2) the difficulty in translating proper names, references and allusions, which underlies how context and intertextuality complicate issues of translatability; and, 3) the constant intralingual translation that even those reading the text in the original are forced to execute. To the extent that the reader of *Ulysses* constantly translates in order to read the text, we see a clear equating of the functions of reading and translation. If, for Borges, reading is writing, for Joyce, reading is translating.

The effect of being made aware of the role of translation in the process of reading, as Senn argues, is to make the reader feel like Bloom: like an outsider, in exile with respect to the English language:[47] "*Ulysses* makes it clear that we are all foreigners in a labyrinth" (49). This process is multiplied and magnified in *Finnegans Wake*, where it is that much more evident that the connections between reading and translation extend to the process of writing: the reader constantly encounters a text constituted of multiple translations, which he/she must in turn retranslate, at least in part, to put some of its meanings in motion. In a text in which nearly every phoneme is a transformation that suggests another transformation, translation quickly becomes synonymous with processes of both writing and reading. As Rosa M. Bollettieri Bosinelli states: "*Finnegans Wake*, as we have it in print, is not written in any kind of 'original,' but is the result of a *process of translation*" (143; emphasis in the original).

Ulysses and *Finnegans Wake* work with processes of "dislocution," as Senn calls it, transformations that disrupt as much as they parallel the source references. In this sense, Joyce's dislocutions are reminiscent of the potential of the periphery to take with irreverence that Borges postulates in "El escritor argentino y la tradición." Joyce's attitudes toward tradition, especially his relationship with canonical writers (e.g., Homer, Dante, Shakespeare), involves an innovative irreverence that is very much analogous to Borges's practice of writing as translation. The idea of creative infidelities, for example, which is so central to Borges's theories of (mis)translation, applies wonderfully well to the entirety of *Ulysses*. Borges's and Joyce's irreverence, their work with dislocution, with mistranslation, represents parallel challenges, from their respective peripheries, to the canons of the center. It is in large part for this reason that Borges always valued the Irishness in Joyce's work, as well as Joyce's problematizing relationship with the English language. But Borges also practices a form of dislocution with respect to Joyce, by establishing both parallels and disruptions with the Irish writer. This leads to the ambivalent and purposefully selective misreading of Joyce that we have seen in this chapter.

The connections between translatability and displacement are crucial in this regard. As Senn points out: "Dislocution is an illustrative synonym for translation: in translating everything is displaced into another culture and speech" (210). But from here Senn concludes that Joyce lies beyond the limits of translation: "What are least translatable are translations . . . : how can dislocutions be dislocuted?" (211). Senn finds translations of Joyce useful, but primarily as readings that contribute to an elucidation of the original.[48] Again we find a privileging of the original, even when that original (i.e., *Ulysses*, *Finnegans Wake*) delights in processes of (mis)translation.

Borges's position toward translating, toward reading/rewriting Joyce, and by implication his position toward the limits of translation, is somewhat different. On the one hand, Borges doubtlessly agrees with the impossibility of translating *Ulysses* and *Finnegans Wake*—translating them in any traditional sense of the word, that is. He states specifically that a "complete/exact" translation is impossible and often repeats the off-handed remarks about *Ulysses* and *Finnegans Wake* being illegible and untranslatable. However, Borges would never argue for the necessity of a "complete" and "exact," totalizing translation/reading/rewriting. The (mis)translations that Borges valorizes and performs always take advantage of multiple displacements that create the potential to rewrite the original (seen as a draft in a series of drafts), through fragmentation, condensation, creative infidelities, and other dislocutions. Borges's thorough irreverence of any idealization of the original undermines the traditional objectives of translation theory, including the delineation of limits of translation meant to protect the sanctity of the original.

In his 1925 translation of Joyce, Borges neatly avoids many of the difficulties that Senn discusses in his study. Omission is not only not a sin for Borges, it is actually an important component of his translations proper.[49] For example, Borges dislocutes a number of specific contextual references by eliminating them as he sees fit, and by recreating the text through the use of a Río de la Plata diction, particularly by putting Molly's monologue in the *voseo*. Even more irreverent is Borges's extreme condensation of Joyce's lengthy *Ulysses* into a one-page fragmentary sample, which functions as an autonomous text: a partial reproduction of the source, now reinscribed as part of Borges's literary production. Borges's solutions, especially this fragmenting move, might strike some Spanish-language readers as frustrating. They may very well yearn for a complete and exact translation; and they may be willing to live with the loss that will necessarily accompany such an attempt, rather than settle for a rewriting of the entirety of *Ulysses* in Joycean Irish English to a one-page Borgesian Argentine Spanish version. These frustrated readers will not find what they are looking for in Borges.[50] Besides, working with frustration, with expectations, can be quite productive. We might think that Borges creates this effect of frustration, of unrest, precisely as he approaches and attempts to go beyond the limits of translation.

Borges's solutions to the problems of translation posed by Joyce's work serve a number of very specific purposes. Borges's moves are important to the degree that they form a part of an aesthetics of irreverence, of displaced fragments, of mistranslation from the margins. This then comes directly into play in Borges's practice of writing as translation, as seen in the example of how Funes reads Joyce. Borges's selective (mis)reading of Joyce reinforces the potential of the periphery. This process serves to equate Borges with Joyce, and make Borges's *argentinidad* a privileged place from which to innovate by taking with irreverence from any and all traditions. And this is applied, somewhat paradoxically, to (mis)translating Joyce, whose work also represents an irreverent challenge to the center, while also conflating writing with reading and translation.

Conclusion: The Last Page / The First Page

The complexity of Borges's textual dialogue with Joyce makes it impossible to speak of a simple model of influence.[51] However, we can use Borges's own ideas on this topic, as presented most clearly in "Kafka y sus precursores," to analyze Borges's ambivalent position on Joyce. This ambivalence, as we have seen, reveals an important point about how Borges wishes to use/create/position Joyce as a possible precursor. Borges repeatedly valorizes Joyce as a polyglot Irish writer, whose most important contribution, in addition to his verbal skills, is his pastiche of multiple narrative styles in a single work (namely in *Ulysses*). Borges takes loose phrases, quotations, and references to specific scenes which he admires out of context. This reinforces a discontinuous, fragmented perception of Joyce's work. And it is precisely this fragmented, multilingual Joyce whom Borges displaces toward, and reinscribes in, an Argentine context.

The other Joyce—the one who Borges parodies by comparing him to Góngora, or by dismissively asserting that Jules Laforgue and Lewis Carroll were more successful in their portmanteau words; the one whose vast, chaotic novels Borges claims never to have read completely; the one whose parallels with Homer in *Ulysses* he find completely uninteresting—is the one from whom Borges tries to disassociate himself as much as possible. Borges wants so much distance from this Joyce that he invents a literary monster, Ireneo Funes, to demonstrate what it would take to read such a version of Joyce. Furthermore, Borges disrupts the totalizing Joyce and his complete novels by recreating them as displaced fragments in a linguistic and cultural Río de la Plata context. These, in turn, through processes of transformation and appropriation, become a part of Borges's own literary discourse.

In the first contact of this imaginary meeting between Borges and Joyce in 1925, Borges states that he has not read all seven hundred pages of Joyce's novel, and he continues to make such remarks throughout his life. If we look beyond Borges's false humility, what we have is an early critique of the form of the long novel, a critique that Borges cultivates with surprising efficacy in all his texts. Rhetorically, Borges's statement is designed to disarm the reader: he sets the reader at ease, assuring him/her that he, too, has not had the patience to persevere through all of *Ulysses*. But then he goes on to write some very erudite comments about the work and finally concludes with the brilliant translation of the last page of *Ulysses*. By the end of this process, Borges and Joyce are on equal planes. The only thing needed, really, was one page (not the seven hundred pages!)—the last page, with its affirmative ending that Borges seems to apply to himself as well—of Joyce's *Ulysses*. The last page of *Ulysses* in English thus becomes the first page of *Ulysses* in Spanish. The last page of Joyce's great work becomes the first page of what would be a long and fascinating textual dialogue that Borges holds with Joyce throughout his life. It also becomes the first page in what can be considered a long line of Ulyssean influence in Latin American fiction throughout the twentieth century.[52]

Borges incorporates Joyce, as he does the many other writers and texts to which he refers, into his literary universe. He does so not quite by manipulating what came before him, but by referring to their work in a manner that allows him to find new ways to dialogue with them. To read a text or to write one—these processes become interchangeable and nearly equivalent in Borges. In some ways, this is not unlike how Joyce is able to write a new version of the *Odyssey*, set it in Dublin, and have all the action occur in just one day, or how Joyce incorporates all previous styles and periods of the English language into his own, as in "Oxen of the Sun," or how he dislocutes all the languages since the collapse of the Tower of Babel into *Finnegans Wake*.

But there are two important differences between Borges and Joyce. First of all, Borges does not work with parody like Joyce does. Joyce, as he incorporates previous styles, seems to want to destroy them, whereas Borges can make previous writers and even entire traditions—especially "minor" ones, as defined by Deleuze and Guattari—come to life (such as the gauchesque, or the Cabalistic traditions). Second, Joyce's work moves consistently toward myth, whereas Borges's moves toward the metaphysical. What I mean by this can be seen if we think about "El inmortal," a story that has a number of similarities with *Ulysses*: Homer and the Wandering Jew, the tension between the personal and the mythical, the references to Vico, and so on.[53] In Borges, the text becomes a contemplation of history and (im)mortality, of the relationship of the individual to time. The myth, the possibility of being Homer, of being immortal, is rejected as a monstrous negation of self—as a "nadería de la personalidad" [nothingness of self]. In Borges, Everyman becomes No man.

As we study how Borges reads Joyce, we witness an aspect of how Borges writes. Borges's textual dialogue with Joyce forces us to think of new ways to theorize translation and, in turn, to rethink the potential of (mis)reading and (mis)translating for different peripheries. Once again, we find that the relationship between reading and translation in Borges is equivalent to the relationship between reading and writing. In theory, translation for Borges accomplishes the same blurring between writer, text, and reader that we have seen numerous times in this book. In this sense, it is a metaphor for writing. Combined with practice, translation and writing, too, become interchangeable and nearly equivalent: as we approach the limits of translation, translation and writing approach a point of undistinguishability.

Conclusions

*B*ORGES *AND TRANSLATION: THE IRREVERENCE OF THE PERIPHERY*
seeks to fill a void in two areas. First, by focusing on the intimate
links between Borges's theories of (mis)translation and his theories
of reading and of writing, this book contributes to the study of Argentine literature; it does so by adding to an understanding of the
development of Borges's aesthetics and to the role that translation
plays in the creation of his texts. Second, my analysis of Borges's
theories of (mis)translation represents a contribution to the field of
translation studies, including consideration of center–periphery dichotomies in the theorizing of translation. In addition, a major aspect of this book has been to show that these two areas need not be
separated, and that translation studies has much to gain by inclusion
of Latin American writers and intellectuals such as Borges, while
literary studies has much to gain by in-depth considerations of the
role of translation in Latin American literatures. In this manner, the
importance of translation in contemporary debates in the humanit-
ies can be expanded to include the ideas of writers from the periphery, as well as the perspectives of what translation means in the
margins, and how it is utilized there.

From a very early age, Borges not only practices the art of translation, he also discovers that thinking about translation can be an
extremely productive way to think about literature in general. As he
states in the opening of "Las versiones homéricas": "There is no
problem as consubstantial to literature and its modest mysteries as
that posed by a translation." In his texts on the topic, Borges observes that every translation is, of necessity, a mistranslation, a deformation of the original, as it is transferred not only from one
linguistic system to another, but also from a specific point in time,
at a specific cultural and geographic location, to another. But this
does not lead Borges to consider translation to be impossible; nor
does he consider mistranslation to be a negative betrayal of a supposedly sacred original. Instead, by suggesting that the notion of a
"definitive text" is a fallacy, Borges holds that there is no reason to

believe that translations are necessarily inferior to the original. This position becomes extremely important as it outlines ways by which Latin American writers can rearticulate their relationships with center and peripheral traditions in the creation of new texts.

An analysis of Borges's theories of (mis)translation leads us to consider the history of Argentine literature as a history of (mis)-translation. Combinations of intralingual and interlingual translation are at the root of the foundation of Argentine literature in the nineteenth century and continue to be a defining characteristic throughout the twentieth century. Borges himself develops his position on the topic in a cultural context rich in avant-garde, polyglot activities. The tensions and contradictions of a duo ancestry—both European and local, cosmopolitan and *criollo*—lie at the core of issues of identity and representation in Argentina. Borges's texts address this problematic, as we saw in our discussion of "El Sur," and illustrate how it can be transformed into a site of potentiality.

Borges's challenge of the concept of originality, articulated from his Argentine periphery, represents one of Borges's main contributions to the theorizing of translation. Debates over the best way to translate a text are nearly as old as the practice itself. In the vast majority of cases, treatises on the topic focus on the most appropriate method to faithfully transpose a text from the source to the target language. Underlying this traditional demand for fidelity is the idea that translation is always accompanied by a loss. Borges's theories of (mis)translation question such privileging of the original. Borges argues that the merits of a translation lie not in how loyal it might be, but rather in the manner by which the translator is able to make use of *creative infidelities* to reinscribe the text in a new context.

Furthermore, Borges suggests that every text is already a rewriting, a mistranslation, of one or more displaced pre-texts. This leads Borges to a practice of writing as translation, which can be seen prominently in the texts of *Historia universal de la infamia*. These stories are composed of a series of (mis)readings and rewritings of acknowledged pre-texts. But the fact that the pre-texts are known does not diminish the value of the new texts, on the contrary. Rather, it highlights a process of appropriation, falsification, and displacement that Borges initiates in the 1930s and develops fully in *Ficciones* and *El Aleph*. As Borges's texts undermine traditional preconceptions of originality, influence, and authorship, they also

introduce a remapping of difference that serves to valorize the periphery in its constant destabilization of the center and its canons.

In this sense, we can argue that Borges's theorizing of translation
focuses on a multiplicity of displacements, as his texts make use
of all manner of shifts—textual, linguistic, temporal, geographic,
cultural, and so on. Change the context, and even the same words,
in the same language, can gain entirely unexpected meanings—
paradoxically without necessarily losing the "original" ones—as
"Pierre Menard, autor del *Quijote*" so elegantly demonstrates.
Time improves texts, according to Borges, as does translation.
Finding ways to make a text "gain" is important for Borges, and
for all of Latin America, given its peripheral geopolitical condition.
Displacement is an important element in any writing, but for writ-
ers/translators in the margins, who are already situated in a displaced location with respect to Western European and U.S. centers,
it is crucial. By validating irreverent rewriting and recontextualization in Argentina—by developing an aesthetics based on a practice
of writing as translation, of mistranslating into a Río de la Plata
language and context—Borges validates his own literary endeavors
and opens the way for other writers to innovate from the periphery.

In his equating of translation with gain, instead of with traditional
loss, Borges rearticulates the practice of translation in such a way
that it becomes rich with potentiality for the margins. Borges does
not bemoan what is left behind; instead, he takes a hold of the past,
of any past tradition, and converts distance and mediation themselves into productive aspects of efficient literary creation. Translation magnifies displacement and reveals disjunctions that are
always present in literature, but are seldom acknowledged. This is
one of the key reasons that Borges is so interested in translation:
displacement in motion. The other key reason is irreverence: the
irreverence of valuing creative infidelities and linguistic and cultural appropriations, the irreverence of placing mistranslation at the
site of the foundation and the renovation of literatures from the periphery.

Borges's texts combine the value and irreverence of creative infidelities and recontextualization, with the value of the temporal
and spatial displacements inherent in the process of translation. As
part of my study I traced how Borges uses this approach with respect to one writer in particular: James Joyce. An important aspect
of this comparison was to present it within the framework of the
Argentine context from which Borges dialogues textually with

Joyce, and as part of Borges's overall literary discourse. This allowed us to see how Borges (mis)reads Joyce to create him as a specific kind of precursor. This approach also helped us locate unexpected parallels and points of contact between the two writers and their respective peripheries.

Joyce's greatest commentary on the topic of translation and translatability may just be the creation of *Finnegans Wake* itself, which, among other things, rewrites the myth of the Tower of Babel. In traditional interpretations of this Biblical story, the language that the citizens of Babylon tried to build with the raising of the Tower is said to be a single, utopic, Adamic tongue, and the confusion ("Babel," literally) is said to come afterward, with the destruction of the Tower. Joyce, for his part, suggests that the language of the Tower is not a single, universal language, but all human languages, at all points in time, merged together in one endless text. In this sense, "Wakese," the language of *Finnegans Wake*, would be the language of the Tower, the outside building pieces that elevate it toward untranslatability. When Joyce writes the language of Babel, he writes in all languages, but he shifts the Tower primarily to Dublin, as it is ciphered through English syntax and Irish history and culture.

If the outside of the Tower of Babel can be said to be, in Joycean terms, all languages spoken/heard at once, the inside, in Borgesian terms, would surely be all books ever written. The inside of the Tower of Babel would then be best described by Borges's "La Biblioteca de Babel," with its endless hexagonal labyrinth of bookshelf after bookshelf of every book ever written, in every language, past, present, and future. But where is the Library located? As the librarian of "La Biblioteca de Babel" explains, "la Biblioteca es una esfera cuyo centro cabal es cualquier hexágono, cuya circunferencia es inaccesible" [the Library is a sphere whose exact center is any one of its hexagons and whose circumference is inaccessible] (*OC* I: 466; *Labyrinths*, 52). The center can be shifted and recontextualized; originality and its values can be questioned; and even the furthest margin, the furthest hexagon, can (re)occupy the center. In this case, Babel is displaced to the shores of the Río de la Plata, where the simulacrum is claimed and validated for all literature, seen as a series of drafts or versions: mistranslations of mistranslations.

In interviews, Borges often repeated that he read *Don Quijote* for the first time in English and that he subsequently found very strange the experience of reading it in Spanish once he realized that its original language was not English. This anecdote, unfortunately, is too often taken at face value,[1] for the veracity of Borges's statement is not nearly as interesting as its implications. What does it mean to read a text in translation that was originally written in one's native tongue, especially when that text is the Spanish foundational *Don Quijote*? How does translation influence the concept of a native tongue? How does a text change with translation? And how does language—as well as culture and all other components that make up the context in which one reads—affect the reading of a text?

This anecdote neatly captures the importance of translation in Borges. There is much poignancy in a South American writer saying that he first read Spain's greatest Golden Age novelist in an English translation, in his house in the neighborhood of Palermo. Borges implies that, from the very beginning, he read with as much irreverence and displacement as he later utilizes in the writing of his texts. The irony is even greater if we consider that *Don Quijote*, arguably the first modern novel, is structured as a translation of an apocryphal Arabic text written by a fictitious author. The very concept of originality begins to fade before our eyes, just long enough for Borges to open a space for himself and other Latin American writers. Asserting that he first read *Don Quijote* in an English translation, regardless of the veracity of this assertion, is an innovative act that highlights how the very condition of marginality—the temporal and spatial distance from Western European and U.S. centers and their canons—can be used to create a site for the production of new texts in the displaced contexts of the periphery.

Epilogue: Reading Argentina, Translating Piglia

As I HAVE SUGGESTED THROUGHOUT THE BOOK, BORGES'S THEORIES of translation are especially significant as they apply not only to his own work, but also to major trends in Argentina's nineteenth and twentieth centuries and to other writers in Latin America. Such an application, I would argue, remains very much relevant in Argentine literature today. To show what I mean by this, I would like to extend the arguments and analyses from my book, in this epilogue, to a discussion of one of Argentina's leading contemporary writers, Ricardo Piglia.[1]

The point of departure for these concluding observations, and one which also influenced significant aspects of this entire study, is a realization I experienced while translating Piglia's *Nombre falso* and *La ciudad ausente*. As I worked on these translations, I became aware of a certain paradox: I was translating texts which were themselves a translation, as they were full of citations, references, allusions, and characters borrowed from other writers; yet Piglia's texts were also undoubtedly original. Upon further reflection, I found this apparent contradiction to be an excellent point of entry into the most important aspects of Piglia's literary production: a rearticulation of the Argentine literary tradition, and the relationship between literature and politics in Argentina. Piglia's project emphasizes the importance of mistranslation, rewriting, and misreading in Argentine literature. In his narratives, Piglia updates the irreverent techniques of his predecessors, especially Borges and Roberto Arlt, and applies them to the contentious sociopolitical context of Argentina's 1970s, 1980s, and 1990s. By questioning literary lineages at times of political and aesthetic uncertainty, Piglia's texts demonstrate how translation can function as an act of resistance in the periphery.

An excellent example of how Piglia works with Arlt and Borges is found in his novella "Nombre falso" (1975). A combination of a

207

fictional literary essay and a detective story, the text is reminiscent of Borges's use of these genres and his blurring of the distinctions between them. But the object of the essay and of the intrigue is an unpublished manuscript by Roberto Arlt. By making the manuscript in question belong to Arlt, Piglia "crosses" Borges with Arlt.[2] In the first part of the novella, "Homenaje a Roberto Arlt," Piglia acts as the protagonist-narrator-detective-literary critic in search of the manuscript. He eventually discovers and includes it as an "Apéndice" after his narrative, as if it belonged to Arlt. But the story, entitled "Luba," is not at all what it appears to be, and its authorship is by no means a simple issue to determine.

As it turns out, "Luba" is Piglia's version of "The Dark," a story by the Russian writer Leonid Andreyev (1871–1919), one of the Russians whom Arlt admired and read—in translation, that is. Piglia rewrites Andreyev's story in a language and style resembling Arlt's, signs Arlt's name to it, and includes it in his own book of fiction. Piglia's version of "The Dark," however, has substantial deviations, as he makes numerous changes, including a long addition that serves as a complete rewriting of the conclusion of the story. In an unexpectedly accurate "Homage to Roberto Arlt," Piglia practices a form of plagiarism reminiscent of the writer to whom he is paying homage. For the origin of "Luba" is an appropriation, a case of creative plagiarism, best exemplified in Argentina by Arlt's troubled (and troubling) relationship to canonical literature.

When *Nombre falso* was first published in Argentina, Mirta Arlt, Roberto Arlt's daughter, telephoned Piglia to tell him that he did not have the right to publish a newly discovered story of her father's without her permission, and wanted to know where he had found it. The Library of Congress was also confounded; it catalogued "Luba" as having been written by Arlt.[3] Critics too were confused about its authorship; one treated it outright as if it were written by Arlt; others only mentioned that the issue of the authorship of "Luba" was problematic, but did not specify how.[4] The confusion between criticism and fiction in *Nombre falso* expanded well beyond the pages of the book, as if reality had begun to imitate art.

A search for a manuscript that does not exist, found within the pages of one author's text, where it is apocryphally attributed to the wrong author? This is reminiscent of the games Borges plays with translation and displacement in stories such as "El acercamiento a Almotásim," "Examinación de la obra de Herbert Quain," or "Pierre Menard: autor del *Quijote*," as we saw in earlier chapters.

But the play of theft and plagiarism in "Nombre falso" also recalls Roberto Arlt's literary economy. As Piglia himself has said: "El robo es la metáfora misma de la lectura arltiana. Se roba como se lee, mejor: robar es como leer" [Theft is the very metaphor of the 'Arltian' reading. You steal in the same way that you read. Better yet: stealing is like reading] ("Roberto Arlt," 24). By crossing Arlt with Borges, to use Piglia's own metaphor, we see that the formulation "stealing is like reading" applies not only to Arlt, but also to Borges, and to other crosses of the two as well.

But the question remains: who is the author of "Luba"? And who is its author once it is in English, as part of *Assumed Name*? The degrees of displacement between one version and another lead to such disorientation, that any semblance of an original is completely lost. Or rather, the originality of Piglia's text lies precisely in a simultaneous veiling and unveiling, through the clues provided in the text, of the authorship of "Luba." The title "Assumed Name" thus takes on added relevance, as the ownership of the text and the roles of the writer, the translator, and the reader (in recreating and seeking to decipher this intrigue) are all thoroughly problematized.

In his creation of "Luba," Piglia recovers and expands the possibilities afforded by Borges's and Arlt's use of irreverence and appropriation and what this reveals about literary property. The series of mistranslations—from a translation of the Russian (by Andreyev), to a certain Río de la Plata Spanish (by Piglia through Arlt and Borges), and back to English (in my translation, as I tried to imagine Arlt through Piglia in late twentieth-century American English)—is like a hall of broken mirrors, or a (per)version of the children's game of telephone. However, as confusing as the connections may get, the line never entirely breaks; it never falls into unintelligible static. It may reveal the condition of Babel, but—or perhaps: because it does—it also points to the core of the creative act.

When I began translating Ricardo Piglia's work in 1993, I did not fully realize what I was getting myself into. At one point, I faxed Piglia in Buenos Aires to ask him how I should handle the numerous citations in *Assumed Name*. Piglia's response is poignant with regards to what happens to a source once it has been quoted and inserted into a new text and context. In his letter, Piglia tells me not to look anything up, to translate his text only, and adds:

Las citas debés traducirlas directamente. . . . Pienso las citas como si fueran personajes (el señor Freud, el señor Melville, el señor Lenin), por

lo tanto no importa si son apócrifas o verdaderas. . . . Cuando el perso-
naje es conocido . . . su nombre funciona de manera distinta a cuando
es desconocido y produce cierto efecto enigmático (¿quién será? ¿será
real o inventado?). No te olvides que el libro se llama 'Nombre falso' y
que en realidad cuenta esa incertidumbre sobre la identidad, la atribu-
ción, la propiedad, etc. (Letter to the author, November 28, 1994)

[You must translate the quotations directly as they are. . . . I think of the
citations as if they were characters (Mr. Freud, Mr. Melville, Mr.
Lenin), so that it does not matter if they are apocryphal or veridical. . . .
When the character is known . . . his name functions in a different manner than when he is someone unknown, in which case it produces a certain enigmatic effect (who could it be? is he real or invented?). Don't
forget that the title of the book is 'Assumed Name' and that this uncertainty about identity, attributions, property, etc. is indeed relevant.]

The complex game of "Assumed Names" in which I now found
myself had broad implications beyond my role in it. In addition to
the challenges these complications represent for a translator in the
U.S., Piglia's use of apocryphal attributions, uncertain authorship,
and unexpected rereadings raise serious ethical and aesthetic issues.
As Ellen McCracken has said: "The . . . crime of plagiarism is not
a moral or literary problem but an economic one because it violates
the laws of private property" (1077). Piglia's texts invite us to reconsider the very basics of the relationship between literature and
identity, between fiction and property, in postcolonial times. And
Piglia's practice of mistranslation takes on added significance for a
Latin American writer in his relationship to a political and cultural
Metropolis. As with his precursors Arlt and Borges, and Sarmiento
before them, irreverence and displacement, theft and falsification,
become a *modus operandi* that serves to problematize every aspect
of the center-periphery dichotomy and to legitimize marginal literary traditions.

These issues take yet another twist as Piglia is translated into English for a U.S. audience. The translator's responsibility in the
U.S.—the ethics of translation from the center, if you will—is to
know what one can betray and what one must not betray. Piglia
himself has commented on the relationship between translation, including of his own texts, and preconceptions of property and appropriation:

A mí siempre me ha interesado la relación que hay entre la traducción
y la propiedad, porque el traductor escribe todo un texto de nuevo que

es de él, pero no es de él. . . . Es una figura extraña la del traductor, está
entre el plagio y la cita. . . . La traducción es un extraño ejercicio de
apropiación.
   En la lengua no hay propiedad privada. . . . El lenguaje es una circula-
ción—es un flujo—común. La literatura corta ese flujo y quizás eso sea
la literatura. ("Lost in Translation")

[I have always been interested in the relationship between translation
and property, since the translator rewrites an entire text that is his, and
yet is not. . . . The translator finds himself in a strange place, somewhere
between plagiarism and citation. . . . Translation is a strange exercise of
appropriation.
   In language there is no such thing as private property. . . . Language
is a circulation with a common flow. Literature disrupts that flow, and
perhaps that is precisely what literature is.]

To this we must add that Piglia's texts always comment upon the
specific sociopolitical and cultural moment in which they are produced. In one of the letters of *Respiración artificial* [Artificial res-
piration] (1980), a character, Roque, writes: "Vivo encerrado todo
el día traduciendo . . ." [I live my life trapped inside, translating]
(76).[5] The censor reading this, trying to search for secret political
messages, does not realize that in this case the message is literal,
since the statement applies as much to him as to the letter writer.
In fact, it applies to much of *Respiración artificial*: being "trapped
inside" history, letters, stories; within an apparently closed system
that all the different writers and readers in the novel, including ourselves, are trying to deal with by interpreting and deciphering "lo
indecible" [the unnamable] as Tardewski calls it near the end of the
novel (209–10).[6] For the continuous work in *Nombre falso* and in
Respiración artificial with displacement and translation corresponds to a questioning of the totality of Argentine history as an
answer to the question—"Hay una historia?" [Is there a story?]—
which opens *Respiración artificial*. From a look back at the nineteenth century, we eventually arrive at the "unnamable" at that time
in Argentina: dictatorship, repression, and the disappeared.
   Respiración artificial unfolds through a series of displacements
and misreadings as it seeks to comment on Argentina's cultural and
sociopolitical situation of the late 1970s. At a time of severe censor-
ship and repression, Piglia utilizes periphrasis, circumlocution, and
substitution—variations of mistranslation—to constantly allude to
the "unnamable." Thus, when Tardewski asks "¿Qué diríamos hoy

que es lo indecible?" [What would we say the unnamable is today?] and answers with "El mundo de Auschwitz" [The world of Auschwitz] (209), the reader realizes that the obvious answer to this question in Argentina is also the "Dirty War" itself. This lends new meaning and implications to Tardewski's comment that: "Hablar de lo indecible es poner en peligro la supervivencia del lenguaje como portador de la verdad del hombre. Riesgo mortal" [To speak about the unnamable is to place in danger the survival of language as the bearer of man's truth. A deadly risk] (210). The "deadly risk" for anyone who spoke out against the military regime in 1980 was very real. Furthermore, the risk is identified in relation to language, a move that places literature as the privileged site where crucial issues—such as the survival of truth in the face of the lies perpetuated by repressive regimes—can be played out. In this sense, whereas mistranslation is seen as a site of national foundation in Sarmiento's nineteenth century, and as a site of innovation in Borges's early and mid-twentieth century, in Piglia's late twentieth century, it becomes a site of political cultural resistance.

When *La ciudad ausente* was published in 1992, now in the transition to democracy, Argentine writers found themselves in an entirely different situation. The main issue they faced was no longer the role of narrative within a context of dictatorship. Rather, the questions that arouse had to do with an inheritance of violence and attempts to reconstruct memory—in both ethical and aesthetic terms. This explains, in part, why *La ciudad ausente* is so concerned with the possibilities of form and representation in the face of an expanding Neoliberal market that masks the individual's isolation and loss.

The machine at the center of *La ciudad ausente* cannot help but remember and produce stories from the uncertain material of memory—her own and that of others. Meanwhile, various governmental agencies—the police, a doctor at a psychiatric clinic that doubles as a prison for political dissidents—try to control the female machine by placing her in a museum and then seeking to disconnect her. The museum, at one level, comes from Macedonio Fernández's *Museo de la Novela de la Eterna* [Museum of the Novel of the Eternal One]: the construction of the novel as an artificial repository for the reader to visit.[7] But the museum in *La ciudad ausente* can also be read as a site where the past is stored and neatly kept in place. The efforts of the official agents to silence the machine fail, however, as her stories are copied and circulated throughout the city. Thus, through a series of reproductions, images, and simulacra, narrative becomes the site of political and aesthetic resistance.

As Francine Masiello has observed:

> *The Absent City* raises representational issues in a world in which an absolute, founding truth is no longer attainable despite our reach back in time. Moreover, this kind of activity is a way to surpass any model for literature described as national allegory, a resistance to any attempt to homogenize local culture. In it, Piglia invites us to see if 'difference' can be analyzed in a more productive way that ultimately facilitates an infinite chain of variants on the themes of exile, isolation, and loss. (*The Art of Transition*, 166)

The way this "difference" is created in the novel is through translation—or, more precisely, through *mis*translation. And the numerous narratives that circulate through *La ciudad ausente*, created by the powerful driving force of mistranslation, constantly challenge "official" hegemonic discourses—where the government's efforts to turn off the machine can be read as a way to impose an official, blanketing version upon Argentina's troubled history.[8]

At stake is a battle over the representation of memory in the aftermath of dictatorship. Underground characters—inventors, journalists, detectives, refugees, exiles, drug users, informants—keep up a duplicitous circulation of copies and versions of narratives that serve to undermine the official discourse. The State is thus unable to get at the root, or origin, of the voice they wish to disconnect. Transformation in *La ciudad ausente*, as Masiello argues, asserts that Latin America is "an active site for the reinvention of literary forms and discourse" (*The Art of Transition*, 168). Variations on the practice of mistranslation multiply and confuse meaning and open the way for a number of muted characters to find a voice.

The enigmatic meaning of the narratives evades Junior, the protagonist seeking to decipher all these stories as he travels through them, as well as the reader. Increasingly, Junior realizes that they originate with the machine. But not only does the machine mistranslate, she is also emptied out ("absent"), in terms of a real origin. In the last part of the novel, Junior fades out, and we hear a monologue by the machine in which we realize that she herself is the composite of numerous literary and historical borrowings. Identity becomes as blurred as the concept of an original text, as the machine channels an irreverent combination of references, including Macedonio Fernández, José Mármol, James Joyce, Roberto Arlt, and William Faulkner. Significantly, the foreign writers in these and other allusions in *La ciudad ausente* are displaced onto a thoroughly Río de la Plata context, in linguistic, literary, geographic, historical, political, and cultural terms.

The mistranslation begins with the machine herself, even before others get hold of her stories. The first story—where one might expect to find an "origin"—is itself a mistranslation. The machine takes the fragments that appear lost and transforms them into something else:

> Primero habían intentado una máquina de traducir. . . . Una tarde le incorporaron *William Wilson* de Poe para que lo tradujera. A las tres horas empezaron a salir las cintas de teletipo con la versión final. El relato se expandió y se modificó hasta ser irreconocible. Se llamaba *Stephen Stevensen*. Fue la historia inicial. . . . Queríamos una máquina de traducir y tenemos una máquina transformadora de historias. . . . Usa lo que hay y lo que parece perdido lo hace volver transformado en otra cosa. Así es la vida. (*La ciudad ausente*, 44–45)

> [At first they had tried to make a machine that could translate texts. . . . One afternoon they fed it Poe's "William Wilson" and asked it to translate it. Three hours later the teletype began to print the final version. The story was stretched out and modified to such a degree that it was unrecognizable. It was now called "Stephen Stevenson." That was the first story. . . . We had wanted a machine that could translate; we got a machine that transforms stories. . . . It takes what is available and transforms what appears to be lost into something else. That is life. (*The Absent City*, 37)]

This machine, who used to be a woman but is now reconstructed from technology and memory, is a strange kind of language machine—which is to say a translation machine. Writers, readers, and critics: we are all translation machines speaking alone in the dark, as she does at the end of the novel, determined to carry on regardless of the hopelessness of the situation. Creating narrative as a form of resistance, as if against fate itself, to postpone the inevitable, a postmodern Sheherazade. Or to fill the empty spaces of the night, of the page, with the fragments of memory that were assumed lost—and that some wish would remain lost.

Like her, we all speak hoping someone will respond and relieve our post-Babel condition. Determined to translate—ourselves, oth-

ers—we participate in the necessary yet impossible task of reconstructing Babel, as Derrida has called it. In this sense,
translation—as a reconstruction of a lost utopia—is an ideal metaphor for the process of reconstructing a collective, lost memory.
And mistranslation is the way by which it can be re-created even
when faced by an "official" discourse that seeks to disconnect such
a process.

The conclusion to Piglia's novel recalls the final affirmation of
Molly Bloom in Joyce's *Ulysses*, as well as a Beckett-like insis-
tence on continuing in the face of any and all physical adversity.
But the context is very importantly a Río de la Plata one:

> Estoy llena de historias, no puedo parar, las patrullas controlan la ciudad
> y los locales de la Nueve de Julio . . . , estoy en la arena, cerca de la
> bahía, en el filo del agua puedo aún recordar las viejas voces perdidas,
> estoy sola al sol, nadie se acerca, nadie viene, pero voy a seguir, en-
> frente está el desierto, el sol calcina las piedras, me arrastro a veces,
> pero voy a seguir, hasta el borde del agua, sí. (*La ciudad ausente*, 178)

In my need to affirm the possibility of translation, I find myself in-
sisting on this affirmation. While I did my best to bring with me
into English the Río de la Plata context (i.e., the Av. Nueve de Julio,
the desert considered the site of "barbarism" in Argentine literary
tradition), I could not help but add an extra "I will" to a text in
dialogue with other texts, to a voice awaiting a confirming ear:

> I am full of stories, I cannot stop, the patrol cars control the city and the
> locales below Av. Nueve de Julio have been abandoned . . . , I am on
> the sand, near the bay, I can still remember the old lost voices where the
> water laps ashore, I am alone in the sun, no one comes near me, no one
> comes, but I will go on, the desert is before me, the stones calcined by
> the sun, sometimes I have to drag myself, but I will go on, to the edge
> of the water, *I will*, yes. (*The Absent City*, 139; emphasis added)

The machine in *La ciudad ausente* is also reminiscent of the final
chapter of *Ulysses* in that she, like Penelope, is constantly weaving
and unweaving stories, stories that come from the memory of others, from other texts, and are transformed into something different.
However, the main Joycean text in *La ciudad ausente* remains *Finnegans Wake*, the modernist text of the night written in all the languages of the world. An immediate point of contact between the
two novels is *The Thousand and One Nights*, which is an important

precursor to both, and also remits us to Borges's theorizing of translation through this medieval text.

In addition, *La ciudad ausente* delineates unexpected similarities between Macedonio Fernández and James Joyce, between the Argentine avant-garde writer as recreated by Piglia, and a branch of modernism that worked from the margins well before it was canonized in the center. This also points to the parallels that can be drawn between Buenos Aires and Dublin, as is already suggested by Borges in "El escritor argentino y la tradición." Piglia, commenting on this connection between Irish and Argentine traditions, observes:

> Dublin and Buenos Aires share the fact that they are both literary cities, in the sense that they have had a large density of writers . . . , who have had a tense relationship with the Metropolis. For example, the tension Stephen Dedalus feels with English, which he considers to be an imperial tongue. The issue of the inheritance of the Spanish language and the struggle to become independent from Spain was, similarly, very much present in Argentina. One can see an analogy between Joyce's relationship with Shakespeare, and Macedonio's with Cervantes. The question becomes: whose language is it? And: how do we overcome the political control associated with this language to reach Shakespeare, for example, thinking of Joyce's parodies in *Ulysses*, and the position that Macedonio takes with respect to Spain's Golden Age? (*The Absent City*, 142–43)

Piglia's cross of Macedonio and Joyce turns out to be very productive, both in *La ciudad ausente* and in the broader context of Argentine literature and culture in the late twentieth century. Piglia reminds us of the extent to which both Macedonio and Joyce, in their respective nations and traditions, represented a major aesthetic and political challenge to the status quo. In this sense, they epitomize a certain project of the avant-garde with which Piglia clearly identifies.[9] Macedonio and Joyce serve as precursors for Piglia, models of writers who establish a problematized position with respect to their societies and cultures. Both Macedonio and Joyce perpetuate "a certain hermetism as a poetics," as Piglia has called it,[10] and rupture preestablished relationships as they challenge the Metropolis and its canons from the margins. This is similar to the irreverent reading that Borges had done of these writers; however, though still highly aestheticized, they are now placed in a much more political position. In *La ciudad ausente*, for example, Piglia places Macedonio's anarchic ideas as an aesthetic and political response to the totalizing narratives of the State and the market, which seek to order and control the individual, and to determine meaning and one's place in society from outside the self.

As a politically committed writer and an avant-garde experimentalist, Piglia creates narratives in *La ciudad ausente* that capture the fragmentation associated with the late twentieth century, the sense of loss and confusion and of picking through the waste heap of history (to borrow a Joycean image). The narratives themselves, as well as their circulation through the society that they seem to both reflect and define, become sites of resistance in a battle that is at once concerned with language and life. By questioning and redefining national traditions, by appropriating with irreverence from traditions outside Argentina, Piglia merges fiction and politics beyond recognition. In the process, his texts suggest the value of literature, and particularly of the aesthetic, in contemporary times.

The end of *La ciudad ausente*, as I mentioned earlier, resonates with the final "yes" of Joyce's *Ulysses*. But this resonance is also mediated by another literary moment from Argentina's past: Borges's one-page translation of *Ulysses*. As we have seen, Borges's 1925 treatment of Joyce's *Ulysses*, much like the opening page of Sarmiento's *Facundo* in 1845, is an "originating" moment based on an act of mistranslation. The machine in *La ciudad ausente*, who takes fragments and memories and processes them into the stories that then circulate through the city, is another such moment, and a crucial one for Argentina's late twentieth century. Piglia's careful reworking of these aspects of Argentine literary tradition reinforces a key practice for writers from the periphery—the practice of mistranslation, of taking with irreverence, of an innovation that can create "fortunate consequences" in new contexts, as Borges suggests.

We must also keep in mind the implications of Piglia's contribution to this practice of mistranslation to the specific sociopolitical reality that his texts navigate. In "The Island," a section of *La ciudad ausente* in which a group of exiles lives in complete isolation, surrounded by a river that could be the Río de la Plata, or the Liffey, or all the rivers of the world, and where the inhabitants study *Finnegans Wake* as if it were the Book, we read: "La nación es un concepto lingüístico" [The nation is a linguistic concept] (128–29; *The Absent City*, 103). The statement suggests not only the end of the so-called master narratives of the West, but also the battle that comes after the death of such beliefs. Or perhaps the aftermath of such a battle, if we want to take Argentina's recent past both figuratively and literally.

Thus, in the aftermath of dictatorship, the concept of the nation is once again at stake. At a time when Neoliberal forces seem to have all but obliterated the traditional role of the intellectual in society, Piglia places language at the center of the definition of the nation, just as it was in the nineteenth century. Piglia's question "Whose language is it?" gains urgency and significance. Language, its role in forming communities, in the balance of what is gained and lost in translation, in expressing memory and articulating loss, is itself at stake in *La ciudad ausente*, much as it is in contemporary times. The relationship between individuals and language, how this relationship circulates through society in narratives, mistranslated against the flow of the discourse of the State and of the market: these are the issues of our times. And the role of literature, Piglia seems to tell us, is to address these questions—ethically and aesthetically, North and South, East and West—today as much as ever.

Notes

Introduction

1. Unless otherwise noted, all translations in the book are mine. A translation is always and quite significantly an interpretation of the text in question. Thus, although translations of the quoted material may exist, I provide my translations as an added element in my readings of the cited texts.

2. For a theoretical framework of the place of translation within literary systems, see Even-Zohar. For a discussion of the importance that cultural context plays in the interpretation of language, see Steiner 32–36. J. Graham also emphasizes the role of the context in any reading when he states: "Just as language is relative to grammar, so grammar is relative to context, in that the real or right grammar for an utterance depends on the context" (28).

3. As Balderston and Schwartz state, and as the essays in their anthology explore: "Translation has become both a mechanism and a metaphor for contemporary transnational cultures in the Americas. . . . Translation continues to be one of the main tools, and defining images, of Latin American culture in its relation to world cultures" (1). Similarly, in his article on the importance of translation in *One Hundred Years of Solitude*, González states: "From Garcilaso Inca to Sarmiento to Borges to García Márquez, the problematics of writing in America and the questions raised by translation have tended to become one and the same, and have generated a literature in which the topic of translation is ever-present, as a reminder of Latin American literature's 'impure' and conflictive origins . . ." (282).

4. Discussing what he terms the "ethics of location," Venuti observes: "The cultural authority and impact of translation vary according to the position of a particular country in the geopolitical economy. In the hegemonic countries, metaphysical concepts of authorial originality and cultural authenticity denigrate translation as second-order writing, derivative and adulterated. . . . In developing countries, translation accrues cultural as well as economic capital" (*The Scandals of Translation*, 187).

5. See, for example, the essays in J. Graham's *Difference in Translation* (which includes texts by Philip E. Lewis, Barbara Johnson, Alan Bass, and Jacques Derrida). Other studies in this branch of translation studies include Quine; Steiner; de Man; Kirk; and A. Benjamin.

6. These studies focus on the sociopolitical and historical implications of translation and on the role of translation in projects of cultural imperialism. See Niranjana; Cheyfitz; Spivak; Robinson; and the essays in Dingwaney and Maier, in Bassnett and Trivedi, and in Budick and Iser.

7. For a study of the role of translation in the history of British and American literature, see Venuti's *The Translator's Invisibility*.

8. The few exceptions to this include Aparicio; the essays in Balderston and Schwartz; the essays in Bradford; Masiello's *The Art of Transition*; and sections of Venuti's *The Scandals of Translation*.

CHAPTER 1. ARGENTINA AND TRANSLATION

1. Sarlo and Molloy (in *Jorge Luis Borges* and *Las letras de Borges*, respectively) argue that Borges must be read within an Argentine context. I agree and extend, here, this position to include Borges's theories of translation as a key aspect of his aesthetics and his overall literary discourse. In addition, I believe that contextualizing a writer's theories and practices of translation is especially important, given the fact that translation constantly forces us to consider differences between languages and cultures, between the local and the global, between center and periphery.

2. Aparicio sums it up well when she states: "Lo que previamente se limitaba a designar una transferencia de una lengua a otra, ahora se ha diseminado como metáfora del acto de lectura y escritura en toda su complejidad fenomológica" [What was previously limited to the designation of a transfer from one language to another, is now disseminated as a metaphor of the act of reading and writing in all of its phenomological complexity] (9). See also J. Graham's "Introduction" to *Difference in Translation*.

3. As the Argentine poet Diana Bellessi has said: "Translation is above all an attempt at alterity. . . . Translation always provokes a meditation on one's own language—on its powers and limits—and on language itself" (26).

4. See Venuti's *The Scandals of Translation*, 186–89.

5. Also applicable here is the concept of "transculturation," first defined in a Latin American context by Fernando Ortiz in the 1930s, and further developed by Ángel Rama, Gustavo Pérez Firmat, and Mary Louise Pratt, among others.

6. In Argentina "criollo" and "criollismo" refer to something inherently local or native; i.e., to something inherently Argentine.

7. The processes of intralingual and interlingual translation to which I refer in this chapter and elsewhere in the book are an expansion of Jakobson's definitions. By intralingual translation I mean not only the rewording of a text within the same language (Spanish, in this case), but also the rereading and rewriting—the transformation—of the language (diction and syntax) and culture of Argentina's past per se. (My use of "intralingual translation," here, is analogous to that used by Pérez Firmat in his analysis of Cuban *"criollismo."*) Likewise, by "interlingual translation" I mean not only "translation proper," but more generally a process of rereading and rewriting—of recontextualizing and appropriating—foreign languages, texts, and traditions.

8. Some of the best, recent work on Sarmiento is found in *Sarmiento: Author of a Nation*.

9. Similarly, Sarlo states: "The fact that [Argentine writers] do not recognize a cultural fatherland in Spain leads them to connect their national literature with those of other European countries. But the fact that there is also a local cultural

tradition does not simplify this connection. . . . Mixture is at once indispensable and problematic" (*Jorge Luis Borges*, 47–48).

10. In addition to Gutiérrez, the members of the Salón Literario included Esteban Echeverría, Juan B. Alberdi, Bartolomé Mitre, and Vicente Fidel López. See Halperín Donghi's *Proyecto y construcción de una nación* and *Una nación para el desierto argentino*.

11. As Altamirano and Sarlo state: "To overcome the barrier of Spanish, rather than to master a foreign language in order to achieve social distinction, is the objective of the *romantic polyglotism program*" ("The Autodidact and the Learning Machine," 163; emphasis added).

12. As Catelli and Gargatagli state: "Gutiérrez, como Sarmiento pocos años después, levanta su pliego de cargos contra España y concluye, como lo harán muchos durante el siglo XIX, con una exhortación a la ruptura lingüística y cultural con la metrópoli. Aquí, la traducción no sólo es vehículo de civilización sino condición para la existencia de un idioma nacional, una literatura nacional, un cielo nacional" [Gutiérrez, like Sarmiento a few years later, raises his list of charges against Spain; he concludes, as many would during the nineteenth century, with an exhortation of a linguistic and cultural break with the Metropolis. Here, translation is not just a vehicle of civilization, but also a condition for the existence of a national language, a national literature, a national sky] (361).

13. As Molloy argues, when Sarmiento says "traducir" [to translate], he means "to read with difference" (*At Face Value*, 24–26). In other words, when Sarmiento reads, he mistranslates, appropriating the foreign to incorporate it, selectively, to his ends on his South American stage.

But Sarmiento also emphasizes the value of "translation proper." For example, towards the end of *Recuerdos*, in the penultimate section entitled "Traducciones" [Translations], Sarmiento lists some of the texts that he has translated, as well as one which he arranged to be translated. This clearly constitutes, for Sarmiento, an important part of his bibliography, which can be seen as the "textual self" (as Molloy calls it) that he leaves behind at the end of *Recuerdos*.

14. As Jagoe states in her analysis of Humboldt's place in Argentina's nineteenth century, for Borges there is no foundational space in Argentina prior to multilingualism. A full reconsideration of Argentina's nineteenth century, as I suggest here, falls outside the scope of this study. This section is intended as an introduction to such a rereading.

15. Sorensen Goodrich—commenting on Sarmiento's "error," which underscores what she calls the "process of transformation typical of cultural annexations"—has tracked down the probable original source, and found that: "The closest one can get to the phrase is Diderot's 'On ne tue pas de coups de fusil aux idées,' a maxim which [Sarmiento] might have encountered in the *Revue Encyclopédique*, read by the members of his generation as a source of European culture. The phrase reached [Sarmiento] in a characteristically mediated way, as the epigraph of an 1832 article written by Charles Didier entitled 'Les doctrines et les idées'" (85).

16. We should note that whereas mistranslation serves as a site of national foundation in Sarmiento's nineteenth century, in Piglia's late twentieth century it will become a site of political cultural resistance. In between the two we have the pivotal work of Borges: Borges's theories of mistranslation and the space Borges

opens through his use of irreverence and displacement. We will return to Piglia's uses of mistranslation in this book's epilogue. See also my article "Ethics and Aesthetics."

17. As Sorensen Goodrich suggests: "*Facundo* is in a way a gloss on the elusive French phrase, proving Sarmiento's determination to help ideas survive the ravages of tyranny during his exile in Chile" (84–85).

Juan Manuel de Rosas (1793–1877) was an Argentine dictator from 1829 to 1852. The *mazorca*, traditionally used to slice melons, was transformed by Rosas into a portable guillotine to intimidate and kill his opponents.

18. Molloy also discusses Sarmiento's misattribution in the epigraph of the *Facundo*, and calls Sarmiento's translation of it "the most digressive of translations"; see *At Face Value*, 29–32. Additionally, we note that Sarmiento's "errors" are not at all limited to this one instance at the beginning of *Facundo*. As Molloy details, one of the epigraphs of *Recuerdos* also has a misattribution, and is accompanied by a "very free translation," both of which turn out to have significant implications (29).

19. There is also the other line of Argentine tradition in the nineteenth century, the line that seeks to found Argentine literature through an intralingual process of translating local speech, traditions, and customs. In other words, the gauchesque, culminating in José Hernández's *Martín Fierro*. But even here there are some interesting crosses, such as Estanislao de Campo's parodic *Fausto criollo*.

20. See Rodríguez Monegal's *Jorge Luis Borges*, 90–93.

21. The Borgeses lived in Geneva, Lugano, Barcelona, Majorca, Seville, and Madrid. They also visited Paris, London, and the North of Italy. A good chronology of Borges's life and work can be found in *Borges: A Reader*, 331–37. See also Maier's *Borges and the European Avant-garde*.

22. See Korn's *Buenos Aires: Los huéspedes del 20*; and *Sectores populares, cultura y política*, by Gutiérrez and Romero.

23. Sarlo states: "Modernidad europea y diferencia rioplatense, aceleración y angustia, tradicionalismo y espíritu renovador; criollismo y vanguardia. Buenos Aires: el gran escenario latinoamericano de una *cultura de mezcla*" [European modernity and Río de la Plata difference, accelaration and anxiety, traditionalism and renovative spirit, *criollismo* and vanguard. Buenos Aires: the great Latin American stage of a *culture of mixture*] (*Una modernidad periférica*, 15; emphasis in the original).

24. In the pages of *Proa* we find, for example, a number of texts by the editors (including several very early poems and essays by Borges); an article entitled "Cubismo, expresionismo, futurismo" by Herworth Walden, translated by Borges; poems by Ricardo Güiraldes, Raúl González Tuñón, Leopoldo Marechal, and Norah Lange; texts by Macedonio Fernández; one poem by Pablo Neruda; drawings by Borges's sister Norah; an article by Guillermo de Torre entitled "Neodadaismo y superrealismo"; an article by Güiraldes on French symbolism, submitted from Paris; the story "El rengo" by Roberto Arlt; a letter from Valéry Larbaud (translated by A. del Carril); and an article by Marinetti, "Contribución al estudio del romanticismo" (translated by Caraffa). In addition, the January 1925 issue contains Borges's essay on, and translation of the last page of, James Joyce's *Ulysses*, both of which we will examine in detail in chapter 5. This same issue contains a translation by Jorge Borges (Borges's father), from English into Spanish, of Ed-

ward FitzGerald's translation of "Rubáiyát" by Omar Khayyám, followed by an article by Borges. We will discuss these in chapter 3.

25. On the importance of *Martín Fierro's* "Manifiesto," see Masiello's *Lenguaje e ideología*, 70–74.

26. The responses include commentaries by Leopoldo Lugones (who, in a positivistic, nationalistic vein, speaks of "la triple influencia de la sangre, el clima y el idioma" [the triple influence of blood, climate and language] that makes up the "Argentine sensibility"); Ricardo Rojas (who refers readers to his nationalistic articles on the subject); Oliveiro Girondo (who states: "Yo creo en nuestra idiosinscrasia . . ." [I believe in our idiosyncrasy . . .]); Roberto Mariani (who focuses on the tango); Ricardo Güiraldes (who recommends that Argentines focus on their "poder de asimilación" [power of assimilation] instead of a practice of "imitación" [imitation], and on their "audacia" [boldness] instead of on their "agresividad" [aggression]); and Pablo Rojaz Paz (who also states that one of the defining characteristics of the "Argentine sensibility" is a "gran capacidad de asimilación" [great capacity to assimilate]) (*Revista Martín Fierro*, 38–40).

27. On the history of the ideological polemics of the Argentine avant-garde, see Prieto's "Boedo y Florida."

28. As Sarlo has said, *Los Pensadores* and *Claridad* "proponen un discurso basado en traducciones que tiene como efecto la democratización, por la difusión masiva, de la cultura europea progresista en el marco rioplatense" [propose a discourse based on translation to effect democratization, through mass distribution, of progressive European culture in a Río de la Plata context] (*Una modernidad periférica*, 27).

29. Translations were also important in the even more revolutionary magazine *Contra*, which had a short run of five numbers in 1933, and in which the poet Raúl González Tuñón published a regular column in addition to some of his poetry. As Sarlo states: "*Contra* esboza . . . una política de traducciones que apoya su programa ideológico-estético" [*Contra* outlines . . . a politics of translation that supports its ideological-aesthetic program] (*Una modernidad periférica*, 148).

For further information on the literary magazines of the time, see, for example, *Las revistas literarias argentinas* by Lafleur, Provenzano, and Alonso; and Salvador's *Revistas argentinas de vanguardia*.

30. See especially King's study of *Sur*'s history. Although *Sur* kept publishing until 1970, and released special issues as late as 1980, its central role in Argentine letters clearly diminishes in the 1960s (King, 166–97).

31. Borges's publications in *Sur,* not included in his *Obras completas* or other books, have been anthologized in *Borges en Sur 1931–1980*.

32. The recognition that Borges began to receive abroad in the 1960s may have happened in any case, although Borges's first French translator, Roger Callois, became acquainted with Borges's work through his participation in *Sur*. Callois spent World War II exiled in Argentina, became involved with Victoria Ocampo and *Sur*, and actively promoted Borges's work when he returned to France (see King, 95–128; and Rodríguez Monegal, 381–82).

33. For a theoretical discussion of the importance of selection processes in considering translated literature as a system, see Evan-Zoher.

34. On Ocampo's political and cultural strategies, see Greenberg's *The Divided Self*; and Sarlo's *La máquina cultural*, 93–194. On the tradition of Latin Americans who have written in English or French, see Díaz.

35. Borges would have disagreed with Reyes's position on translation, as the Mexican writer strongly favored a literal approach. See Reyes's *Mallarmé entre nosotros* and Aparicio, 54–63. For a study of the relationships between Reyes and Borges, see Barili.

36. Ortega, like a number of other twentieth-century thinkers (from Benjamin to Venuti), goes back to the early nineteenth-century German Romantics, such as Schleiermacher, to support his argument in favor of literal translations. As we will see in chapter 2, this is one of the lines of translation theory with which Borges most disagrees and which he most directly challenges.

37. For an analysis of Gombrowicz, his work, and his presence in Argentina, see Larkosh's *The Limits of the Foreign*; and García's *Gombrowicz, el estilo y la heráldica*. During his exile in Argentina, Gombrowicz also wrote *Transatlantyk* (1953), a novel written in Polish which is as much about Argentina as it is about Poland, and which constantly works with issues of identity and language in marginal literatures. On the relationship between Gombrowicz and Argentine literature, see Saer's "La perspectiva exterior"; and Piglia's "¿Existe la novela argentina?"

Chapter 2. Borges on Translation

1. In translation studies, there is minimal inclusion of Borges's essays in anthologies on the topic, and almost no analysis to speak of. One of the only anthologies that includes one of Borges's essays is Venuti's *The Translation Studies Reader*. But Borges is not included, for example, in Schulte's and Biguenet's *Theories of Translation*; in Santoyo's *Teoría y crítica de la traducción: antología*; in Munday's *Introducing Translation Studies*; in Bassnett's and Lefevere's *Translation, History and Culture*; or in Gentzler's *Contemporary Translation Theories*. The main critical anthologies, such as J. Graham's *Difference in Translation*; Dingwaney's and Maier's *Between Languages and Cultures*; Budick's and Iser's *The Translatability of Cultures*; and Bassnett's and Trivedi's *Post-Colonial Translation*, do not include any analysis of Borges's contributions to translation studies either. Even Steiner, who presents an insightful reading of the importance of translation in "Pierre Menard" in *After Babel* (73–76), completely leaves out Borges's essays about translation in his otherwise thorough list of key texts on the topic ("Select Bibliography," 500–516).

2. The existing bibliography by Latin Americanists on Borges and translation, which is far from exhaustive, includes: Olea Franco's "Borges y el civilizado arte de la traducción"; Willson's "La fundación vanguardista de la traducción"; Bravo; Gargatagli and López Guix; Danielson; and Aparicio, 107–48. Also relevant and very useful is Balderston's and Schwartz's recent anthology, *Voice-Overs*, which includes Borges's "The Homeric Versions" and a brief piece on Borges and translation by W. Costa.

The book on Borges and translation to which I refer is Kristal's recent *Invisible Work*. The main contribution of Kristal's book is to bring attention to the importance of translation in Borges; the most useful sections of *Invisible Work* are those that discuss some of Borges's translations. Kristal, however, misses an opportunity to place Borges's theories of translation in context: either within the context of

Argentine literature, or in a broader translation studies context. With respect to Argentine literature, Kristal insists on the dated view that Borges is a "universal" writer (e. g., "Borges remains the most universal of Latin American writers," 136), without probing into what this actually means in the case of Borges, nor why such a claim may be problematic (both of which Sarlo does in *Borges, un escritor en las orillas*). With respect to a translation studies context, Kristal's book contains very little translation theory. In fact, Kristal uses a very limiting definition of translation, especially in light of recent critical theory, which has looked at translation as a thoroughly complex process with broad cultural, philosophical, and political implications. (See, for example, J. Graham's "Introduction"; or Venuti.) Kristal, for example, states that: "A translator rewrites a sequence of words with a different sequence of words" (2). Although this is certainly true, it is also only a part of what occurs in the process of translation.

3. Cited in Pastormerlo (1). In most interviews in which translation is discussed, however, Borges comments on the two main approaches to translation (the literal or the paraphrase) and suggests that both are legitimate and potentially valuable, albeit for very different reasons (see, for example, the interviews with Alifano; or Sorrentino). This is entirely consistent with Borges's main essays on translation, as we see in this chapter.

4. Although "The Task of the Translator" was first published in 1923, as the "Introduction" to Benjamin's translation of Baudelaire's *Tableaux parisiens*, its recent influence dates from the late 1960s and from Hannah Arendt's translation of Benjamin in the volume *Illuminations* (1968). It is mostly at this point that thinkers such as Derrida and de Man take Benjamin as a point of departure to further develop their ideas on translation. But the original date of Benjamin's essay is relevant in another sense: namely in its proximity to Borges's first essays on translation.

5. I am referring especially to Venuti; Niranjana; Cheyfitz; and the essays in Dingwaney and Maier, and in Budick and Iser.

6. See Helft's *Bibliografía completa* for a complete listing of Borges's translations.

7. Borges's theories are clearly informed by his own practice as a translator, and vice versa. We should actually consider to what extent the entirety of Borges's literary production—or perhaps that of any writer—is an act of translation. We will explore this idea in chapter 3.

8. On this first period of Borges's work, see Olea Franco's *El otro Borges*.

9. In his brief commentary on this essay, Kristal gets this part exactly backwards, as he states that Borges associates himself with a Romanticist approach to translation, instead of the other way around (15–16).

10. See Steiner, especially his chapter "The Claims of Theory" in *After Babel* (248–311), for a historical overview of the topic.

Borges's comments in "Las dos maneras de traducir" correspond with what he says about Classicism and Romanticism in other texts around the same time. In "La nadería de la personalidad" (*Inquisiciones*, 1925), for example, Borges fervently attacks the adoration of a unified subject in literature, as exemplified by Romanticism. This stance also corresponds with the problematizing of the subject in Borges's own work at that time, and to issues of subjectivity as they were treated in the Argentine avant-garde. See Masiello 95–106 and 147–63. An interesting parallel also exists between Borges's stance here (his attack on the Romantic subject, his essay "La nadería de la personalidad," his position on translation) and T. S. Eliot's "Tradition and the Individual Talent."

11. The terminology utilized by Schleiermacher and other German thinkers of the time transposes the letter/spirit dichotomy into the "image of the appropriate distance a translation should achieve between its own tongue and the original" (Steiner, 280). More recently, Venuti has used Schleiermacher's formulation for his definitions of domesticating and foreignizing translations, strongly arguing in favor of the latter; see, for example, *The Translator's Invisibility*, 19–42.

12. As Peter France states: "If in the 18th c. fluent domestication was the norm, it would seem that the pendulum has since then swung the other way, at least as far as translation theory is concerned. By the end of the 20th c. it has become normal to advocate 'taking the reader to the author,' as Schleiermacher put it . . ." (5).

13. See Molloy's chapter "Rúbricas textuales," in *Las letras de Borges* (49–71). See also Monegal's chapter "Reading as Writing," in *J. L. Borges* (323–38).

14. As Aparicio states: "La imagen de 'borradores' . . . no admite distinciones entre original y traducción" [The image of 'drafts' . . . does not allow for distinctions between original and translation] (112).

15. Stating that a translation is always an "operación literaria" [literary operation], Octavio Paz explains that: "La traducción implica una transformación del original. Esa transformación no es ni puede ser sino literaria porque todas las traducciones son operaciones que se sirven de los dos modos de expresión a que, según Roman Jakobson, se reducen todos los procedimientos literarios: la metonimia y la metáfora" [Translation always implies a transformation of the original. This transformation cannot but be literary because all translations are operations that utilize the two modes of expression to which, according to Roman Jakobson, all literary procedures can be reduced: metonymy and metaphor] (*Traducción*, 13–14.).

The concept of Lefevere's to which I refer is outlined in "Literary Theory and Translated Literature." There, Lefevere defines "refracted texts" as those that find their way into traditions or canons through multiple rewritings—such as, for example, how readers may be familiar with the stories of the classics from having encountered them in different manifestations, even if they have never read the "originals" of said classics.

16. We will return to a discussion of the role of translation in "El acercamiento a Almotásim" in chapter 5.

17. J. Graham, discussing the relationship between text and context, states: "Just as language is relative to grammar, so grammar is relative to context, in that *the real or right grammar for an utterance depends on the context*" (28; emphasis added).

18. As Steiner states: "Whatever treatise on the art of translation we look at, the same dichotomy is stated: as between 'letter' and 'spirit,' 'word' and 'sense'" (275).

19. Arnold and Newman's polemic is found in *Essays by Matthew Arnold* (1914). In addition to his literal translation of the *Iliad*, Newman also did a literal translation of the *Odes* of Horace. See also *The Oxford Guide to Literature in English Translation* 64–73.

20. In these essays by Newman and Arnold, Borges finds what would certainly have been an obscure reference for his Argentine readers.

21. In his comparison of these versions, Borges translates the samples into Spanish himself. Borges's skills as a translator truly shine here, as he demonstrates his ability to reproduce (recreate) linguistic constructions (the letter) from one language to another. As Levine has observed, the piece provides Borges with: "An excuse . . . to give a virtuoso performance of different styles and eras of Homer" ("Some Versions of Homer," 1135). By seeking archaic effects at times, or using Gongoresque inversions and hyperboles for Pope, for example ("Some Versions of Homer," 1138), Borges beautifully recreates the vocabulary and syntax of the various translators, as well as of the language of their specific time periods, into Spanish. See also Olea Franco's "Borges y el civilizado," 444.

22. Jakobson states: "No lack of grammatical device in the language translated into makes impossible a literal translation of the entire conceptual information contained in the original" (147). Nabokov states: "The clumsiest literal translation is a thousand times more useful than the prettiest paraphrase" (127).

23. The first paragraph and a half of the "Prólogo," dated November 23, 1931 (about six months before the publication of "Las versiones homéricas"), is a slightly earlier and rougher version of the same material that Borges would use for the beginning of "Las versiones homéricas." After this point the texts diverge and go on to cover quite different ground (the rest of the "Prólogo" discusses specifics of Valéry's poem). "Las versiones homéricas" is the better known and by far the more influential of the two, especially for the theorizing of translation (the "Prólogo" was not included in book form until *Prólogos con un prólogo de prólogos,* 1975).

24. See Venuti's "Introduction" in *Rethinking Translation,* 6–7.

25. As González states: "One fundamental difference between Borges's and Benjamin's approaches to translation appears here: while Borges reflects upon translation with an ironic detachment that takes its cue from Bertrand Russell's analytical philosophy, Benjamin's approach is neo-Hegelian, emphasizing as it does a vitalistic notion of language and art, and an idea of translation as a movement towards transcendence" (275–76).

26. See, for example, *The Ear of the Other* and "Des Tours de Babel."

27. Aparicio also states that: "Cabe añadir que Derrida, y algunos críticos desconstruccionistas, estiran y extienden estos conceptos de complemento y diferencia hasta su máximo potencial. Derrida va más allá de Borges en su discusión radicalizadora del concepto de original, afirmando que si acaso hay adeudamiento en una traducción, la deuda la tiene el autor del primer texto con sus traductores eventuales, en vez del traductor con el autor" [We should add that Derrida, and some deconstructionist critics, stretch and extend these concepts of complement and difference to their maximum potential. Derrida goes beyond Borges in his radicalizing discussion of the concept of the original, arguing that if there is any indebtedness in translation, it is the author of the first text who owes a debt to his eventual translators, instead of the translator with the author] (23). I disagree with Aparicio on this point. As I argue in these pages, I believe that Borges in fact goes further than Derrida in severing the ties of determination between original and translation.

28. The essay is divided into three parts, the first two of which first appeared in

the popular Argentine magazine *Crítica* in 1934. The entire essay is dated 1935 and appears in *Historia de la eternidad* (1936). As we will see in chapter 3, these dates are important as they coincide with the production of the stories in *Historia universal de la infamia* (1935).

29. The same might be said about readers in the Orient in modern times as well, as the text has "reentered" the Arab world through fairly recent translations of the European versions. See, for example, Knipp, 47–48; or Armistead and Monroe, 7.

30. The Orientalism discussed by Said (in *Orientalism*) is especially marked in the translations of *The Thousand and One Nights*, particularly in those by Galland and Burton. For critiques of Burton's Orientalism, see Kabbani; and Carbonell Cortés, 63–70.

31. Borges always claimed that *The Thousand and One Nights* was one of the first books he read as a child in his father's library. The version he found there, and the one he always preferred, is the one by Richard F. Burton. *The Thousand and One Nights* also appears frequently in Borges's texts. For a complete list of references to the *Nights* in Borges's work, see Balderston, *The Literary Universe*, 219; for a list of references to Burton, see Balderston, *The Literary Universe*, 25–26. For a discussion of Borges's references to the *Nights* in interviews and in his "Autobiography," see Rodríguez Monegal, 71–72. See also my article "*The Thousand and One Nights* in Argentina."

32. The two audiences, in their respective times and locations, represent the two different horizons (in Jauss's terms), which effect the interpretation of the text. In this respect, the fact that each "horizon" represents not only a temporal difference, but also a linguistic one, only serves to complicate the matter further. This strongly suggests the importance of studying translation for reader response theories.

33. Borges's position is in stark contrast with accepted scholarship, which has tended to criticize Richard F. Burton's version of the *Nights*, focusing on his alleged plagiarism, his inconsistent style, and his nearly pornographic rendering of some of the stories. See, for example, Knipp, 49–51.

34. I mean this in the same sense that Balderston studies Stevenson as a precursor of Borges in *El precursor velado*.

35. Derrida also finds Jakobson's scheme problematic, mainly because Derrida does not see such a clear distinction between intralingual and interlingual translation ("Des Tours de Babel," 173–74). Borges and Derrida coincide here, especially in light of what "Pierre Menard" teaches us about translation. See my discussion of "Pierre Menard" in chapter 3.

36. The first major move in this direction is found in J. Graham's aforementioned anthology of 1985, *Difference in Translation*.

37. Despite the proximity in thought between Lewis and Borges, Lewis's essay is published in yet another anthology on translation theory, and a key one at that (*Difference in Translation*, 1985), which all but ignores Borges (who of course articulated his ideas about half a century before Lewis).

38. Borges writes about cummings: "Sabemos, ¡ay!, que a la literatura suele preferir la tipografía. En efecto, lo primero que llama la atención en la obra de cummings son las travesuras tipográficas: los caligramas, la abolición de signos de puntuación. Lo primero, y muchas veces lo único. Lo cual es una lastima, porque el lector se indigna (o se entusiasma) con esos accidentes y se distrae de la poesía, a veces espléndida, que Cummings le propone" [We know, alas, that he tends to

prefer typography over literature. In effect, the first thing that draws our attention in Cummings's work is his typographic mischief: the calligrams, the abolition of punctuation marks. The first, and often the only thing. Which is a shame, because the reader becomes indignant (or enthusiastic) with these accidents and is distracted from the poetry, at times splendid, which Cummings proposes to him] (*Textos cautivos*, 162).

39. Borges give as an example of this the verse: "La cara terrible de Dios, más resplandeciente que una cuchara" [gods' terrible face,brighter than a spoon] (*Textos cautivos* 163). Borges points out that "cuchara" [spoon] is completely unexpected; one might anticipate something like "espada" [sword] or "estrella" [star], he says. It is important to note that what Borges rescues from cummings in this reading reflects Borges's views and preferences in poetry at the time, as he had already largely distanced himself from his young "*ultraista*" days.

40. [God's terrible face, brighter than a spoon, summarizes the image of a single fatal word; until my life (which liked the sun and the moon) resembles something that has not occurred. I am a birdcage without any bird, a collar in search of a dog, a kiss without lips; a prayer lacking knees; but something beats within my shirt providing that he is undead, who living, is no one. I have never loved you, my dear, as I now love.]

This is my translation of Borges's translation of the cummings strophe. As this "back translation" shows, Borges's version is actually fairly literal at the level of vocabulary and syntax; his irreverence, as outlined above, resides in the complete recontextualization and reformatting of cummings's verses.

Here is the corresponding strophe from cummings's original:

> gods' terrible face, brighter than a spoon,
> collects the image of one fatal word;
> so that my life(which like the sun and the moon)
> resembles something that has not occurred:
> i am a birdcage without any bird,
> a collar looking for a dog,a kiss
> without lips; prayer lacking any knees
> but something beats within my shirt to prove
> he is undead who,living,noone is.
> I have never loved you dear as now i love. (*Poems*, 259)

41. Another notable moment in Borges's translation comes in the last line, as Borges renders "I have never loved you dear as now i love" as "Nunca te he querido, querida, como ahora quiero." Here Borges magnifies the effect of the repetition of variations on "love"/"querer" by translating "dear" as "querida," thus adding to the original even as he undoes cummings's signature lower case "I."

42. See Civantos's *Between Argentines and Arabs*.

43. A similar argument to the one I present here is made by Pires Vieira's "New Registers for Translation in Latin America" with regard to the role of translation in Brazilian literature.

CHAPTER 3. WRITING AS TRANSLATION

1. The one story included in the book not previously published in *Crítica* is "El asesino desinteresado Bill Harrigan." Borges also reviews one of the texts

later included in the "Índice de las fuentes" of *Historia universal de la infamia*, Herbert Asbury's *The Gangs of New York* (the pre-text for "El proveedor de iniquidades Monk Eastman"). "El puntual Mardrus," which would become the second part of "Los traductores de *Las 1001 Noches*" ("2. El doctor Mardrus"), was published in *Crítica* on February 3, 1934; and "Las 1001 Noches," which would become the first part of "Los traductores de *Las 1001 Noches*" ("1. El capitán Burton") was published there on March 10, 1934. The third and final part of "Los traductores de *Las 1001 Noches*" ("3. Enno Littmann"), for its part, did not appear until its inclusion in the final version of the essay in *Historia de la eternidad* in 1936. I draw this bibliographic information from Helft's *Bibliografía completa*; Zangara's edition of *Borges en Revista Multicolor*; and *Revista Multicolor de los Sábados, 1933–1934*.

2. In addition to the translations Borges publishes in *Crítica* from 1933 to 1934, around this period Borges also translates André Gide's *Perséphone* (1936), Virginia Woolf's *Un cuarto propio* (1936) and *Orlando* (1937), Franz Kafka's *La metamorfosis* (1938), G. K. Chesterton's "Lepanto" (1939), the *Antología de la literatura fantástica* (1940, with Adolfo Bioy Casares and Silvina Ocampo), Henri Michaux's *Un bárbaro en Asia* (1941), *Los mejores cuentos policiales* (1943, with Bioy Casares), Herman Melville's *Bartleby* (1943), William Faulkner's *Las palmeras salvajes* (1944), and numerous translations in *El Hogar* between 1936 and 1939 (including poems and fragments of texts by Carl Sandburg, Wallace Stevens, T. S. Eliot, Arthur Waley, as well as the poems by e. e. cummings that we looked at in the previous chapter). See Helft's *Bibliografía completa*.

3. Critics have mostly paid attention exclusively to temporal shifts in accounting for the difference between Menard and Cervantes. See, for example, Steiner, 73–76. Although this displacement is certainly important, as we will see it is only one of several factors that contribute to creating the difference which then creates new meaning.

4. For a discussionn of the role of Cide Hamete Benengeli's role in the *Quijote*, see Américo Castro.

5. As Molloy states: "En la ficción borgeana se abre y se dinamiza, con obvio placer, un mensaje narrativo que está lejos de ser inerte y fijo: mensaje que integra, como letras del libro, a quienes lo redactan, lo narran, y lo leen, y a la vez se dispersa en ellos. Las nadas entre escriba y lector poco difieren; tampoco difieren las nadas entre escriba y texto, entre texto y lector, entre el texto 'visible' y el pretexto: son dialogantes permutables en plano de igualdad" [In Borges's fiction, a narrative message, which is far from being inert and fixed, is opened and made dynamic with obvious pleasure: a message that integrates, like the signs of a book, those who write, narrate, and read it, while dispersing itself through them. There is little difference in the nothingness between scribe and reader; nor is there any difference in the nothingness between scribe and text, between text and reader, between 'visible' text and pre-text: they are all moveable dialoguers on equal planes] (52).

6. See also the translation of "El atroz redentor Lazarus Morell" in *Borges a Reader*, 41–42.

7. As Ramona Lagos observes: "Primera conclusión no explícita, aunque sugerida en el relato, es: *Las Casas es también un redentor atroz*. . . . [Borges] está invitando . . . a la observación crítica de la interpretación oficial de la historia hu-

mana. Está invitando a ejercer la agresión intelectual, en su mejor sentido, de cues-
tionar, de ver lo aceptado, desde otro punto de vista, desde otros ángulos no
previstos. . . . El rasgo de estructura abierta que ofrece la literatura borgeana reside
en que el nuevo posible que él postula no ofrece características definitivas o inmu-
tables" [The first conclusion, non-explicit though suggested by the story, is: *Las
Casas is also a dread redeemer*. . . . Borges invites the critical observation of the
official interpretation of human history. He is inviting us to practice intellectual
aggression, in the best sense, of questioning, of looking at the accepted from another point of view, from other unexpected angles. . . . The trait of an open structure offered by Borges's literature resides in that the new possibility that he
postulates does not offer definitive or immutable characteristics] (120; emphasis in
original).

8. In the opening paragraph of "El atroz redentor Lazarus Morell" cited above,
for example, we find terms such as "oriental" to refer to someone from Uruguay;
a reference to Antonio Ruiz (who fought in the Wars of Independence and died in
1824 [*The Literary Universe*, 52]) by his nickname "Falucho"; the questions about
the origins of the tango; a mention of "el candombe," the name of a dance as
well as a political maneuver in Argentina; references to "Pedro Figari," Uruguayan
painter and lawyer, 1861–1938 (*The Literary Universe*, 54); "Vicente Rossi," Argentine critic and historian, author of *Cosas de Negros* (1926) and *Folletos lengu-
araces* (*The Literary Universe*, 132); and Miguel Estanislao "Soler": Argentine
general and politician, 1783–1814 (*The Literary Universe*, 143); and, most important, the allusion to José Hernández's *Martín Fierro* ("el moreno que asesinó
Martín Fierro").

9. I am thinking of texts such as "La forma de la espada" [The Shape of the
Sword], "Tres versiones de Judas" [Three Versions of Judas], "El muerto" [The
Dead Man], and especially "Tema del traidor y del héroe" [Theme of the Traitor
and the Hero].

10. Another infamy in *Historia universal de la infamia* is that the "Índice de
fuentes" is not entirely factual, but contains an apocryphal entry: the fictional
source *Die Vernichtung der Rose*, supposedly by Alexander Schulz, as a pre-text
for "El tintorero enmascarado Hákim de Merv." Alexander Schulz is a masked
rephrasing of the name of Borges's friend, the Argentine artist Xul Solar, who
never wrote such a text, and especially not in German. This invented source suggests how the technique of taking selectively from existing pre-texts can be expanded, as Borges does in future stories, in which he cites apocryphal as well as
veridical sources. We can think, for example, of "Tlön, Uqbar, Orbis Tertius," in
which Borges expands the pre-text of the *Encyclopedia* to include a fictional section that then opens up into a fantastic other world.

Incidentally, the "Index" of *Historia universal de la infamia* is not "un Índice
más o menos apócrifo," as María Esther Vázquez claims (142). If anything, it is a
more or less veridical Index, with the one apocryphal inclusion. The distinction is
important. Borges works mostly, as critics in recent years have finally begun to
demonstrate, with real (even if at times very obscure) pre-texts, and interpolates
fictional creations onto these. Borges's texts cannot, therefore, be summed up (i.e.,
dismissed) as "a-political, fantastic" stories; this would entirely miss the crucial
sociohistorical and cultural issues with which they constantly challenge the reader.

11. The stories included in "Etcétera" are: "Un teólogo en la muerte," taken

from *Arcana Coelestia* by Emanuel Swedenborg; "La cámara de las estatuas" and "Historia de los dos que soñaron," both drawn from Richard F. Burton's translation of the *Arabian Nights*; a version of "El brujo postergado," from don Juan Manuel's *Libro de Patronio*; "El espejo de tinta," taken from *The Lake Regions of Equatorial Africa* by Richard F. Burton; and "Un doble de Mahoma," drawn from *Vera Christiana Religio* (1771) by Emanuel Swedenborg.

With respect to the two texts that Borges recreates from Burton's *Nights*, Kristal is only partially correct when he says that Borges: "Secretly participates in the process of transforming Arab stories" (26). Borges does indeed contribute to the reproduction and circulation of certain tales from *The Thousand and One Nights*, but an important aspect of Borges's process is precisely that he does *not* do so secretly: Borges always openly and significantly reveals his pre-texts as part of his complex rewriting of them.

12. I disagree with Montgomery's assessment that Borges's "adaptation, considered as a part of Borges's writing, does not stand out" and that "the tale still belongs to the Infante [Don Juan], as it always has, for he, for his part, was highly independent in his use of sources. Borges's adaptation amounts to a very warm appreciation of his model" (464). Montgomery admits that the "modernization is of interest" (464). I would argue that this "modernization," combined with the taking of one "Exemplo" out of the *Conde Lucanor* and recontextualizing it within Borges's own book, represents a violent displacement from the past and the center toward the present and the periphery. Variations need not be enormous for their effects to be.

13. Whenever he stated that "Pierre Menard" was his first story, Borges would recount the anecdote of the accident on Christmas Eve 1938 which, according to him, led him directly to deciding to write something different than what he had done before (see Irby, 37; Rodríguez Monegal, 320–25; Vázquez, 161; or Borges's "Autobiographical Essay").

14. We should never feel compelled to accept Borges's claims at face value, as his statements in interviews, and even more so in his "Autobiographical Essay," are often related to the fictional image that he wishes to construct of himself and his work. Rodríguez Monegal points out that "Pierre Menard" is not Borges's first story, but he seems to assume that Borges simply made a mistake in his retelling of how things happened (*J. L. Borges*, 325), instead of it being a conscious move on Borges's part to establish "Pierre Menard" as *the* inaugurative fictional text of his literary career.

In fact, it is not hard to see that "Pierre Menard" is not at all Borges's "first story," especially if we look back at Borges's work in *Crítica* from 1933–34, or the texts of *Historia universal de la infamia* (1935), or "El acercamiento a Almotásim" (first published in *Historia de la eternidad*, 1936), or even at certain aspects of the narratives in *Evarristo Carriego* (1930). As Molloy has said: "Más que una ruptura, 'Pierre Menard' marca una clara continuación de las Ficciones previas, reconocidas o no como relatos. . . . 'Pierre Menard' no inaugura la ficción borgeana, simplemente la afirma" [More than a rupture, 'Pierre Menard' marks a clear continuation of the previous Fictions, recognized or not as stories per se. . . . 'Pierre Menard' does not inaugurate Borgesian fiction, it simply affirms it] (*Las letras de Borges*, 53).

If we really had to choose a story that separates Borges's early work from the beginning of his more mature work (i.e., the stories in *Ficciones* and *El Aleph*), that text would undoubtedly be "El acercamiento a Almotásim," written two full years before "Pierre Menard." "Almotásim" not only marks a crucial step in the development of Borges's fiction, it also connects *Historia universal de la infamia* (as well as the essays in *Discusión* and *Historia de la eternidad*) with Borges's stories in *Ficciones* and everything that follows. See my discussion of "El acercamiento a Almotásim" in chapter 5.

15. See Molloy's *Las letras de Borges*, 52–59.

16. Early in the reception of the "Pierre Menard," Bioy Casares advised that the list was not arbitrary (Bioy Casares, 63; Olaso, 87). But it was not until several decades later that Molloy fully considered the importance of the list (*Las letras de Borges*, 52–59). More recently, Olaso discusses each item on the list, contributing valuable bibliographical information about Menard's writings. Also important is Balderston's situating of Menard within his cultural and sociohistorical milieu in *Out of Context*.

17. Balderston points out that *La conque* had already been out of circulation for seven years by the time Menard supposedly publishes his poems there (*Out of Context*, 18–19). This falsification warns us from the beginning that the apocryphal and the veridical will be interlaced in Menard's "visible work," and that we must read this list very carefully.

18. Item (a) also resonates with Valéry's dictum that one does not finish a poem, but rather abandons it. Was the first version perhaps abandoned by Menard? Is the second, revised version the final one, or has it, too, been abandoned?

19. Items (c) and (d), respectively, are: "Una monografía sobre 'ciertas conexiones o afinidades' del pensamiento de Descartes, de Leibniz y de John Wilkins . . ." [A monograph about "certain connections or affinities" between the thinking of Descartes, Leibniz and John Wilkins]; and "Una monografía sobre la *Characteristica Universalis* de Leibniz . . ." [A monograph about Leibniz's *Characteristica Universalis*] (*OC* I: 444–45).

20. This monograph also summarizes the "ejecución deliberada y metódica del programa que enunció Valéry" [deliberate and methodical execution of Valéry's program] (Olaso 91), and thus corresponds to Menard's tutelage within symbolism.

21. About this item, Steiner correctly states that it demonstrates: "[Menard's] (and Borges's) awareness of the connections between the seventeenth century pursuit of an inter-lingua for philosophic discourse and the 'universalism' of modern symbolic and mathematical logic" (73).

22. Borges emphasizes the connections between mathematical and alphabetical symbolic systems in both "El idioma analítitco de John Wilkins" and "Funes el memorioso." See my analysis of "Funes el memorioso" in chapter 5.

23. And there is a third echo in Menard's interest in chess, which, as Balderston points out, recalls Valéry: "The article Menard wrote on possible changes in the game of chess . . . parallels Valéry's discussion of a card game . . . [in which] 'the rules of the game change with every deal'" (*Out of Context*, 19).

24. As is explained in *Borges: Una enciclopedia*: "La preocupación por el lenguaje fue otro centro de interés compartido [entre Borges y Xul]. Al deslumbramiento temprano de Borges por el idioma artificial del obispo Wilkins (1928) y la saturación criollista de *El tamaño de mi esperanza* (1927), Xul suma la creación

de una *panlingua* y del *criol* o neocriollo, reflejo vanguardista del cocoliche que atravesaba la lengua porteña de inmigración y ejercicio de brevedad con el que Xul intentó textos literarios para su difusión, pues consideraba que el *criol* iba a ser 'futur lenguo del Contenente'" [The preoccupation of language was another area of interest shared between Borges and Xul. To Borges's early bewilderment about the Bishop Wilkins's artificial language (1928) and to the *criollo* saturation in *El tamaño de mi esperanza* (1927), Xul adds the creation of a *panlingua* and of *criol* or *neocriollo*, an avant-garde reflection of the '*cocoliche*' found in the *porteño* language of immigration; with these exercises in brevity Xul tried to disseminate literary texts, as he considered that *criol* would become '*futur lenguo del Contenente*'] (344). Borges's humorous comments about Xul's "Pan juego" are also quite interesting (*Conversaciones*, 38; Olaso, 96).

25. In addition to references to the seventeenth century, "El idioma analítico de John Wilkins" also refers to a number of other efforts to create a universal language, including those of the nineteenth century, such as Johann Martin Schleyer's Volapuk or Giuseppe Peano's *Interlingua*, both precursors to Esperanto.

26. Menard's use of Saint-Simon (French soldier, diplomat and writer, 1675–1755) as his example is extremely ironic, as Fishburn points out: "Saint-Simon's flair for character-drawing, love of gossip, combination of prejudice and superstition and talent for catching the atmosphere of the historical moment make him unique among French diarists. . . . These qualities, however, are not matched by style and grammar, which hardly make him a suitable candidate for an 'examination of the essential metric laws of French prose'" (211). What is relevant here is the manner in which Saint-Simon's writing marks a certain historical moment, an issue that will come up again in Menard's rewriting of Cervantes.

27. Olaso completely misses the irony in his discussion of this item, where he calls Menard's choice of "précieux" for "cultos" "impecable" (100–102). On the other hand, does this mean that Menard's word choice is inaccurate? This is not so clear, for there are numerous points of contact drawn throughout the text between the seventeenth century and symbolism. Menard's translation of "boussole" for "aguja de navegar" (both meaning a compass), for its part, is fairly straight forward.

28. See also Olaso's discussion of this item (112–14). Steiner, for his part, says that: "*Pace* the suave authority of the memorialist, I incline to believe that 'a literal translation of Quevedo's literal translation' of Saint François de Sales was, indeed, to be found among Menard's papers" (73).

29. Maurice Barrès (1862–1923) was a French writer whose books include a text on bullfighting and a biography of El Greco (Fishburn, 28). Argentine writer Enrique Larreta's (1875–1961) novels include *La gloria de Don Ramiro* (1908), set in Ávila and Toledo at the time of Philip II. As Fishburn suggests: "A contrast may be established between *La gloria de Don Ramiro* [by Enrique Larreta], in which the author sets out to recreate the historic atmosphere of the sixteenth century by using archaic Spanish for the dialogues, and Pierre Menard's version of *Quixote*" (137). Balderston, Gallo and Helft state that: "Su prosa castiza [Rodríguez Larreta's], de inusual riqueza léxica y pletórica de giros españoles nunca interesó a Borges . . ." (*Borges: Una enciclopedia*, 203).

Fishburn also argues that: "The allusion to *Salammbô* should be considered in the light of Borges's comment that, no matter how rich Carthaginian literature may have been, it could never have included a novel like Flaubert's, for 'every writing belongs to its own time' (second prologue to *Luna de enfrente* [*OC* I: 55]). Pierre Menard's rewriting of *Quixote* as a 'document' of Nîmes in the twentieth century reflects that view by way of parody" (211–12).

30. In addition, "Pierre Menard" reminds us of the importance of historicizing translation, and how translation historicizes literature. On the historicity of translation, see Niranjana.

31. As Beatriz Sarlo has said: "La paradoja de Pierre Menard pone en escena el proceso de la escritura llevándolo al límite del absurdo y la imposibilidad, pero haciéndolo, al mismo tiempo, visible. Esto, en el margen del Río de la Plata, equivale a reivindicar un nuevo tipo de colocación para el escritor y la literatura argentina. . . . Si ninguna originalidad puede ser reclamada por ningún texto, si todo sentido nuevo surge de la lectura o de la escritura en contexto, la inferioridad de 'las orillas' se desvanece: el escritor periférico tiene las mismas prerrogativas que sus predecesores o sus contemporáneos europeos" [The paradox of Pierre Menard brings to the forefront the process of writing, taking it to the limit of the absurd and the impossible, while making it simultaneously visible. This, on the edge of the Río de la Plata, is equivalent to a recovery of a new kind of placement for the Argentine writer and tradition. . . . If no form of originality can be claimed by any text, if every new meaning arises from reading or writing in context, then the inferiority of "the margins" disappears: the writer from the periphery has the same prerogatives as his European predecessors or contemporaries] (*Borges, un escritor*, 81).

32. See also Rabell, 205–6.

33. As Murillo notes: "Se da titulo de la supuesta versión original. Nótese que la llama *historia*. El libro de Cervantes, y el del *segundo* autor, se supone ser interpretación, relato o nueva versión de un original. Puede pensarse, pues, que *la historia* de don Quijote es el libro "original" dentro del libro de Cervantes, que sería una novela en nuestro sentido moderno" [The title of the supposed original version is given. Note that it is called a *history*. The book by Cervantes, and by the *second* author, is supposedly an interpretation, a retelling or a new version of an original. One can think, then, that the *history* of don Quijote is the "original" book within Cervantes's book, which would be a novel, in the modern sense of the word] (143 n. 18; emphasis in the original).

34. On Menard and William James, see Balderston's *Out of Context*, 18–24.

35. I am grateful to Ricardo Piglia for suggesting this idea to me. In a recent conversation, Piglia states: "¿Qué quiere decir 'El examen de la obra de Herbert Quain'? Quiere decir algo que también tiene que ver con la determinación. Es decir, yo estoy aquí escribiendo una novela de dos amigos que están en un bar en Buenos Aires, y entonces nosotros podemos irnos juntos al cine, o yo me puedo volver a mi estudio y vos te volvés a tu lugar, o puede aparecer otro amigo que se sienta con nosotros. . . . Herbert Quain [elige] las tres, [sin excluir ninguna de ellas]. . . .

"Esta red de posibles alternativas es clásica en la traducción. . . . La traducción es una decisión respecto a alternativas que están [marcadas] . . . ; es como un mapa la traducción. A diferencia de la ficción, donde vos no conocés el mapa de las alternativas, en definitiva no hay una red que te lleva en una dirección. En cambio la traducción sería un lugar donde vos tenés que elegir siempre la palabra con la que vas a trasladar, y por lo tanto estás siempre tomando decisiones . . ." (Piglia, interview by author, August 16, 1999).

[What does "An Examination of the Work of Herbert Quain" mean? It means something that is also related to determinism. That is to say, I am here writing a novel about two friends in a café in Buenos Aires, and then we can go together to the movies, or I can return to my study and you can go back to your place, or another friend can show up and join us. . . . Herbert Quain chooses all three, without excluding any of them. . . .

This web of alternative possibilities is classic in translation. . . . Translation is a decision with respect to the alternatives that are marked . . . ; translation is like a map. Unlike fiction, where you do not know the map of alternatives, there is no definitive net that takes you in a specific direction. Translation, instead, would be a place where you always have to choose the word that you are going to transpose, and you are therefore always making decisions. . . .]

36. See *A Thousand Plateaus*, 31–32.

37. Borges considers similar issues in "La supersticiosa ética del lector" (*Azul*, January–February 1931, then included in *Discusión*, 1932).

38. Beckford (1760–1844), known as the wealthiest man in England during his lifetime, became infamous for the enormous Gothic estate he built on Fonthill, and for the rumors of hedonism surrounding his life, which eventually led to him being ostracized and dubbed "The Fool of Fonthill." The biography to which Borges alludes in the essay is Guy Chapman's *Beckford: A Biography* (1932).

39. Seeking to analyze the context of Borges's statement that "the original is unfaithful to the translation," Kristal says: "Borges thinks that the French original is unfaithful to the translation because it was rendered with sloppy haste, whereas the English version was crafted with thoughtful care and attention to detail" (24). As I try to show in this section, Borges's statement is considerably more complex and provocative than this.

40. I am grateful to Michelle Hamilton for helping me track down many of the specific Persian and Arabic references in this section of the text.

41. Borges uses Omar's Persian name in this first paragraph (Umar ben Ibrahim al Khayyami), his Spanish name through most of the essay (Umar instead of Omar), and then his English name and Arabic surname (Omar Khayyám) in the next paragraph, when he discusses FitzGerald's version of the *Rubáiyát*.

Something similar occurs with the translation of the name of Averroes in "En busca de Averroes." In that story, it is directly related to the narrator's attempt to reach Averroes through translation. See my discussion of "La busca de Averroes" in chapter 4.

42. It is no coincidence that Borges emphasizes the role of the *Quijote* as part of the literary and linguistic trek that leads FitzGerald to Omar. The *Quijote* leads FitzGerald to Omar, we assume, through the presence of Cide Hamete Benengeli, and the fact that the novel is itself constructed on the premise that it is a translation of a supposed Moorish "original" text. As is the case in "Pierre Menard," the reference to the *Quijote* in the midst of a discussion about translation adds depth and irony, and points at the fiction of the concept of originality.

43. As Fishburn explains: "FitzGerald maintained that to be readable a translation must be a paraphrase and wrote: 'It is an amusement to me to take what liberty I like with these Persians, who as I think are not poets enough to frighten me from

such excursions, and who really do want a little care to shape them.'" FitzGerald's translation of the *Parliament of Birds* is also extremely free: "The original is a lengthy poem, which FitzGerald condenses into a few pages, selecting particularly apologues, or little stories with obvious morals" (90).

See also my discussion of the role of the translation of the *Parliament of Birds* in "El acercamiento a Almotásim" in chapter 5.

44. I am referring in particular to Alazraki's *La prosa narrativa* (especially 74–100). See also my response to Alazraki's reading of pantheism in my discussion of "El acercamiento a Almotásim" in chapter 5.

45. The specific terminology that Borges uses in his discussion of Omar and FitzGerald also reinforces the idea of collaboration. The term "conjunción," for example, contains the astronomical reference to the fortuitous alignment of celestial objects; the grammatical connotation of a term that connects clauses or sentences; and the medieval resonances of the word, when it was used to connote a mixing or union of dissimilar substances in alchemy, but also the physical union between two people in marriage. "Configuración" is also interesting, again with its astronomical and astrological connotations about the relative position, apparent or actual, of celestial objects; but also, in general terms, its definition regarding how elements are arranged to shape the outer form of an object or body.

46. See Molloy, 78–95 on the role of the double in this and other stories by Borges.

47. See Sarlo's *Borges, un escritor*, 85–93 for a discussion of how these stories dialogue and rework the *Martín Fierro*.

48. See Balderston's "The Mark of the Knife" for a good start to a contextual discussion of this story.

49. See Sarlo's *Borges, un escritor*, 98–99, and Balderston's *Out of Context*, 81–97.

CHAPTER 4. THE AESTHETICS OF IRREVERENCE

1. The central place of "El escritor argentino y la tradición" in Borges's aesthetics is evidenced by Borges's manipulation of its publishing history. First delivered as a conference in 1951, the essay appears in print in 1953 (*Cursos y conferencias*); Borges then places it in *Discusión* (beginning with the 1957 edition), a collection of essays first published in 1932, and keeps it there in the various editions of the *Obras completas*, as if to suggest that the text had been written in the early 1930s. By including it in *Discusión*, Borges creates the illusion that "El escritor argentino y la tradición" is an early articulation of his aesthetics.

2. Borges does not consider it a "problem" at all. This is clear from the skepticism he professes from the beginning of the essay: "Quiero formular y justificar algunas proposiciones escépticas sobre el problema del escritor argentino y la tradición. Mi escepticismo no se refiere a la dificultad o imposibilidad de resolverlo, sino a la existencia misma del problema. Creo que nos enfrenta un tema retórico, apto para desarrollos patéticos; más que una verdadera dificultad mental entiendo que se trata de una apariencia, de un simulacro, de un seudoproblema" [I wish to formulate and justify here some skeptical proposals concerning the problem of the Argentine writer and tradition. My skepticism is not in relation to the difficulty or

impossibility of solving the problem, but rather to its very existence. I believe that we are faced with a rhetorical theme, which lends itself to pathetic elaborations; rather than with a true mental difficulty, I take it we are dealing with an appearance, a simulacrum, a pseudoproblem] (*OC* I: 267).

3. On this period, see, for example, Altamirano's and Sarlo's "La Argentina del Centenario"; and Olea Franco's *El otro Borges*, 23–76.

4. As an example, Borges discusses *La urna*, the 1911 book of poems by Enrique Banchs (1888–1968). Borges argues that even though this poem does not contain any local Argentine imagery per se, it still conveys a sensibility that is unquestionably Argentine (*OC* I: 269–70). On Borges and Banchs, see *Borges: Una encyclopedia*, 29–30.

5. See also the translation of "El escritor argentino y la tradición" in *Labyrinths*, 177–85.

6. We need only think of the numerous Jewish and Irish writers who Borges accesses in his texts (e.g., Baruj Spinoza, Gustav Meyrink, Martin Buber, Franz Kafka, Rafael Cansinos Assens, and Alberto Gerchunoff, among other Jewish writers; Berkeley, Swift, Shaw, Dunsany, Joyce, among other Irish writers), to realize the importance of Jewish and Irish letters in Borges's work. For the importance of the Jewish tradition in Borges, see Aizenberg. Unfortunately, there is no thorough study of the importance of the Irish tradition in Borges. For a partial discussion, see Leddy; Murillo; and my analysis of Borges and Joyce in chapter 5.

7. Although his readership and influence was already significant in Argentina and throughout Latin America at the time of "El escritor argentino y la tradición" (1951), Borges was still far from the international sensation he would become in the 1960s. As a handful of critics have observed, this recognition and canonization, Borges's status as a so-called universal writer, often comes at the expense of his "*argentinidad*." In other words, in their readings of Borges, Europeans and North Americans often erase the very marginality he claimed in his work, and from which he dialogued with multiple traditions to problematize issues of canon formation, influence, authorship, originality, and center–periphery hierarchies. On how Western Europe and the U.S. have tended to translate and read Borges, see Molloy's "Lost in Translation"; Sarlo's *Jorge Luis Borges* 1–6; and Balderston's "Borges: The Argentine Writer."

8. For a good study of Güiraldes and *Don Segundo Sombra*, see the essays in the critical edition of the English translation of *Don Segundo Sombra* (1995).

9. I am referring specifically to Bloom's *The Anxiety of Influence* (1973).

10. Borges also provides "a few topological elucidations" in the commentary that accompanies the English translation of the collection *The Aleph* (268–69).

11. Piglia discusses these kinds of substitutions in "Emma Zunz" and "Tema del traidor y del héroe," among others, in "Nueva tesis sobre el cuento" (*Formas breves*, 101–34).

12. See, for example, "Des Tours de Babel."

13. As Fishburn and Hughes observe, Averroes: "Became the principal source of Greek thought for medieval Christian and Jewish theology" (24).

14. See, for example, Stewart's "Borges on Language and Translation"; and Balderston's "Borges, Averroes, Aristotle" and *Borges, realidades y simulacros*, 151–70.

15. See Dapía for a discussion of the concepts of "context," "framework," "conceptual scheme," and "paradigm" in Borges's text.

16. The story has been translated as "Averroes' Search"; this includes the otherwise excellent translation by James E. Irby, from which I quote in this section.

17. As Fishburn and Hughes state: "Much of what is said about him [Averroes] in 'Averroes' Search' stems from Renan's *Averroès et l'Averroïsme*" (24).

18. The "resistance to closure and to system," as Balderston calls it ("Borges, Averroes, Aristotle," 206), is clearly part of what Borges finds so "beautiful" about Averroes's failed search.

19. As Octavio Paz has said: "Eliot believed in fidelity to tradition and authority; others of us believed in subversion and change" ("Ceremonies," 11).

Borges's process of taking with irreverence, of a practice of writing that is synonymous with rereading and mistranslation, resonates with a number of modernist writers. Ezra Pound and James Joyce come immediately to mind. I will discuss the similarities and differences in the uses of translation between Borges and Joyce in chapter 5. I discuss Eliot instead of Pound in this section in part because Eliot worked to appropriate and define the canonical Metropolis in a more consistent fashion than Pound. For a discussion of translation in Pound, see Venuti's *The Translator's Invisibility*, 187–205; and Kenner. A comparative study of Borges and Pound remains to be done.

20. I disagree with Jon Thiem, who looks at Borges's relationship with Dante in "El Aleph" through Bloom's model of an anxiety of influence. As we have seen several times in this study, influence does not lead to anxiety for Borges; rather, it is transformed through the lens of mistranslation and recontextualization into a field of potentiality. In "El Aleph," Borges is clearly playing irreverently with his influence, the Dantean pre-text, and delighting in the potential realized by displacement and mistranslation in/to/from the periphery.

21. A number of Dahlmann's characteristics resonate with Borges's own personal history. On the biographical parallels between Dahlmann and Borges, see Bell-Villada, 78–79.

22. As we saw in chapter 2, Borges's only comments about Weil's version (dated 1839–42) in "Los traductores de *Las 1001 Noches*" have to do with Weil's infidelities, which Borges highly praises. He states: "Sus interpolaciones me merecen todo respeto" [His interpolations deserve all my respect]; and after giving several brief examples of these, he adds: "Esas buenas apocrifidades no son indignas de Burton o Mardrus" [These good falsifications are not unworthy of Burton or Mardrus] (*OC* I: 410).

23. Commenting on the fact that, as he rides the train to the Pampas and to the *pulpería* where he will meet his destiny, Dahlmann is reading the *Arabian Nights* in translation, Sarlo states: "In a way translation is also the problem of Latin American literature, at least from Borges's point of view: his country is a marginal space compared with the Western literary tradition, and the position of its writers is in itself problematic" (*Jorge Luis Borges*, 47).

24. Borges states that "El Sur" is "acaso mi mejor cuento" [perhaps my best story] from its first publication in *Artificios* (in the "Prologue" to this book; *OC* I: 483). See also *Borges: A Reader*, 357.

25. "El oficio de traducir" was first published in *La Opinión* on September 21, 1975, and reproduced that same year in a special edition of the journal *Sur* entitled "Problemas de la traducción" [Problems of Translation]. The text also includes reflections on the task of translating by the Argentine writers/translators José

Bianco (1908–86), Alberto Girri (1919–91), and Enrique Pezzoni (1926–89). Borges's sections from this issue have since been reproduced in *Borges en Sur*.

26. Borges also goes on to warn us that this should not be taken to an extreme; that it should not be a justification for the excessive use of local color or other regionalisms. However, it is clear from Borges's statements here, as in his previous texts, that Borges believes that there is such a thing as an "Argentine Spanish," and that this has great potential especially when it comes to translation.

27. Part of the work that needs to be done is to include an analysis of translation proper in Latin America as part of Latin America's overall literary production. This is especially the case when translations are done by writers, as has been the case in Latin America for hundreds of years, from the Inca Garcilaso de la Vega to Andrés Bello, Gertrudis Gómez de Avellaneda, and José María de Heredia; from José Martí, Rubén Darío, Julián de Casal, José Asunción Silva, Gutiérrez Nájera, to Guillermo Valencia; and from Borges, Julio Cortázar, Haroldo de Campos, to Octavio Paz and José Emilio Pacheco—to name some of the most prominent ones.

The existing important studies on the role of translation in Latin America include Aparicio; Balderston and Schwartz; Levine's *The Subversive Scribe*; Pérez Firmat; Pires Vieira; Ortega; Colombi; and Pera.

CHAPTER 5. BORGES READS JOYCE

1. In "Kafka y sus precursores," Borges states: "El hecho es que cada escritor *crea* a sus precursores. Su labor modifica nuestra concepción del pasado, como ha de modificar el futuro" [The fact is that every writer *creates* his precursors. His work modifies our conception of the past, just as it will modify the future] (*OC* II: 89–90; emphasis in the original). In this same essay, Borges enumerates a series of texts that he identifies as "Kafkaesque," all written before Kafka, and not resembling each other at all. Borges then states that this last point is "el más significativo" [the most significant one], since it is Kafka himself who allows us to see what is "Kafkaesque" about his precursors, as "created" by his very work: "En cada uno de esos textos está la idiosincrasia de Kafka, en grado mayor o menor, pero si Kafka no hubiera escrito, no la percibiríamos; vale decir, no existiría" [Each one of those texts contains, to a major or minor degree, the idiosyncrasy of Kafka, but if Kafka had not written, we would not perceive it; which is to say, it would not exist] (*OC* II:89). In a sense, as Borges "creates" his precursor Joyce, we see certain "Borgesian" elements in Joyce which we would perhaps not perceive—which perhaps do not even exist—prior to Borges's work.

2. The commentary part of the article, without the translation, is then included in *Inquisiciones* (1925). I should mention that Borges indeed appears to be the first Hispanic "adventurer," or at least the first Argentine, to tackle *Ulysses*. A survey of key journals of the time in Argentina (including *Martín Fierro, Nosotros, Síntesis*, and *Caras y Caretas*, as well as earlier numbers of *Proa*) reveals only one previous mention of Joyce, in the May 1922 issue of *Nosotros*. It is a brief, unsigned note, entitled "James Joyce," containing biographical information about the writer, announcing the publication of *Ulysses*, and advising that a potential reader would have the need to "ser dueño de considerable cultura clásica" [know a considerable amount of classical culture] to be able to understand it. It also mentions

the intervention of the Society for the Prevention of Vice in the publication of *Ulysses* in the U.S., but assures us that, "Sin embargo, el libro de Joyce no es licencioso, sino obsceno" [However, Joyce's book is not licentious, but obscene].

3. I note, in passing, the importance of a connection to Larbaud in introducing Joyce and other avant-garde writers of the period to Argentine writers. This topic is studied by Blasi in *Güiraldes y Larbaud*.

4. As Murillo states: "Both have worked on their respective cities, Dublin and Buenos Aires, like mythographers resurrecting from sounds, local sights, houses, and streets, a timeless vision of their inhabitant" (ix). Similarly, Schwartz observes: "Tanto Dublin quanto Buenos Aires sâo ficcionalmente construídas como centros geográficos de arquitectura labiríntica" [Both Dublin and Buenos Aires are fictionally constructed as geographic centers of labyrinthic architecture] ("Borges e Joyce," 143).

5. The perspective of "ausencia" [absence] and the comments about the "yo" [I] that Borges identifies in *Ulysses* resonate with Borges's ideas in "La nadería de la personalidad" [Nothingness of Self] (first published in *Proa*, August 1922, then included in *Inquisiciones*, 1925).

As Masiello observes in *Lenguaje e ideología*, in his early essays, Borges: "Describió al sujeto hablante como una autoridad confiada pero dispersa, que infecta el orden del discurso mediante sus formas abundantes y fragmentadas. La creación, la originalidad, y el privilegio especial del 'yo' literario se explican en términos de la más pequeña cogenrencia espacio-temporal. En su comentario al *Ulises* de James Joyce, Borges expone estos problemas esenciales" [Described the speaking subject as a confident, but dispersed authorial voice, which infects the order of discourse through its many fragmented forms. Creation, originality, and the special privilege of the literary 'I' are explained in terms of the smallest spatial-temporal relationship. In his commentary of Joyce's *Ulysses*, Borges presents these essential problems] (104). See also Masiello's *Lenguaje e ideología*, 95–106 and 147–63 on the issue of Borges and subjectivity.

6. Note Borges's use of the word "proa" [prow], which literally denotes the front of a ship, but figuratively refers to the front, the leading edge, the avant-garde of literary movements. This connects directly with the name of the journal in which this essay appears (*Proa* was one of the most avant-garde publications in Argentina at the time).

7. Neuquén is a province in the South of Argentina.

8. See, for example, Schwartz's "Borges y la primera," 721; or Salgado, 66–67.

9. A similar timeliness of Borges's dialogue with Joyce is true, incidentally, of his review of *Finnegans Wake*, which appeared immediately after its publication (in *El Hogar* on June 16, 1939—on Bloomsday!), and of his article about neologisms in the *Wake* (in *Sur* 62, November 1939).

10. Very much as he had said in "Las versiones homéricas," Borges now states: "Presuponer que toda recombinación de elementos es necesariamente inferior a un arreglo previo es presuponer que el borrador 9 es necesariamente inferior al borrador H ya que no puede haber sino borradores. El concepto de *texto definitivo* no corresponde sino a la superstición o al cansancio" [To presuppose that every recombination of elements is necessarily inferior to a previous arrangement is to presuppose that draft 9 is necessarily inferior to draft H, as there can be only drafts.

The concept of the *definitive text* corresponds only to superstition or fatigue] ("Nota," 49; emphasis in the original).

11. As Fiddian suggests, it is necessary to keep in mind the notion of intertextuality (even and especially as it was shaped by Borges and Joyce) in any comparative study of the influences of Joyce's work on Latin American writers (27–28). I would add that what is at stake here are some of the basic tenets of literature, of influence and tradition, and of the role of translation in relation to them.

12. In other words, the translator must reproduce the "(ab)use" already present in the original, as Philip E. Lewis calls it.

13. As Schwartz has said, these ideas imply that: "La posibilidad que una traducción tiene de superar al original, coloca al traductor en posición de verdadero recreador" [The possibility that a translation can be superior to the original, places the translator in the position of a true recreator] ("Borges y la primera," 722).

14. As Schwartz argues, Borges's translation is much less literal than Salas Subirat's, especially in situations where a literal translation would miss the idiomatic meaning of the original. Schwartz discusses how Borges, in comparison with Salas Subirat: "Aprieta y torna el lenguaje más coloquial—siendo este último un rasgo esencial para el tipo de discurso en cuestión: el monólogo interiorizado de Molly Bloom (corriente de la conciencia)" [Tightens and makes the language more colloquial—this latter being an essential trait for the type of discourse in question: Molly Bloom's internal monologue (stream of consciousness)]; how he manages to avoid literal translation for poetic language and for local idiomatic expressions; and how he avoids artificial solutions that fall outside the style of the original language (such as using literary written expressions to translate dialogued language) ("Borges y la primera," 723–24).

15. Schwartz also points out a moment in Borges's translation, which he terms paronomastic equivalency, in which an original effect is removed and dislocated to another place where it is not in the original but can be recreated in the translation. The phrase in question is the repetition of "the sea the sea," which Borges displaces to another place earlier in the monologue: "y las castañuelas y aquella noche en Algeciras cuando perdimos el vapor las castañuelas . . . ," whereas the "castanets" appears only once in the English version. ("Borges y la primera" 723–24).

16. It is somewhat surprising that Borges would choose this particular moment of *Ulysses* to translate at all. One might think that Stephen's stream of consciousness in the first part of the novel, or some of the moments from "Ithaca," might have suited him better. For "Penelope," and this last moment in particular, deals with sexual desire much more explicitly than most of Borges's own work ever does.

17. As opposed to something more literal, such as "sí lo haré Sí" or "sí deacuerdo Sí." Ellmann describes how Joyce may have been influenced by the French translation, under process even as Joyce was making final revisions to *Ulysses*, to add the final "Yes" to the conclusion of his novel in English (536).

18. In this sense, Borges's aesthetic of the fragment is much more than just a critique of the realist or the modernist novel, as some critics have suggested. See, for example, Salgado, 70–72.

19. For the comprehensive list of the Borgesian texts in which Joyce is mentioned, see Balderston's *The Literary Universe*.

20. See Concha, 475–79.

21. Some critics have taken Borges's references to pantheism and metempsychosis, here and elsewhere, too literally and have sought there a solution to the many enigmas found in all of Borges's texts (see especially Alazraki, 74–100). It seems extremely hard to believe that Borges, the consummate skeptic, however, would actually believe in the transmigration of souls and reincarnation.

22. Borges's contributions to *El Hogar* are collected in *Textos Cautivos: Ensayos y reseñas en El Hogar (1936–1939)* and in *Borges en El Hogar 1935–1958*.

23. One could think of all of these texts, and of *Ulysses* or *Finnegans Wake*, as being literary representations of the world of the kind the narrator glimpses in "El Aleph."

24. This position stands in sharp contrast with T. S. Eliot's assessment of *Ulysses*, as expressed in "*Ulysses*, Order, and Myth" (1923). Eliot, of course, is also dialoguing with Joyce, and executes a similar process of reading *Ulysses* in terms of what he wants to find, and not necessarily in terms of all it contains.

25. Borges's article concludes with the unusual magazine-feature tone: "James Joyce, ahora, vive en un departamento en París, con su mujer y sus dos hijos. Siempre va con los tres a la ópera, es muy alegre y muy conversador. Está ciego" [James Joyce currently lives in an apartment in Paris, with his wife and two children. He often takes the three of them to the opera, he is very happy and loves to talk. He is blind] (*Textos cautivos*, 84).

26. The first copy of the *Wake* from Faber & Faber reached Joyce in Paris on January 30, 1939 (Ellman, 728).

27. Among other places, Borges mentions Lewis Carroll in the "Prólogo" to *Ficciones*, and includes an epitaph from *Through the Looking Glass* in "Las ruinas circulares." He also writes a "Prologue" to Carroll's *Obras completas* in Spanish in 1976. For a complete listing of Borges's texts that include references to Lewis Carroll, see Balderston's *The Literary Universe*, 30.

There is some debate about when exactly Joyce read Carroll. For a discussion on this issue, see Atherton, 127–36.

28. I am grateful to the Berkeley Tuesday *Finnegans Wake* Reading Group for the insights in which they allowed me to share during my participation with the group in 1999–2000.

29. As Atherton states many years later in his study on Joyce's sources: "Many of the wildest and most startling features of *Finnegans Wake* are merely the logical development, or the working out on a larger scale, of ideas that first occurred to Lewis Carroll" (124). Of these, Atherton goes on to say: "The most obvious, and the most important, of Joyce's verbal borrowing from Carroll is the portmanteauwords" (126). See Atherton's chapter "Lewis Carroll: The Unforeseen Precursor" for a more in-depth discussion of the "borrowings" Joyce made from Carroll (124–34).

30. While explaining the meaning of "The Jabberwocky" to Alice, Humpty Dumpty says: "Well, 'slithy' means 'lithe and slimy.' 'Lithe' is the same as 'active.' You see *it's like a portmanteau—there are two meanings packed up into one word*" (Carroll, 187; emphasis added).

31. The first stanza of "The Jabberwocky" is: " 'Twas brillig, and the slithy toves / Did gyre and gimble in the wabe: / All mimsy were the borogoves, / And the mome raths outgrabe" (Carroll, 187). In Borges's adaptation, we see that

"Coesper" is the burlesque Latin amalgamate of "vesper" (evening) and "coena" (dinner), just as "brillig" is a compound of "broiling" and "dinner." Similarly, in the footnote, "lubricus" (slippery) + "graciles" (slender, graceful) = "lubriciles," just as in "The Jabberwocky" "lithe" + "slimy" = "slithy."

32. Joyce also referred to the *Wake* as a "monster" around the time it was first published (Ellmann, 729).

33. The relevant lines from Milton's poem are:

> . . . And lay e're while a Holocaust,
> From out her ashie womb now teem'd
> Revives, reflourishes, then vigorous most
> When most unactive deem'd,
> *And though her body die, her fame survives,*
> *A secular bird ages of lives.* (lines 1702–7; emphasis added)

34. *The Egyptian Book of the Dead* that Joyce most consulted is the one from Thebes (Bishop, 90–91).

35. I am grateful to Dan Schiff for helping me gloss these lines. I also consulted McHugh for his annotations to this section.

36. *Urn Burial* (1658) is a treatise: "Written in the form of a discourse inspired by the discovery of ancient sepulchral urns in Norfolk. Following the discovery of this unsuspected 'subterranean world,' Browne praises the custom of commending man's ashes to the anonymity of an urn 'not much unlike the Urns of our nativity,' as opposed to the fallacy of monuments and the 'folly of posthumous memory'" (Fishburn, 251). Borges translated chapter 5 of *Urn Burial* into Spanish with Bioy Casares; this translation was published in *Sur* (January 1944, 15–26). There is also an interesting reference to *Urn Burial* at the end of "Tlön, Uqbar, Orbis Tertius," when the narrator mentions that he is working on a Quevedian translation of it, which he does not intend to publish—an act worthy of Pierre Menard.

37. On the overlaps between Funes's and Borges's biographies, see, for example, Rodríguez Monegal, 58.

38. As Salgado has observed, this valorization of the fragment is expressed in the article's very title. From Borges's point of view, Salgado argues, "Joyce's genius is for pastiche and for precise, choice phrasing, not for the wide, unruly canvases of novelistic writing. This perspective explains Borges's conviction—explicit in the essay's title—that Joyce's work can only be appreciated through an aesthetic of the fragment" (70).

39. I am grateful to Daniel Balderston for suggesting this overlap between "Funes el memorioso" and this particular moment from *Don Quijote*. I am also grateful to Anthony Cascardi for discussing this parallel with me.

40. Fiddian, in his discussion of "Fragmento sobre Joyce," calls Funes: "A monstrous hyperbole of the totalizing faculty" (29).

41. References to Joyce are found in the following essays from *Otras inquisiciones*: "La flor de Coleridge," "La creación y P.H. Gosse" (around the theme of omphalus), "Quevedo" (where Joyce is listed, along with Goethe, Shakespeare, Dante, as examples of authors whose work encompass entire literatures), and in "Del culto de los libros" (as one of several authors whose writing is an ends in and of itself). For a complete list of Borges's references to Joyce, see Balderston's *The Literary Universe*.

42. Another useful way to think of Borges's ambivalence to Joyce is with Molloy's term "vaivén" [fluctuation] and the uncomfortableness ("inquietud" [anxiety]) that such a technique creates in Borges's texts (Molloy, 9–14).

43. On the importance of Vico in the *Wake*, see Bishop, 206–15.

44. Borges also adds that Joyce's greatest talent is verbal: "El innegable genio de Joyce era puramente verbal; lástima que lo gastó en la novela" [Joyce's undeniable genius is purely verbal; it is too bad that he wasted it on the novel]; and he concludes with a borrowed barb: "Virginia Woolf dijo que el *Ulises* es una gloriosa derrota" [Virginia Woolf has called *Ulysses* a glorious defeat] (*OCC*, 854).

45. Joyce's greatest accomplishment might be said to be to translate all languages into Wakese, as his own form of Irish English. Joyce has also been credited with doing wonders in Italian in his translation of the ALP section of the *Wake*. See, for example, Bollettieri Bosinelli's "Beyond Translation."

46. Discussing whether Joyce is translatable, Senn argues that *Ulysses* is a "borderline case," whereas *Finnegans Wake* falls "out of the translator's province" (4–5). According to Senn, a translator is often forced to make an interpretive choice where the original text allows for multiple options, thus sacrificing the polyvalencies of the original: "In any foreign tongue *Ulysses* becomes less interstructured. . . . What translation can deal with least is translation itself" (48). See also the essays in Lawrence's *Transcultural Joyce*.

47. At one point in "Eumeus," Leopold Bloom bemoans the excess number of languages in the world. Thinking of the men he overheard earlier speaking in Italian, he comments to Stephen on the beauty of that language. Stephen informs Bloom that the men were in fact arguing over money, to which Bloom replies: "—Is that so? Mr Bloom asked. Of course, he subjoined pensively, at the inward reflection of there being more languages to start with than were absolutely necessary, it may be only the southern glamour that surrounds it" (*Ulysses*, 622). The reader cannot help but sympathize with Bloom, as his experience is quite similar to ours when we try to read Joyce. A little later on, Stephen comments on the deceptive nature of language, in a progression that encompasses the history of Europe, and concludes by trying to make Shakespeare sound Irish: "Sounds are impostures, Stephen said after a pause of some little time. Like names, Cicero, Podmore, Napoleon, Mr Goodbody, Jesus, Mr Doyle. Shakespeares were as common as Murphies. What's in a name?" (*Ulysses*, 622).

This exchange is also indicative of the problematics of representation at the site of a multiplicity of languages, an effect that is exponentially magnified in the confusion of languages (i.e., in the Babylonic ruins) of *Finnegans Wake*.

48. According to Senn, although translation involves a set of compromises and a balancing of priorities that lead to inevitable sacrifices and losses, they are still useful because they represent "A complete running commentary of the original" (2).

49. Despite the many difficulties that Senn identifies in his study, he sees silence as an alternative that is forbidden to the translator, because "omission [of any part of the original] would mutilate the text even more [than] the loss of overtones and ambiguities . . . normally taken for granted" in translation (11).

50. Luckily, we do have the attempts of other translators: Salas Subirat's 1945 translation, and, more recently, of José Maria Valverde (1976). See Conde-Parrilla for a commentary of a few aspects of these translations.

51. In this regard, I disagree with Rice, in his otherwise useful "Subtle Reflections of/upon Joyce in/by Borges," in which he looks at Borges's relationship with Joyce in terms of Bloom's anxiety of influence.

52. I am thinking of the kind of tracing of *Ulysses* in Latin American fiction that Gerald Martin has done in his *Journeys Through the Labyrinth*. We can think, for example, of certain elements in the novels of Juan Rulfo, José Lezama Lima, Alejo Carpentier, Miguel Angel Asturias, Joao Guimarães Rosa, Gabriel García Márquez, and Carlo Fuentes, among others. In the case of Argentine literature alone, we could speak of a series of Joycean moments, beginning with Borges's 1925 partial translation, and extending through Leopoldo Marechal's *Adán Buenosayres*, certain aspects of Julio Cortázar's *Rayuela*, some of Manuel Puig's narrative techniques, the presence of Joyce in Ricardo Piglia, etc.

53. For an initial analysis of the importance of translation in "El inmortal," see Kristal, 98–103. See also Murillo's in-depth discussion of Borges's story in *The Cyclical Night*.

CONCLUSION

1. This is the case, for example, in Rodríguez Monegal's interpretation, who focuses on the importance of English in Borges. Although English, and multilingualism in general, is definitely a key component of Borges's texts, reading the anecdote literally leaves us a little short-handed. Furthermore, the veracity of Borges's statement is placed in doubt by his comments about *Don Quijote* in "Las versiones homéricas," as we saw in chapter 2.

EPILOGUE

1. An expanded version of the arguments in this "Epilogue" can be found in my article "Ethics and Aesthetics North and South: Translation in the Work of Ricardo Piglia."

2. Borges and Arlt arguably represent the two pivotal aesthetics of twentieth-century Argentine literature. As Piglia himself has said: "Cruzar a Arlt con Borges, para usar una metáfora positivista, es una de las grandes utopías de la literatura argentina. Creo que esa tentación, más o menos consciente, está en Onetti, en Cortázar y en Marechal. Arlt y Borges son los dos grandes escritores argentinos, y en algún sentido a partir de ellos se arman todas la genealogías, los parentescos y las intrigas de la literatura argentina contemporánea" [To cross Arlt with Borges, to use a positivistic metaphor, is one of the great utopias of Argentine literature. I think that this temptation is found, more or less consciously, in Onetti, in Cortázar, and in Marechal. Arlt and Borges are the two great Argentine writers; in a certain sense they constitute the point of departure for all genealogies, relationships, and intrigues in contemporary Argentine literature] (Costa, 42).

On this issue, see also Fornet; and Jitrik.

3. Within the "fiction" of the novella, the story is by Arlt—by Arlt as a fictional character. In the "real" world, of course, the story is not by Arlt. To date,

"Luba" still appears in the Library of Congress database as if it had been written by Arlt.

4. This persisted among critics until McCracken helped reveal what she termed Piglia's "metaplagiarism" in her 1991 *PMLA* article. The matter was then further clarified and explored by Fornet in his 1994 *Nueva Revista de Filología Hispánica* article. The critic who reads "Luba" as if it had been written by Arlt is Hayes; Lindstrom and Gnutzmann mention the uncertainties surrounding the authorship of "Luba," but go no further. See McCracken, 1081.

5. *Respiración artificial* is available in English, as *Artificial Respiration*, thanks to Balderston's excellent translation. On this section of the novel, see Bratosevich, 216.

6. Tardewski, incidentally, is meant to resonate with Gombrowicz, which adds another level to the themes of exile and displacement in the novel.

7. Macedonio Fernández (1874–1952) is one of the most unusual characters in Argentine literary history. Much celebrated by Borges and others for his ingenuity, a key figure in Argentina's avant-garde movements, he is mostly ignored outside Argentina. For a discussion of his work see, for example, García's *Macedonio Fernández*; or Prieto's *Desencuadernados*. For further analysis of the role of Macedonio in *La ciudad ausente*, see my article "Piglia entre Joyce y Macedonio."

8. Significantly, in *La ciudad ausente* the potential of reproduction and translation in the periphery is located before the forces of the Neoliberal market. As Masiello also observes: "Piglia . . . situates this relationship between the original and its copy, between the source text and its translations in the heart of the mass-media age and the process of globalization. It is the 'delirium of simulation' (15) that motivates characters of *La ciudad ausente*. The novel is composed through different copying machines: cassettes, walkmen, radios, television monitors, maps, and mirrors—even tattoos—reproduce in miniature the larger representations of life and feelings" (*The Art of Transition*, 166).

9. The return to this aspect of the avant-garde, found in other contemporary South American writers such as Cristina Peri Rossi, Diamela Eltit, and Juan José Saer, just to name a few, seems to be a conscious move on the part of a handful of intellectuals as a response to the Neoliberal project in their respective societies. As Masiello has observed, "Only the aesthetic can respond to Neoliberal times" ("Translating History," 13).

10. In his "Afterword" (*The Absent City*, 143).

Bibliography

Abadi, Marcelo. "Averroes y su trémula esclava pelirroja." *Variaciones Borges* 7 (1999): 166–77.

Aizenberg, Edna. *Borges, el tejedor del Aleph y otros ensayos: Del hebraísmo al poscolonialismo*. Frankfurt am Main: Vervuert & Madrid: Iberoamericana, 1997.

Alazraki, Jaime. *La prosa narrativa de Jorge Luis Borges*. 2d ed. Madrid: Gredos, 1974.

Alifano, R. *Twenty-four Conversations With Borges: Including a Selection of Poems*. Housatonic, MA: Lascaux Publishers, 1984.

Altamirano, Carlos and Beatriz Sarlo. "La Argentina del Centenario: Campo intelectual, vida literaria y temas ideológicos." *Hispamérica: Revista de literatura* 25–26 (1980): 33–59.

———. "The Autodidact and the Learning Machine." In *Sarmiento: Author of a Nation*, edited by Tulio Halperín Donghi, Iván Jaksic, Gwen Kirkpatrick, and Francine Masiello, 156–68. Berkeley, Los Angeles, London: University of California Press, 1994.

Andreev, Leonid. *The Dark*. Translated by L. A. Magnus and K. Walter. Richmond, England: The Hogarth Press, 1922.

Aparicio, Frances R. *Versiones, interpretaciones, creaciones: Instancias de la traducción literaria en Hispanoamérica en el siglo veinte*. Gaithersburg, MD: Ediciones Hispamérica, 1991.

Arlt, Roberto. *El juguete rabioso*. Buenos Aires: Centro Editor de América Latina, 1981.

Armistead, Samuel G., and James T. Monroe. "Celestina's Muslim Sisters." *Celestinesca* 13.2 (November 1989): 7–31.

Arnold, Matthew. "On Translating Homer, 1861–62." In *Essays by Matthew Arnold*, 245–426. London: Oxford University Press, 1914.

Atherton, James S. *The Books at the Wake: A Study of Literary Allusions in James Joyce's* Finnegans Wake. New York: The Viking Press, 1960.

Balderston, Daniel. "Borges: The Argentine Writer and the 'Western' Tradition." In *Borges and Europe Revisited*, edited by Evelyn Fishburn, 37–48. London: Institute of Latin American Studies, University of London, 1998.

———. "Borges, Averroes, Aristotle: The Poetics of Poetics." *Hispania* 79.2 (1996): 201–7.

———. *Borges, realidades y simulacros*. Buenos Aires: Biblos, 2000.

———. "Fundaciones míticas en 'La muerte y la brújula.'" *Variaciones Borges* 2 (1996): 125–36.

———. *The Literary Universe of Jorge Luis Borges: An Index to References and Allusions to Persons, Titles, and Places in His Writings.* New York and Westport: Greenwood Press, 1986.

———. "The Mark of the Knife: Scars as Signs in Borges." *Modern Language Review* 83.1 (1988): 67–75.

———. *Out of Context: Historical Reference and the Representation of Reality in Borges.* Durham and London: Duke University Press, 1993.

———. *El precursor velado: R.L. Stevenson en la obra de Borges.* Translated by Eduardo Paz Leston. Buenos Aires: Editorial Sudamericana, 1985.

Balderston, Daniel, Gastón Gallo, and Nicolás Helft. *Borges: Una enciclopedia.* Buenos Aires: Grupo Editorial Norma, 1999.

Balderston, Daniel, and Marcy E. Schwartz, eds. *Voice-Overs: Translation and Latin American Literature.* Albany, NY: State University of New York Press, 2002.

Barili, Amelia. *Jorge Luis Borges y Alfonso Reyes: la cuestión de la identidad del escritor latinoamericano.* México: Fondo de Cultura Económica, 1999.

Barth, John. "The Literature of Exhaustion." *The Atlantic Monthly* 220.2 (Aug. 1967): 29–34.

Bassnett , Susan, and André Lefevere. *Translation, History and Culture.* New York: Cassell, 1995.

Bassnett, Susan, and Harish Trivedi, eds. *Post-Colonial Translation: Theory and Practice.* London and New York: Routledge, 1999.

Bell-Villada, Gene H. *Borges and his Fiction: A Guide to His Mind and Art.* Chapel Hill: The University of North Carolina Press, 1981.

Bellessi, Diana. "Gender and Translation." In *Voice-Overs: Translation and Latin American Literature*, edited by Daniel Balderston and Marcy E. Schwartz, 26–29. Albany: State University of New York Press, 2002.

Benjamin, Andrew. *Translation and the Nature of Philosophy: A New Theory of Words.* London: Routledge, 1989.

Benjamin, Walter. "The Task of the Translator." In *Theories of Translation: An Anthology of Essays from Dryden to Derrida*, edited by Rainer Schulte and John Biguenet, 71–82. Chicago: The University of Chicago Press, 1992.

Bioy Casares, Adolfo. Rev. of *El jardín de senderos que se bifurcan*, by Jorge Luis Borges. *Sur* 92 (May 1942): 60–65.

Bishop, John. *Joyce's Book of the Dark, Finnegans Wake.* Madison: The University of Wisconsin Press, 1986.

Blasi, Alberto. *Güiraldes y Larbaud: Una amistad creadora.* Buenos Aires: Editorial Nova, 1970.

Bloom, Harold. *The Anxiety of Influence: A Theory of Poetry.* New York: Oxford University Press, 1973.

Bollettieri Bosinelli, Rosa Maria. "Beyond Translation: Italian Re-writings of *Finnegans Wake*." *Joyce Studies Annual* (1990): 142–61.

Borges, Jorge Luis. *The Aleph and Other Stories, 1933–1969.* Edited and translated by Norman Thomas di Giovanni in collaboration with the author. New York: E. P. Dutton, 1978.

———. *Borges en El Hogar 1935–1958*. Buenos Aires: Emecé Editores, 2000.

———. *Borges: A Reader: A Selection From the Writings of Jorge Luis Borges*. Translated and edited by Emir Rodríguez Monegal and Alastair Reed. New York: E. P. Dutton, 1981.

———. *Borges en Sur 1931–1980*. Buenos Aires: Emecé Editores, 1999.

———. "Fragmento sobre Joyce." *Sur* 77 (Feb. 1941): 60–62.

———. "Joyce y los neologismos." *Sur* 62 (Nov. 1939): 59–61.

———. *Labyrinths: Selected Stories and Other Writings*. Translated and edited by Donald A. Yates and James E. Irby. New York: New Directions, 1964.

———. "Nota sobre el *Ulises* en español." *Los Anales de Buenos Aires* 1.1 (Jan. 1946): 49.

———. *Obras Completas I–IV*. Barcelona: Emecé Editores España, 1996.

———. *Obras Completas en Colaboración*. Barcelona: Emecé Editores España, 1995.

———. *Textos Cautivos: Ensayus y Reseñas en "El Hogar" (1936–1939)*. Barcelona: Tusquets, 1986.

———. *Textos Recobrados 1919–1929*. Buenos Aires: Emecé Editores, 1997.

———. "El *Ulises* de Joyce." *Proa* 6 (Jan. 1925): 3–6.

———. "La última hoja del *Ulises*." *Proa* 6 (Jan. 1925): 8–9.

Bosworth, C. E., E. van Donzel, W. P. Heinrichs, and G. Lecomte, eds. *The Encyclopaedia of Islam*. New Edition. Vols. 3 and 8. London: Luzac & Co., 1979.

Bradford, Lisa. "La visión de las versiones: Un estudio de diferencias/resistencias en Emily Dickinson." *Celehis: Revista del Centro de Letras Hispanoamericanas* 4.4–5 (1995): 117–32. La Plata, Argentina.

———, ed. *Traducción como cultura*, 13–24. Buenos Aires: Beatriz Viterbo Editora, 1997.

Bratosevich, Nicolás. *Ricardo Piglia y la cultura de la contravención*. Nicolás Bratosevich y grupo de estudio. Buenos Aires: Atuel, 1997.

Bravo, María Elena. "Borges traductor: el caso de *The Wild Palms* de William Faulkner." *Insula* 40:462 (May 1985): 11–12.

Budick, Sanford, and Wolfgang Iser. *The Translatability of Cultures: Figurations of the Space Between*. Stanford, Calif.: Stanford University Press, 1996.

Burton, Richard F. *The Book of the Thousand Nights and a Night: A Plain and Literal Translation of the Arabian Nights Entertainments*. Volume 4. London: The Burton Club, 1885. 100–104 (Night 272) and 288–90 (Night 351).

Bush, Ronald. *T. S. Eliot: A Study in Character and Style*. New York and Oxford: Oxford University Press, 1983.

Carbonell Cortés, Ovidio. "Orientalism in Translation: Familiarizing and Defamiliarizing Strategies." In *Translator's Strategies and Creativity: Selected Papers From the 9th International Conference on Translation and Interpreting, Prague, September 1995*, edited by Ann Beylard-Ozeroff, Jana Kralova, and Barbara Moser-Mercer, 63–70. Amsterdam: Benjamins, 1998.

Carroll, Lewis. *Alice's Adventures in Wonderland and Through the Looking-Glass.* New York: The New American Library, 1960.

Castro, Américo. "El cómo y el porqué de Cide Hamete Benengeli." In *Hacia Cervantes.* 3rd edition, 409–19, Madrid: Taurus, 1967.

Catelli, Nora, and Marietta Gargatagli. *El tabaco que fumaba Plinio: Escenas de la traducción en España y América: relatos, leyes y reflexiones sobre los otros.* Barcelona: Ediciones del Serbal, 1998.

Cervantes, Miguel de. *El Ingenioso Hidalgo Don Quijote de la Mancha.* Part I. Edited by Luis Andrés Murillo. Madrid: Clásicos Castalia, 1978.

Cheyfitz, Eric. *The Poetics of Imperialism: Translation and Colonization From* The Tempest *to* Tarzan. Philadelphia: University of Pennsylvania Press, 1997.

Civantos, Christina. *Between Argentines and Arabs: The Writing of National and Immigrant Identities.* Ph.D. diss. Berkeley: University of California, 1999.

Colombí, Beatriz. "José Martí: traducir, transpensar." *Inti: Revista de cultura hispánica* 49–50 (Spring–Fall 1999): 59–69.

Concha, Jaime. "*El Aleph*: Borges y la historia." *Revista Iberoamericana* 49:123–24 (April–September 1983): 471–85.

———. "On the Threshold of *Facundo*." In *Sarmiento: Author of a Nation.*

Conde-Parrilla, Ma Ángeles. "James Joyce's *Ulysses*: The Obscene Nature of Molly's Soliloquy and Two Spanish Translations." *James Joyce Quarterly.* 33(2) (1996): 211–36.

Connolly, Thomas E. *The Personal Library of James Joyce: A Descriptive Bibliography.* Buffalo: Dept. of English, University of Buffalo, 1957.

Costa, Marithelma. "Entrevista: Ricardo Piglia." *Hispamérica: Revista de Literatura* 15.44 (Aug. 1986): 39–54.

Costa, Walter Carlos. "Borges, the Original of the Translation." In *Voice-Overs: Translation and Latin American Literature,* 182–93.

Cummings, E. E. *Poems 1923–1954.* New York: Harcourt, Brace & World, Inc., 1968.

———. "Poem / Poema." Translated by A. Bioy Casares y J. L. Borges. *Sur* (Marzo–Abril 1944, "Número dedicado a la literatura norteamericana"): 113–14.

Danielson, David J. "Borges on Translation: Encoding the Cryptic Equation." *The Comparatist* 11 (May 1987): 76–85.

Dapía, Silvia. "The Myth of the Framework in Borges' 'Averroes' Search.'" *Variaciones Borges* 7 (1999): 147–65.

De Man, Paul. "Conclusions: Walter Benjamin's 'The Task of the Translator.'" *The Resistance to Theory,* 73–105. Minneapolis: University of Minnesota Press, 1986.

Deleuze, Gilles, and Félix Guattari. *Kafka: Toward a Minor Literature.* Translated by Dana Polan. Minneapolis: University of Minnesota Press, 1986.

———. *A Thousand Plateaus: Capitalism and Schizophrenia.* Translated by Brian Massumi. Minneapolis: University of Minnesota Press, 1987.

Derrida, Jacques. "Des Tours de Babel." In *Difference in Translation,* edited by Joseph Graham, 165–207. Ithaca, NY: Cornell University Press, 1985.

———. "Roundtable on Translation." In *The Ear of the Other*, translated by Peggy Kamuf, 91–161. New York: Schocken Books, 1985.

Dingwaney, Anuradha, and Carol Maier, eds. *Between Languages and Cultures: Translation and Cross-cultural Texts*. Pittsburgh: University of Pittsburgh Press, 1995.

Duff, Charles. "*Ulises* y otros trabajos de James Joyce." *Sur* 5 (Summer 1932): 86–127.

Eliot, T. S. "Ulysses, Order, and Myth." Review of *Ulysses* by James Joyce. *The Dial* 75.5 (Nov. 1923): 480–83.

———. *The Wasteland and Other Poems*. New York: Harcourt, Brace & World, Inc., 1962.

Ellmann, Richard. *James Joyce*. New York: Oxford University Press, 1982.

Even-Zohar, Itamar. "The Position of Translated Literature Within the Literary Polysystem." In *The Translation Studies Reader*, edited by Lawrence Venuti, 192–97. London and New York: Routledge, 2000.

Fernández Moreno, César. "C. G. Jung: *¿Quién es Ulises?*" *Sur* 120 (Oct. 1944): 79–82.

Ferrari, Gustavo and Ezequiel Gallo, eds. *La Argentina del ochenta al centenario*. Buenos Aires: Editorial Sudamericana, 1980.

Fiddian, Robin W. "James Joyce and Latin American Fiction." *Estudos Anglo-Americanos* 5–6 (1981–1982): 48–49.

———. "James Joyce and Spanish-American Fiction: A Study of the Origins and Transmission of Literary Influence." *Bulletin of Hispanic Studies* 66: 23–39.

Fishburn, Evelyn, and Psiche Hughes. *A Dictionary of Borges*. London: Duckworth, 1990.

Fondebrider, Jorge, ed. *La Buenos Aires ajena: Testimonios de extranjeros de 1536 hasta hoy*. Buenos Aires: Emecé Editores, 2001.

Fornet Jorge. "'Homenaje a Roberto Arlt': O, la literatura como plagio." *Nueva Revista de Filología Hispánica (NRFH)* 42.1 (1994): 115–41.

France, Peter. "Translation Studies and Translation Criticism." In *The Oxford Guide to Literature in English Translation*, edited by Peter France, 3–10. Oxford and New York: Oxford University Press, 2000.

Friedrich, Hugo. "On the Art of Translation." In *Theories of Translation: An Anthology of Essays from Dryden to Derrida*, 11–16.

García, Germán. *Gombrowicz, el estilo y la heráldica*. Buenos Aires: Atuel, 1992.

———. *Macedonio Fernández, la escritura en objeto*. Buenos Aires: Siglo Veintiuno Editores, 1975.

Gargatagli, Ana, and Juan Gabriel López Guix. "Ficciones y teorías en la traducción: Jorge Luis Borges." *Livius: Revista de Estudios de Traducción* 1 (1992).

Gentzler, Edwin. *Contemporary Translation Theories*. London and New York: Routledge, 1993.

Gilbert, Stuart. "El fondo latino en el arte de James Joyce." *Sur* 122 (Dec. 1944): 11–24.

Gillet, Louis. "Recuerdos de James Joyce (Conclusión)." *Sur* 88 (Jan. 1942): 53–65.

————. "Recuerdos de James Joyce." *Sur* 87 (Dec. 1941): 28–42.

Gnutzmann, Rita. *Roberto Arlt o el arte del calidoscopio.* Bilbao: Universidad del País Vasco, 1984.

González, Aníbal. "Translation and the Novel: *One Hundred Years of Solitude.*" In *Gabriel Garcia Marquez*, edited by Harold Bloom, 271–82. New York: Chelsea House, 1989.

Goodrich, Diana Sorensen. *'Facundo' and the Construction of Argentine Culture.* Austin: The University of Texas Press, 1996.

Graham, Joseph. Introduction to *Difference in Translation*, 13–30.

Greenberg, Janet Beth. "The Divided Self: Forms of Autobiography in the Writings of Victoria Ocampo." Ph.D. diss. Berkeley: University of California, 1986.

Güiraldes, Ricardo. *Don Segundo Sombra.* Translated by Patricia Owen Steiner. Critical editor Gwen Kirkpatrick. Pittsburgh: University of Pittsburgh Press, 1995.

Gutiérrez, Leandro, and Luis Alberto Romero. *Sectores populares, cultura y política: Buenos Aires en la entreguerra.* Buenos Aires: Editorial Sudamericana, 1995.

Halperín Donghi, Tulio. *Una nación para el desierto argentino.* Buenos Aires: Centro Editor de América Latina, 1982.

————. *Proyecto y construcción de una nación.* Caracas: Ayacucho, 1980.

Hayes, Aden W. "La revolución y el prostíbulo: 'Luba' de Roberto Arlt." *Ideologies and Literature: A Journal of Hispanic & Luso-Brazilian Studies* 2.1 (1987): 141–47.

Helft, Nicolás. *Jorge Luis Borges: Bibliografía completa.* Buenos Aires: Fondo de Cultura Económica, 1997.

Irby, James E., Napoléon Murat, and Carlos Peralta. *Encuentro con Borges.* Buenos Aires: Galerna, 1968.

Jakobson, Roman. "On Linguistic Aspects of Translation." In *Theories of Translation: An Anthology of Essays from Dryden to Derrida*, 144–51.

"James Joyce." *Nosotros* 156 (May 1922): 139–41.

Jitrik, Noé. "En las manos de Borges el corazón de Arlt. A propósito de *Nombre falso*, de Ricardo Piglia." *Cambio* 3 (1976): 85–91.

Johnson, Barbara. "Taking Fidelity Philosophically." In *Difference in Translation*, 142–48.

Joyce, James. "Una escena de *Desterrados.*" Translated by A. Jiménez Fraud. *Sur* 35 (Aug. 1937): 68–86.

————. *Finnegans Wake.* New York: Penguin Books, 1976.

————. *Ulysses.* Vintage International Edition. New York: Random House, 1990.

Kabbani, Rana. *Europe's Myths of Orient.* London: Pandora Press, 1988.

Kenner, Hugh. Introduction to *Ezra Pound: Translations*, 9–14. New York: New Directions, 1963.

King, John. *Sur: A Study of the Argentine Literary Journal and its Role in the Development of a Culture, 1931–1970.* Cambridge: Cambridge University Press, 1986.

Kirk, Robert. *Translation Determined*. New York: Oxford University Press, 1986.

Knipp, Christopher. "The *Arabian Nights* in England: Galland's Translation and its Successors." *Journal of Arabic Literature* 5 (1974): 46–54.

Korn, Francis. *Buenos Aires: Los huéspedes del 20*. Buenos Aires: Grupo Editor Latinoamericano, 1989.

Kristal, Efraín. *Invisible Work: Borges and Translation*. Nashville: Vanderbilt University Press, 2002.

Lafleur, Héctor, Sergio Provenzano, and Rodolfo Alonso. *Las revistas literarias argentinas: 1893–1967*. Buenos Aires: Centro Editor de América Latina, 1967.

Lagos, Ramona. *Jorge Luis Borges, 1923–1980: Laberinto del espíritu, interjecciones del cuerpo*, 99–165. Barcelona: Editores del Mall, 1986.

Larkosh, Christopher Edward. "The Limits of the Foreign: Translation, Migration and Sexuality in 20th-Century Argentine Literature." Ph.D. diss. Berkeley: University of California, 1996.

Lawrence, Karen R., ed. *Transcultural Joyce*. Cambridge and New York: Cambridge University Press, 1998.

Leddy, Annette. "Borges and Swift: Dystopian Reflections." *Comperative Literature Studies* 27:2 (1990): 113–23.

Lefevere, André. "Literary Theory and Translated Literature." *Dispositio* 7.19 (1982): 3–22.

Levine, Suzanne Jill. "Some Versions of Homer." *PMLA* 107.5 (Oct. 1992): 1134–38.

———. *The Subversive Scribe: Translating Latin American Fiction*. St. Paul, Minn.: Graywolf Press, 1991.

Lewis, Philip E. "The Measure of Translation Effects." In *Difference in Translation*, 31–62.

Lindstrom, Naomi. "The Aguafuertes of Roberto Arlt: Reprises of an Idiosyncratic Genre." *Revista canadiense de estudios hispánicos* 12 (1987): 134–40.

Maier, Linda S. *Borges and the European Avant-garde*. New York: Peter Lang Publishing, 1996.

Martí Alanis, Antonio. "La función epistomológica del traductor en *El Quijote*." *Anales Cervantinos* 23 (1985): 31–46.

Martin, Gerald. "Into the Labyrinth: *Ulysses* in America." In *Journeys Through the Labyrinth: Latin American Fiction in the Twentieth Century*, 121–70. London: Verso, 1989.

Masiello, Francine. *The Art of Transition: Latin American Culture and Neoliberal Crisis*. Durham, N.C.: Duke University Press, 2001.

———. *Lenguaje e ideología: Las escuelas argentinas de vanguardia*. Buenos Aires: Hachette, 1986.

———. "Translating History: Politics, Identity, and Conversation in *La ciudad ausente*." Unpublished.

Matamoro, Blas. *Genio y figura de Victoria Ocampo*. Buenos Aires: Editorial Universitaria de Buenos Aires, 1986.

McCracken, Ellen. "Metaplagiarism and the Critic's Role as Detective: Ricardo Piglia's Reinvention of Roberto Arlt." *PMLA* 106.5 (Oct. 1991): 1071–82.

McHugh, Roland. *Annotations to Finnegans Wake.* Rev. edition. Baltimore and London: The John Hopkins University Press, 1991.

Molina, César Antonio. "Las primeras traducciones españolas del *Ulises.*" *Insula: Revista de Letras y Ciencias Humanas* 39.447 (Feb. 1984): 1, 14.

Molloy, Sylvia. *At face value: Autobiographical Writing in Spanish America.* Cambridge, and New York: Cambridge University Press, 1991.

———. *Las letras de Borges.* Buenos Aires: Editorial Sudamericana, 1979.

———. "Lost in Translation: Borges, the Western Tradition and Fictions of Latin America." In *Borges and Europe Revisited,* 8–20.

Moner, Michel. "Cervantes y la traducción." *NRFH* 38: 513–24.

Montgomery, Thomas. "Don Juan Manuel's Tale of Don Illán and its Revision by Jorge Luis Borges." *Hispania-A Journal Devoted to the Teaching of Spanish & Portuguese* 47 (1964): 464–66.

Mosquera, Daniel O. "*Don Quijote* and the Quixotics of Translation." *Romance Languages Annual* 6 (1994): 546–50.

Munday, Jeremy. *Introducing Translation Studies: Theories and Applications.* London and New York: Routledge, 2001.

Murillo, L. A. *The Cyclical Night: Irony in James Joyce and Jorge Luis Borges.* Cambridge: Harvard University Press, 1968.

Nabokov, Vladimir. "Problems of Translation: *Onegin* in English." In *Theories of Translation,* 127–43.

Newman, Francis W. "Homeric Translation in Theory and Practice. A Reply to Matthew Arnold by Francis W. Newman, 1861." In *Essays by Matthew Arnold,* 313–76. London: Oxford University Press, 1914.

Niranjana, Tejaswini. *Siting Translation: History, Post-Structuralism, and the Colonial Context.* Berkeley: University of California Press, 1992.

Olaso, Ezequiel de. *Jugar en serio: aventuras de Borges.* México, D.F.: Paidós Mexicana: Facultad de Filosofía y Letras, Universidad Nacional Autónoma de México, 1999.

Olea Franco, Rafael. "Borges y el civilizado arte de la traducción: una infidelidad creadora y feliz." *Nueva Revista de Filología Hispánica (NRFH)* 44.2 (2001): 439–73.

———. *El Otro Borges. El Primer Borges.* México: Fondo de Cultura Económica, 1993.

Ortega, Julio. "Transatlantic Translations." *PMLA (Publications of the Modern Language Association of America)* 118.1 (January 2003): 25–40.

Ortega y Gasset, José. "Miseria y esplendor de la traducción." In *Obras Completas.* Volume V, 431–52. Madrid: Revista de Occidente, 1961.

Pastormerlo, Sergio. "Borges y la traducción." In *Borges Studies on Line.* J. L. Borges Center for Studies & Documentation. http://www.hum.au.dk/romansk/borges/bsol/pastrom1.htm.

Paz, Octavio. *Los hijos del limo: del romanticismo a la vanguardia.* 2d ed. Barcelona: Seix Barral, 1974.

———. *El signo y el garabato.* México: J. Mortiz, 1973.

———. *Traducción: literatura y literalidad.* Barcelona: Tusquets Editores, 1981.

Pera, Cristóbal. "'Three Trapped Tigers' or Literature as Translation." In *Translation Perspectives: Selected Papers* 6, 249–57. Binghamton, NY: 1984.

Pérez Firmat, Gustavo. *The Cuban Condition: Translation and Identity in Modern Cuban Literature*. Cambridge: Cambridge University Press, 1989.

Petitjean, Armand. "El tratamiento del lenguaje en Joyce." *Sur* 78 (March 1941): 42–59.

Piglia, Ricardo. *The Absent City*. Translated by Sergio Waisman. Durham, N.C.: Duke University Press, 2000.

———. *Assumed Name*. Translated by Sergio Waisman. Pittsburgh: Latin American Literary Review Press, 1995.

———. *Artificial Respiration*. Translated by Daniel Balderston. Durham, N.C.: Duke University Press, 1994.

———. *La ciudad ausente*. Buenos Aires: Editorial Sudamericana, 1992.

———. "¿Existe la novela argentina?" *Espacios de crítica y producción* 6 (1987): 13–15.

———. *Formas breves*. Buenos Aires: Temas Grupo Editorial, 1999.

———. *Nombre falso*. Buenos Aires: Siglo Veintiuno Editores, 1975.

———. Letter to the author. 28 November 1994.

———. "Lost in Translation: Ricardo Piglia, Daniel Balderston, Sergio Waisman in Dialogue." Berkeley, March 4, 1998.

———. *Respiración artificial*. Buenos Aires: Editorial Sudamericana, 1988.

———. "Roberto Arlt: una crítica de la economía literaria." *Los libros* (Marzo–Abril 1973): 22–27.

———. "Sarmiento the Writer." In *Sarmiento: Author of a Nation*, 127–44.

Pires Vieira, Else Ribeiro. "Liberating Calibans: Readings of *Antropofagia* and Haroldo de Campos' poetics of transcreation." In *Post-Colonial Translation: Theory and Practice*, edited by Susan Bassnett and Harish Trivedi, 95–113. London and New York: Routledge, 1999.

———. "New Registers for Translation in Latin America." In *Rimbaud's Rainbow: Literary Translation in Higher Education*, edited by Peter Bush and Kirsten Malmkjaer, 171–95. Amsterdam and Philadelphia: John Benjamins Publishing Co., 1998.

Pratt, Mary Louise. *Imperial Eyes: Travel Writing and Transculturation*. London and New York: Routledge, 1992.

Prieto, Adolfo. "Boedo y Florida." In *Estudios de literatura argentina*, 29–56. Buenos Aires: Editorial Galerna, 1969.

Prieto, Julio. *Desencuadernados: vanguardias ex-céntricas en el Río de la Plata: Macedonio Fernández y Felisberto Hernández*. Rosario, Argentina: Beatriz Viterbo Editora, 2002.

Quine, Willard V.O. "Meaning and Translation." In *The Translation Studies Reader*. London and New York: Routledge, 2000. 94–112.

Rabell, Carmen R. "Cervantes y Borges. Relaciones intertextuales en 'Pierre Menard, autor del *Quijote*.'" *Revista Chilena de Literatura* 42 (Aug. 1993): 201–7.

Rama, Ángel. *Transculturación narrativa en América Latina*. México: Siglo Veintiuno, 1982.

Revista Martín Fierro 1924–1927 Edición Facsimilar. Estudio preliminar de Horacio Salas. Buenos Aires: Fondo Nacional de las Artes, 1995.

Rice, Thomas J. "Subtle Reflections of/upon Joyce in/by Borges." *Journal of Modern Literature* 24.1 (2000): 47–62.

Robinson, Douglas. *Translation and Empire: Postcolonial Theories Explained*. Manchester, U.K.: St. Jerome Press, 1997.

Rock, David. *Argentina 1516–1987: From Spanish Colonization to Alfonsín*. Berkeley and Los Angeles: University of California Press, 1987.

———, ed. *Argentina in the Twentieth Century*. London and Pittsburgh: Duckworth, 1975.

Rodríguez Monegal, Emir. *Jorge Luis Borges: A Literary Biography*. New York: E.P. Dutton, 1978.

Romano-Sued, Susana. "Borges y la ficción como crítica: ficción, abismo y metatextualidad." In *Traducción como cultura*, 167–84.

Romero, José Luis. *El desarrollo de las ideas en la sociedad argentina del siglo XX*. Buenos Aires: Ediciones Solar, 1983.

Saer, Juan José. "La perspectiva exterior." *Punto de vista 35* (1989): 14–19.

Said, Edward. *Orientalism*. New York: Pantheon Books, 1978.

Salgado, César Augusto. "*Barroco* Joyce: Jorge Luis Borges's and José Lezama Lima's antagonistic readings." In *Transcultural Joyce*, 63–96.

Salvador, Nélida. *Revistas argentinas de vanguardia (1920–1930)*. Buenos Aires: Ediciones culturales argentinas, 1962.

Sánchez Robayna, Andrés. "Borges y Joyce." *Insula: Revista de Letras y Ciencias Humanas* 38.427 (April 1983): 1, 12.

Santoyo, Julio-César, ed. *Teoría y crítica de la traducción: antología*. Barcelona: Publicaciones de la Universitat Autònoma de Barcelona, 1987.

Sarlo, Beatriz. "Borges en *Sur*: un episodio del formalismo criollo." *Punto de Vista 16* (1982): 3–6.

———. *Borges, un escritor en las orillas*. Buenos Aries: Editora Espasa Calpe / Ariel, 1995.

———. *Jorge Luis Borges: A Writer on the Edge*. London and New York: Verso, 1993.

———. *La máquina cultural: Maestras, traductores y vanguardias*. Buenos Aires: Grupo Editorial Planeta, 1998.

———. *Una modernidad periférica: Buenos Aires, 1920 y 1930*. Buenos Aires: Ediciones Nueva Visión, 1988.

Sarmiento, Domingo F. *Facundo, Civilización y Barbarie: Vida de Juan Facundo Quiroga*. México: Editorial Porrúa, 1991.

———. *Mi defensa*. 1843; rpt. in *Obras*, III. Buenos Aires: Imprenta y Litografía Mariano Moreno, 1896.

———. *Recuerdos de provincia*. 1850; rpt. in *Obras*, III. Buenos Aires: Imprenta y Litografía Mariano Moreno, 1896.

Schopenhauer, Arthur. "On Language and Words." In *Theories of Translation*, 32–35.

Schulte, Rainer and John Biguenet. Introduction to *Theories of Translation*, 1–10.

Schwartz, Jorge. "Borges e Joyce (via Salas Subirat, Antônio Houaiss e Haroldo de Campos)." *Boletim Bibliográfico Biblioteca Mário de Andrade* 45.1–4 (1984): 143–55.

———. "Borges y la Primera Hoja de *Ulysses*." *Revista Iberoamericana* 43 (1977): 721–28.

Senn, Fritz. *Joyce's Dislocutions: Essays on Reading as Translation*. Baltimore: The John Hopkins University Press, 1984.

Sorrentino, Fernando. *Seven Conversations With Jorge Luis Borges*. Translated by Clark M. Zlotchew. Troy, N.Y.: Whitston Publishing Co., 1982.

Spivak, Gayatri Chakravorty. "The Politics of Translation." In *The Translation Studies Reader*, 397–416.

Steiner, George. *After Babel: Aspects of Language and Translation*. Oxford and New York: Oxford University Press, 1992.

Stewart, Jon. "Borges on Language and Translation." *Philosophy and Literature* 19.2 (1995): 320–29.

Sur 338–339 (Jan.–Dec. 1976). "Problemas de la traducción" Special Issue. Buenos Aires: Sur, 1976.

Vázquez, María Esther. *Borges: Esplendor y derrota*. Buenos Aires: Tusquets Editores, 1996.

Venuti, Lawrence. Introduction to *Rethinking Translation: Discourse, Subjectivity, Ideology*, edited by Lawrence Venuti, 1–17. London and New York: Routledge, 1992.

———. *The Scandals of Translation: Towards an Ethics of Difference*. London and New York: Routledge, 1998.

———, ed. *The Translation Studies Reader*. London and New York: Routledge, 2000.

———. *The Translator's Invisibility*. London and New York: Routledge, 1995.

Waisman, Sergio. "Ethics and Aesthetics North and South: Translation in the Work of Ricardo Piglia." *MLQ (Modern Language Quarterly)* 62–63 (September 2001): 259–83.

———. "Piglia entre Joyce y Macedonio: Una revalorización estética y política." *Revista de Estudios Hispánicos* (2004). Forthcoming.

———. "*The Thousand and One Nights* in Argentina: Translation, Narrative, and Politics in Borges, Puig, and Piglia." *Comparative Literature Studies*, 40–44 (2003): 351–71.

Willson, Patricia. "La fundación vanguardista de la traducción." *Borges Studies on Line*. J.L. Borges Center for Studies & Documentation. http://www.hum.au.dk/romansk/borges/bsol/pw.htm.

———. "Traductores en *Sur*: teoría y práctica." In *Traducción como cultura*, 133–40.

Zangara, Irama, ed. *Borges en Revista Multicolor: Obras, reseñas y traducciones inéditas de Jorge Luis Borges*. Buenos Aires: Editorial Atlantida, 1995.

Zavala, Iris M. *Colonialism and Culture: Hispanic Modernisms and the Social Imaginary*. Bloomington: Indiana University Press, 1992.

Index

Aizenberg, Edna, 238n. 6
Alazraki, Jaime, 237n. 44, 243n. 21
Alberdi, Juan B., 221n. 10
Alberti, Rafael, 38
Alfonso X, 107
Altamirano, Carlos, 25, 221n. 11
Anales de Buenos Aires, 163
Andreyev, Leonid: "The Dark," 208
Angel Asturias, Miguel, 246n. 52
Aparicio, Frances, 21, 53, 63–64, 220n.
  2, 226n. 14, 227n. 27, 240n. 27
Arabian Nights. See *Thousand and One
  Nights, The*
Argentina: and Buenos Aires's cultural
  mixtures, 14, 29, 30, 37–39, 107,
  122, 135–36, 139, 222n. 23; as colony, 19; contemporary literature of,
  16–17, 207; as context for Borges's
  theories on translation, 13–15, 19–
  23, 28–31, 34–39, 74, 78–83, 84, 91,
  203; democracy in, 212; dictatorship
  in, 211–12, 222n. 17; and French
  culture, 24–28, 30, 36, 38, 127, 128,
  133, 152; gauchesque tradition of,
  32, 127–28, 133, 151–52, 200, 222n.
  19; and identity/subjectivity, 22, 28,
  31, 33–34, 126–28, 149–51, 203,
  223n. 26; Independence Movement
  of, 24; journals and magazines of, 22,
  29, 30–37, 85, 222–23n. 24, 223nn.
  28 and 29, 240–41n. 2, 241n. 6; linguistic difference from Spain of,
  153–54, 167–69, 198, 209, 240n. 26;
  and modernization, 29; and nation
  foundation in the nineteenth century,
  14, 19, 22–27, 29, 128, 212, 221n.
  12, 221–22n. 16; on the periphery,
  19, 28, 35, 37, 40, 74, 80–83, 92,
  126, 134, 148, 156, 203–4, 235n. 31,

239n. 23; polyglossia in, 14, 22–25,
  28, 32–34, 38, 122, 203, 221n. 14;
  repression in, 211–12; tension between foreign and local/*criollo* traditions of, 22, 25, 26, 28–33, 37, 126,
  127–28, 133–34, 149–51, 203, 222n.
  23; twentieth-century/avant-garde literature of, 11, 14, 17, 22, 25, 28–35,
  216, 217, 223n. 27, 225–26n. 10,
  247nn. 7 and 9; visitors to, 37–40
Aristotle, 125, 156, 175; *Poetics*,
  139–46
Arlt, Mirta, 208
Arlt, Roberto, 16, 207–10, 214, 222–
  23n. 24, 246n. 2, 246–47n. 3
Arnold, Matthew, 54–55, 57, 67–68,
  165, 226n. 19, 227n. 20
Asbury, Herbert: *The Gangs of New
  York*, 87, 229–30n. 1
Asunción Silva, José, 240n. 27
Atherton, James S., 243n. 29
Attar, Ferid Eddin, 171–73
Averroes, 125, 139–46, 156, 172, 236n.
  41, 238n. 13
Azul, 236n. 37

Babel, Tower of, 12, 30, 39, 43, 44, 59–
  60, 64–65, 96, 99, 122, 156, 180–83,
  200, 205, 209, 214–15, 245n. 47
Balderston, Daniel, 94, 101, 104, 106,
  143, 219n. 3, 224–25n. 2, 228nn. 31
  and 34, 233nn. 16, 17, and 23, 234–
  35n. 29, 237n. 48, 238n. 7, 239n. 18,
  240n. 27, 242n. 19, 244n. 30
Banchs, Enrique: *La Urna*, 238n. 4
Barrès, Maurice, 103, 234–35n. 29
Barthes, Roland, 51
Baudelaire, Charles, 113
Beckett, Samuel, 215

259